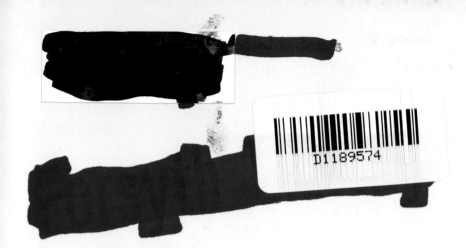

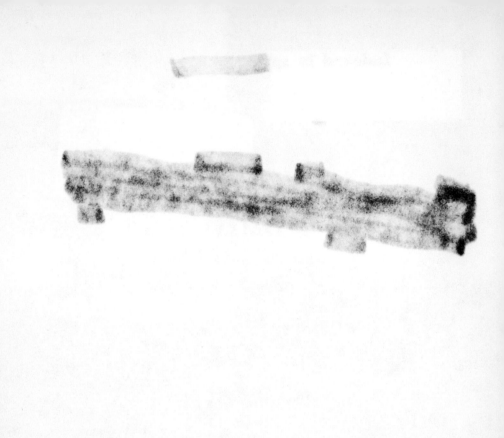

THEATRE
in DADA
and SURREALISM

THEATRE
in DADA
and SURREALISM

J. H. MATTHEWS

1974 SYRACUSE UNIVERSITY PRESS

Library of Congress Cataloging in Publication Data

Matthews, J. H.
    Theatre in Dada and surrealism.

842.9109
$M439t$
1974

    Includes bibliographical references.
    1. French drama—20th century—History and
criticism.   2. Dadaism.   3. Surrealism.   I. Title.
PQ558.M3   842'.9'1091   73-16286
ISBN 0-8156-0097-6

Manufactured in the
United States of America

i Sian

Adeiniog pob chwant

J. H. Matthews is Professor of French at Syracuse University. Since 1965 he has been editor of *Symposium: A Quarterly Journal in Modern Foreign Literatures*. He is editor of a selection of stories by Guy de Maupassant (1959), as well as two special issues of *La Revue des Lettres Modernes*, and author of *Les Deux Zola* (1957) and numerous articles on nineteenth- and twentieth-century French literature. His interest in surrealism has led him to write also *An Introduction to Surrealism* (1965), *Péret's Score/Vingt Poemes de Benjamin Péret* (1965), *An Anthology of French Surrealist Poetry* (1966), *Surrealism and the Novel* (1966), *André Breton* (1967), *Surrealist Poetry in France* (1969), and *Surrealism and Film* (1971).

Contents

Preface

Ours is a century that has brought the structure and function of theatre, together with the playwright's obligations to his public, under self-conscious critical scrutiny such as was never known before 1900. Yet in discussions about where drama is going, and why, the contribution of Dada and surrealism to dethroning traditional and inherited assumptions and to opening up new perspectives has been distorted, when it has not been ignored. Hence it is the purpose of the following investigation to show what Dada and surrealist writers have sought when turning to the stage and, at the same time, to make a contribution to the history of avant-garde theatre through examination of representative plays and dramatized texts expressive of Dada and surrealist ambitions.

There is no denying that there has seemed to be some excuse, in the past, for disregarding Dada and surrealist practice in the theatre. It is only too evident that the immediate impact made by Dada playwrights before 1920 was severely limited. It is just as clear that we have no occasion to plead that these playwrights were unfortunate victims of circumstance, denied the opportunity to meet a wide audience. By and large, more than one performance of their works for the stage would not have seemed to these men favorable treatment of their material so much—paradoxical as it sounds, at first—as betrayal of it. As for certain surrealist writers, from around 1920 to the 1960s they might have had reason to envy the chance of just one stage presentation. To other authors, no less faithful to surrealism, the prospect of being produced offers so little appeal that adoption of dramatic format represents something quite different from admitting a need to meet an audience across the footlights, or even consenting to do this.

At this point one might interject that the history of drama—even avant-garde drama—must give precedence to plays that have benefited from stage presentation. While the question of precedence cannot be disputed, the work of drama historians will remain incomplete so long as they decline to consider theatrical works that have never been put on or that have reached only a restricted public, perhaps under less than desirable conditions.

All the same, anyone who, admitting the validity of this argument, undertakes to examine Dada and surrealist texts in dramatic form soon runs into special difficulties. It does not take him long to notice that plays written under Dada or surrealist inspiration really have had little chance to attract public attention. Rarely if ever performed, all too often, if published at all, they have appeared initially in out-of-the-way magazines or in limited editions that seem to have exerted a fascination for bibliophiles rather than for students of contemporary drama. In more than a few instances, where accessible printings do exist, these have reached the public years after the works in question were composed, at a time when their originality necessarily has earned them less credit than they deserve.

At all events, a number of significant texts are available at last. It is not too soon, therefore, to ask what Dada and surrealism really have attempted to do with the theatre. We can ask, now, how and why they turned to drama. And we can hope to reach balanced answers; so long, that is, as we are prepared to examine the results obtained in relation to the ends Dada and surrealist writers have had in view—not in the light of theatrical tradition and certainly not upon their supposed merits as literature, which both Dada and surrealism hold in contempt.

In the study that follows, an effort will be made to keep in sight the creative impulses and, where these apply, the theoretical edicts that have guided individual writers in their effort to extend expression of Dada or surrealism to the theatre. So far as possible, the arrangement of the chapters takes a chronological course. This presents the opportunity to retrace the gradual, hesitant emergence of surrealist ambitions from Dada's literary terrorism. It offers, too, the chance to observe what kinds of imperatives influence experiments with drama conducted by Dada and surrealist authors. It permits us to detect parallels, possible influences, important new departures, and evolving concerns. So it will show how surrealism in the theatre can reach its culmination in the unperformable play and—at the same time, without being inconsistent with itself—the essentially dramatic spectacle of *Cérémonial pour . . . Sade*, by Alain-Valery Aelberts and Jean-Jacques Auquier.

Preparation of this book, completed with the assistance of my wife, was made possible by a grant-in-aid from the American Council of Learned Societies, supplemented by financial support from Syracuse University. I am grateful to Anna Balakian for reading and criticizing my manuscript. Special thanks are due to Alain-Valery Aelberts and Jean-Jacques Auquier, to Radovan Ivsic, and to Jehan Mayoux. The chapter on Julien Gracq appeared originally in *The Romanic Review* and is reprinted by kind permission of Columbia University Press.

JHM

Fayetteville, New York
Summer 1973

THEATRE
in DADA
and SURREALISM

Introduction

You don't construct sensibility upon
a word; any construction converges
upon boring perfection, the stagnant
idea of a gilded bog,
a relative human product.[1]

DADA made its presence felt in Europe around 1916 as a negative spirit at odds with cultural values that, on a war-torn continent, no longer seemed attuned to the times. Dada's attack upon consecrated forms found expression quite readily in the area of artistic creation. However the iconoclastic effort that was Dada was by no means confined to the media of painting and sculpture. It embraced also denial of inherited literary modes and styles. Thus, for example, Dada implemented protest through a new conception of poetry, divorced from principles of style, scornful of traditional sentiments, and contemptuous of rational discourse.

Today, though, to the public at large, mention of Dada means opening up discussion of art—or, as they might prefer to say, of anti-art. And there seems to be ample excuse for this. It was, after all, essentially the contribution made by Dada on the artistic plane that received publicity in a major exhibition at the Dusseldorf Kunsthalie in September and October 1958 and at the Stedelijk Museum, Amsterdam, between December 1958 and February 1959. The same was true of the magnificent show celebrating the fiftieth anniversary of the launching of Dada, first at the Kunsthaus in Zurich—where European Dada was born—from October 8 through November 17, 1966, and then at the

1. Tristan Tzara, "Manifeste Dada 1918," *Sept Manifestes Dada* (Jean-Jacques Pauvert, n. d. [1963]), p. 21. Unless otherwise indicated, the place of publication for all books in French is Paris.

Musée National d'Art moderne, Paris, from November 30 through January 30, 1967. Moreover, the general public's knowledge of surrealism has been subject to similar limitations. We can discount all the exhibitions held without the backing of the surrealist movement, many of which betray the phenomenon they purport to represent. But even if we concentrate upon the international surrealist exhibitions organized by the surrealists themselves, since surrealism became autonomous with the publication of André Breton's *Manifeste du Surréalisme* in 1924, we have to admit that these shows invariably risk leaving outsiders with the impression that painting, objects, and sculpture are just as much the main preoccupation of surrealist creative endeavor as they appear to have been in Dada.[2]

This fact needs stressing, then. From the first, subversion of artistic criteria was accompanied in Dada as much as in surrealism by opposition to established literary values. For surrealism no less than for Dada, subversion betokened dissatisfaction with tradition and hence an impulse to explore new means of expression in all areas of creative endeavor. Thus it is particularly unfortunate that, by the process of simplification that hastens the assimilation of new ideas, Dada, for instance, has survived in popular memory as the anti-artistic movement that seems to have been born simply to father more recent experiments in self-liberation among painters, some of whom, indeed, have been labeled neo-Dadaist.

If we choose to move a little closer to our subject and proceed to ask whether someone wishing to know more of Dada and surrealism than can be learned from attending an exhibition has the chance to do so, we find, of course, that he has such an opportunity. The special merit of Robert Motherwell's *The Dada Painters and Poets*, for example, is that it gives as much space to poetry as to painting, while it chronicles the history of Dada.[3] No work comparable with Motherwell's exists for surrealism. Yet it might be argued that we need not regret that this is so. Those who want information upon the nature of surrealism's contribution to poetry have no difficulty finding what they

2. The last surrealist show to be labeled Exposition internationale du Surréalisme, the eleventh, was held in Paris in 1965 under the title *L'Ecart absolu* (*Absolute Divergence*). One more exhibition on the international scale was held in 1968 in Brno, Prague, and Bratislava, under the title *Princip Slasti* (*The Pleasure Principle*).

3. Robert Motherwell, ed., *The Dada Painters and Poets* (New York: Wittenborn, Schultz), 1951.

need.[4] The trouble starts when one feels curious about Dada's attitude toward the theatre, or about surrealism's experiments with drama. Relatively little has been said on the subject, so that one may be forgiven for concluding that Dada's approach to the stage, and surrealism's too, is unworthy of attention. By and large, it appears, the whole question has been pushed aside, and for good reasons, it seems at first glance.

The fact of the matter is that it is as unfruitful as it is foolhardy to speak of Dada theatre or of surrealist drama. Even a preliminary consideration of the available evidence recommends that we limit ourselves, instead, to acknowledging the existence of a certain number of texts by writers of Dada or surrealist persuasion which, sometimes for want of a better definition, may be called plays. To begin with, at all events, our inquiry appears not merely unpromising, but denied definite orientation.

When we take up the question of theatre in the perspective of Dada or surrealism, our initial impression is that the best guidelines may well be of the most unsophisticated kind. Thus, it would appear, the plays of Tristan Tzara could be considered an expression of Dada primarily because their author was one of the founders of Dada in Switzerland. As for Georges Ribemont-Dessaignes, his *L'Empereur de Chine* could be termed a Dada text because it was the first piece of writing in dramatic form to be published in France—during 1921—in the "Collection Dada." Results are likely to be less than satisfactory, though, if we go about things in this fashion. Tzara's plays and Ribemont-Dessaignes's plainly have little in common. What is more, the theatrical works of neither of these authors offer very clear affinities with, shall we say, *S'il vous plaît* by André Breton and Philippe Soupault, performed on March 27, 1920.

But our problems do not end here. *S'il vous plaît* was presented under Dada aegis. The fact is especially worthy of note because Breton and Soupalt had co-authored, a year earlier, a series of texts they called *Les Champs magnétiques*. The historical importance of these texts is that they

4. They can begin with the following anthologies, all assembled by surrealists: Georges Hugnet, *Petite Anthologie poétique du Surréalisme* (Editions Jeanne Bucher, 1934); Benjamin Péret, *La Poesia surrealista francese* (Milan: Schwartz editore, 1959); Aldo Pellegrini, *Antología de la poésia surrealista de lengua francesa* (Buenos Aires: Compañia general Fabril editora, 1961); Jean-Louis Bédouin, *La Poésie surréaliste* (Editions Seghers, 1965). They may consult also Juan José Ceselli, *Poesia Argentina et Vanguardia: Surrealismo e Invencionismo* (Buenos Aires: Ministerio de Relaciones exteriores y Culto Argentina, 1964); Christian Bussy, *Anthologie du Surréalisme en Belgique* (Gallimard, 1972).

were produced by the very process of verbal automatism which, in his 1924 surrealist manifesto, Breton was to salute as basic to surrealist expression. In fact, *Les Champs magnétiques* has never ceased to be considered, in surrealist circles, the first attempt to explore the surrealist potential of language, to adapt language to purposes quite different from those that interested Dada. The existence of *Les Champs magnétiques* is proof, then, that chronology offers no safe-conduct through the confusing and sometimes apparently conflicting evidence that has come down from the period when Dada was active and surrealism in gestation. *L'Empereur de Chine* was written at the beginning of 1916, before its author had ever heard the word "Dada." While one critic at least gives precedence to surrealism over Dada in this play,[5] Ribemont-Dessaignes speaks in his memoirs of merely having "flirted" with surrealism. He did not find it to his liking at all to cast off his Dada identity, when Dada yielded to surrealism. Yet we cannot attach too much importance to his hesitations, since there is reason to suspect his actions of being motivated by personal antipathy for André Breton, far more than by deeply held convictions, aesthetic or anti-aesthetic. As for Breton, his respect for *L'Empereur de Chine*, we should notice, was in no way diminished by its author's aversion to surrealism. Breton and Soupault, meanwhile, wrote *S'il vous plaît* before they made Tzara's acquaintance. At that time, Tzara had not yet left Zurich for Paris, where Dada really took root only after his migration from Switzerland to France. Later, after the demise of Dada, Tzara joined the surrealists, freely associating for a while in surrealism's program of revolt, which had replaced Dada's.

Unfortunately, no guaranteed criterion exists that, cutting across misleading chronological boundaries, would permit us to classify this play as unquestionably of Dada inspiration and that play as of purely surrealist derivation. The thesis advanced by Michel Sanouillet, who contends in his *Dada à Paris* that surrealism in France is merely an extension of Dada, is no less tendentious than arguing that Dada is surrealism in disguise or in search of its true identity. Progress is likely to be more sure if the liberty granted all creative writers within Dada is recognized as having direct consequences for the theatre: absence of a consistent and consecutive approach to drama as well as absence of a unified program for the stage.

5. P. Blanchard, cited by Michel Corvin in "Georges Ribemont-Dessaignes et le Laboratoire 'Art et Action,'" *Cahiers Dada surréalisme*, No. 1 (1966), p. 166.

To begin with, at any rate, avoidance of dogmatism and rigid controls on the part of Dada writers of plays bids us be wary of attempting to determine where Dada in the theatre stops and where surrealism begins. It is advisable to note, rather, how often attitudes taken by writers in the Dada tradition were adopted by the first surrealists also. Iconoclasm, for instance, is fundamental to theatre as understood and practiced both in Dada and in surrealism. Hence the exuberant aggressiveness of the following notes by Tristan Tzara represents equally the approach of the latter and of the former:

> Première: "Sphynx and Straw Man" by O. Kokoschka. Firdusi, Rubberman, Anima, Death.
>   This performance decided the role of our theatre, which will entrust the stage direction to the subtle invention of the explosive mind, scenario to the audience, visible direction, grotesque props: the DADAIST theatre. Above all masks and revolver shots, the effigy of the director. Bravo! & Boom boom![6]

Naturally, it would be difficult to deduce from these few phrases any theory destined to modify or question playwriting constructively, in the name of Dada. At best, one senses that certain ideas on the methods and purposes of dramatic composition were to grow only incidentally out of a distinctive conception of communication and expression, affecting the drama among other literary modes. These ideas reflected no preconceived intent, no concerted effort by Tzara and his associates—either those he knew in Zurich during the First World War or encountered later in Paris—to improve, update, or otherwise revitalize the playwright's art. On the contrary, it is in its negative aspects that Dada treatment of theatre can be said to manifest the greatest measure of unity. At the same time, there is no occasion to speak of a sudden and intentional change of emphasis, subject matter or style, deliberately adopted once Dada gave way to surrealism. Since Breton's outlook upon life was basically incompatible with Tzara's, during the early days of surrealist activity temperamental differences contributed more to indicating where boundaries eventually would be erected than did distinctions on the plane of theory. Hence estimates of the theatre could not be characterized as marking an entirely new departure, during the middle twenties; or so it seems at first. After all, Breton had

6. Tristan Tzara, "Zurich Chronicle (1915–1919)," cited in Motherwell, ed., *The Dada Painters and Poets*, pp. 237–38.

been motivated to join Dada largely by disgust for literature as nothing more interesting than a succession of aesthetic exercises carried out in accepted literary forms. His eventual disagreement with Dada's philosophy of nihilism, as expressed by Tzara, did not dispose of that disgust altogether. Disgust continued to nourish many of the attitudes we identify as typical of the surrealist posture.

Surrealism agrees with Dada in opposing any compromise with rational, emotional, and moral preoccupations of the kind traditionally underlying the theatre in France, no less than elsewhere. Instead of these, Dada developed a form of spectacle—the word *manifestation* ("demonstration," "celebration," "outburst," "revelation") being used in French to describe performances put on before the public by those militating for Dada—that was essentially a deliberate act of provocation. From the first, an instinct for showmanship in Tzara guided Dada toward exhibitionism. And this, for a time anyway, fascinated those in Paris who were not to declare themselves surrealists until after brief but impassioned association with Dada. We find Breton beginning a lecture at the Ateneo in Barcelona on November 17, 1922, with the following words: "In general, I consider that a critical study is quite out of place in the present circumstances and that the smallest theatrical effect would serve my purposes better." Significantly, he went on to speak of Alfred Jarry, seated at a table with a bottle of absinthe in front of the curtain at the Salle du Nouveau Théâtre in 1896, on the first night of his *Ubu Roi*. Breton mentioned also Arthur Cravan in wartime New York, having to be dragged in a state of intoxication onto the rostrum from which he was supposedly to lecture about modern humor, and where he started to undress before his audience. Breton's conclusion was unequivocal: "All things considered, the sense of provocation is still what is to be appreciated most in this matter. A truth will always gain from taking an outrageous turn when finding expression."[7]

In his essay entitled "Après Dada," Breton dates the "funeral" of Dada from about May 1921.[8] Yet there is no immediately observable difference between the statement just taken from his 1922 address in Barcelona and an affirmation of Tzara's, the next year: "Dadaism has

7. André Breton, "Caractères de l'Evolution moderne et ce qui en participe," *Les Pas perdus* (Editions de la N.R.F., 1924), pp. 181–82.
8. See *Les Pas perdus*, p. 124.

never rested on any theory and has been only a provocation."[9] Before the days of surrealism, Dada recognized the theatre as a valid expression of the principle of provocation, when it is treated as somewhat self-contradictory, when, for example, the form of drama is adopted to nondramatic ends. In part, this is what Tzara's *1918 Dada Manifesto* implied: "Let every man cry out: a great destructive negative work needs to be accomplished. To sweep away, to clean up." All things considered, one might hope, then, to begin dealing quite practically with the question of drama in Dada by identifying what drama is not, for Dada—categorizing the things Dada writers do not wish to do and noting what they reject. For elements of negativity are paramount, even when they engender innovative features leading in some cases to distinctly positive results, as Dada gives way to surrealism. All the same, consistency is far from the Dada playwright's mind, and concerns the surrealist little if any more. Tzara neglects plot entirely in two plays (1916 and 1920) about the celestial adventures of someone he calls Monsieur Antipyrine. In *S'il vous plaît* Breton and Soupault handle plot with undisguised irony. Ribemont-Dessaignes, though, develops a relatively firm plot line in *L'Empereur de Chine*, as he does also in *Le Bourreau du Pérou* (1926). In addition, he declares that all his plays—even the enigmatic playlet *Le Serin muet* (1919)—have a philosophical import patently lacking in, for example, Louis Aragon's *L'Armoire à Glace un beau Soir* (written between 1922 and 1923) and in Aragon's *Au Pied du Mur* (first performed in 1925), as it is absent, too, from the Breton-Soupault sketch *Vous m'oublierez* (1920).

The only truly common feature of early surrealist playwrighting, one thinks at first, is certainly its most durable link with drama of Dada inspiration: denial of the right of conventional and conservative forces to inhibit free expression in the theatre. As is the case with Dada, it is in the nature of surrealism to cast down sacrosanct forms, repudiate established aesthetic principles, and be wary of all rules in deference to the spirit of revolt and iconoclasm. This is why theatre *per se* is of no more value to Breton and his companions than to Tzara and his. The defenders of Dada and those of surrealism are far from being concerned with making a memorable contribution to the literature of the stage. To borrow a phrase used in 1968 by José Pierre, as

9. Cited by Roger Vitrac in "Tristan Tzara va cultiver ses Vices," *Le Journal du Peuple*, April 14, 1923.

a title for a volume of surrealist short stories and plays, they have *D'autres Chats à fouetter:* other fish to fry. In surrealism as much as in Dada, the idea of a play as a conventional form is valid only so long as the drama provides a framework into which writers can conveniently pour their material. It is a matter of indifference to them if this material does not quite fill the mold where it has been cast, or if it overspills the limits we are accustomed to see dramatists respect. Indeed, in the theatre perhaps more than anywhere else, one is made aware of the things that Dada and surrealism have done *to* a given literary form, rather than *for* it.

When we have said this much, we still cannot point, either in Dada or in surrealism, to proof of a well-planned, concerted attack upon the medium of theatre. The most we can do, at this juncture, is indicate certain characteristic trends that appear common to both.

In writers to whom the idea of professionalism in literary or artistic production is abhorrent, it is only to be expected that distaste for ordained approaches and perspectives should provoke striking departures from the norm of playwriting. When bringing people on stage before an audience, neither Dada nor surrealism displays consistent regard for characterization. In fact, the very idea of character is ridiculed quite frequently, as in the dramatis personae of Tzara's *Le Cœur à Gaz.* In surrealism, notably, skepticism about the unity of character in theatrical presentation is plain to see. No doubt this reflects, at least in part, Breton's marked dislike for conventional drama and the roles it offers as exemplary. "Oh eternal theatre," he exclaims in his *Introduction au Discours sur le Peu de Réalité* (1927), "you demand that not only to play the role of another but also to dictate this role, we mask ourselves in his resemblance, that the mirror before which we pass send back a foreign image of ourselves. Imagination has every power except that of identifying ourselves in spite of our appearance with a personage other than ourselves." What could be more logical to Breton than this conclusion, which deeply influences the surrealists' conception of drama: "Literary speculation is illicit as soon as it sets up, facing an author, personages he declares to be in the right or in the wrong, after having created them out of nothing"?

In his *Nadja* (1928), Breton confided, "I who never go to the theatre [. . .]." The revised version of his text (1963) changes the phrasing of this admission without betraying its meaning, or suggesting even a minor modification in attitude: "Braving my distaste for the boards [. . .]." The realistic prejudice of conventional drama held as little appeal for him as for Tzara. Indeed Breton preferred to give attention to the "question of reality, in its relationship to possibility, a question which remains the great source of anguish."[10] The general orientation of his thinking thus dictated his views upon theatre. In Paul Palau's *Les Détraquées,* performed at the Théâtre des Deux Masques, following one of the fundamental principles of surrealism Breton was responsive to the "latent content" that he detected behind the "manifest content" of a lurid drama. In his *Anthologie de l'Humour noir,* reviewing various interpretations of Synge's *Playboy of the Western World,* he asserted that a most satisfying explanation of the play rested, to his mind, on the Oedipus complex. He added, "The important thing is that exploration of the 'latent content' leads here to confronting a rosette of meanings tending to have value on several planes at once and to have value for everyone, as if, with *The Playboy,* we were dealing with a precipitate of the universal dream" (p. 347).

Where Breton consistently distinguishes latent content from manifest content, Tzara separates the spirit from technique in a manner that strengthens, rather than weakens, the parallel between Dada and surrealism in matters pertaining to theatre. "It is not a new technique that interests us, but the spirit," averred the Dada leader in a lecture delivered in 1922.[11] From both Dada and surrealism, respect for theatrical form, convention, and technique draws nothing but suspicion, because it endorses submission to temptations of a literary nature. As a result, if we try to evaluate the plays examined below on their literary merits, we are in danger of losing sight of what is essential, as much to practitioners of Dada as to defenders of surrealism. So long as we confine ourselves to estimating the supposed worth of these texts as works of literature, we must expect to find ourselves not only less than pleased with the quality of the material we are handling, but actually engaged in diverting it from its true purpose. For, in surrealism no less than in Dada, the conflict between form and technique, on the one hand, and expression of latent content and a nonliterary anti-artistic spirit, on the other, is resolved invariably to the detriment of formal and technical requirements, and in disregard of aesthetic standards.

10. André Breton, *Anthologie de l'Humour noir* [1940], rev. ed. (Jean-Jacques Pauvert, 1966), p. 468.
11. Tristan Tzara, "Conférence sur Dada," *Sept Manifestes Dada,* p. 140.

The theatregoer tends to find established dramatic forms reassuring and considers technical competence essential in the playwright. But Dada and surrealism believe it salutary to outrage their public by refusing to meet expectations or to abide by specifications. It is not enough to notice that, coming to plays written in the spirit of Dada or surrealism with the hope of seeing some tangible contribution made to the art of the theatre or the technique of dramatic presentation, spectators and readers are more in danger of being disappointed than they are likely to be rewarded. At the very least, Dada and surrealist writing for the stage demonstrates indifference to the medium of the play. In its most aggressive forms, such writing constitutes a frontal attack upon the very idea of dramatic communication. For this reason, it casts the audience in an unaccustomed and disconcerting role.

It was typical of Dada to challenge its audience in direct confrontation. Mounting a Dada spectacle meant putting on a public show. Success depended, therefore, upon the presence of spectators who would find themselves witnessing a performance for which they were unprepared. Surprise was a key element in Dada provocation and could be replaced effectively by no other ingredient. This largely is why the manner of making contact with audiences favored in Dada was destined to have a limited potential. It was just a matter of time before participants ran out of ideas for taking the public off guard. It was equally predictable that, quick to learn from experience, the public soon would be alerted to Dada's methods. Discovering that Dada used terrorist tactics to ridicule good taste, culture, reason, and even the spirit of inquiry, people either stayed away from the next spectacle or returned in a state of mind quite different from before and even prepared, in some cases, to enjoy what was intended to aggravate. There seems little doubt, therefore, that the distinctive posture of the surrealists, who for more than forty years took care to keep their distance from the public, resulted from one of the lessons Dada taught Breton and several of the friends who followed him out of the Dada camp into surrealism.[12]

12. In his *Second Manifeste du Surréalisme*, published in *La Révolution surréaliste* in 1929 and published separately the following year, Breton made the best-known declaration on this subject when he asserted, "We absolutely must stop the public *entering* if we want to avoid confusion." See André Breton, *Manifestes du Surréalisme* (Jean-Jacques Pauvert, n. d. [1962]), p. 211. Cf. Paul Eluard's letter to Breton, September 2, 1931: "We always have in reality done without a public,

So far as they relied upon the audience's trust in the playwright's responsibility to his craft, those undertaking to express the mood of Dada on the stage paid the drama a compliment, in a roundabout fashion. But when doing so, they indicated how little, really, their interest in plays had to do with dramatic ambition. Within the framework of a Manifestation Dada held at the Théâtre de la Maison de l'Œuvre (Salle Berlioz) on March 27, 1920, Tzara's *La Première Aventure céleste de Monsieur Antipyrine* was termed a "double quatrologue." But *Le Serin muet* was presented as a one-act play and *S'il vous plaît* called a comedy. The program of the Festival Dada at the Salle Gaveau on May 26 listed Tzara's *La Deuxième Aventure céleste de Monsieur Antipyrine* without explanatory subtitle, while *Vous m'oublierez* was classified as a sketch. Viewed by traditional standards, classifications in this manner represented an act of literary piracy. Dada-affiliated writers were providing their public with a yardstick for measuring the distance separating their theatre from familiar dramatic forms. So they invited the audience to ponder the significance and implications of that distance, just as the surrealist Georges Hugnet was to do when giving his play *Le Droit de Varech,* published in 1930, the subtitle of melodrama.

In advance of surrealism, Dada had this as one of its essential qualities: it guaranteed individual writers the greatest possible liberty. "The work of art is never beautiful by degrees, objectively, for everyone," declared Tzara's 1918 Dada manifesto. "Criticism is therefore useless, it exists only subjectively, for each person, [. . .]. Thus DADA was born from a need for independence, for mistrust before community of of ideas. Those who belong with us retain their liberty. We recognize no theory."

Although formulating no positive theory of drama, those who elected to speak for Dada or surrealism from the stage necessarily had to face the consequences of having chosen the theatre as their means of expression. Drama poses a special problem for any writer, that of communication with an audience seated beyond the footlights. Release from the necessity to face this problem cannot be obtained by the simple expedient of denying that the audience is present. However grudging it may be, adoption of theatrical form betrays the assumption that an assembled group of people are listening and reacting to what

---

we have done everything to discourage the public!" (cited in Michel Sanouillet, *Dada à Paris* [Jean-Jacques Pauvert, 1965], p. 393).

they hear. The author has agreed to meet his public collectively, to solicit the attention of a number of persons at once. He therefore anticipates certain reactions more or less consciously, and writes accordingly. And so, when one is dealing with a theatrical mode as unconventional and self-consciously anti-conformist as is the case in Dada and surrealism, the question of justification for presentation in dramatic form is of central concern. More especially, one must ask what the author is free to do, what the audience is justified in expecting—and with what results.

To answer this question with some degree of accuracy demands that we raise others: What kind of audience does the playwright foresee? Is it preferably a reading public, making contact with Dada and surrealist works on an individual basis, or rather one brought together for the occasion by a theatrical presentation, benefiting to a greater or lesser extent from the cooperation of a stage designer? How does the Dada or surrealist writer envisage his audience, then? Is it perhaps as a collectivity to be challenged, seduced, or mocked by what he places before them? Does he treat the footlights as an impassible barrier, or as a merely conventional obstacle that, for purposes of his own, he is entitled to ignore or cast down? And when can he be said to betray a need for an audience, indicative of promptings other than those to which he responds knowingly?

Michel Sanouillet remarks that all those participating in Dada and surrealism who became concerned with the problems of the theatre postulated a change of attitude in the public: "The passive consenting spectator was to give way to a hostile participant, constantly fustigated by the author and actors."[13] Although Sanouillet cites only Ribemont-Dessaignes, Tzara, Roger Vitrac, and Antonin Artaud (without, by the way, indicating whether the last two belonged to Dada or to surrealism), his observation is generally valid. Underlying the approach to drama we may regard as typical of Dada and surrealism is a fundamental question: What is to be the nature of communication in the theatre, and to what desired or anticipated effects will it lead? Handling this question calls for more than just being aware, in each case, of admissible philosophical assumptions and projections, or even of tendencies having immediate or long-term technical consequences. It requires in addition some acquaintance with impulses and compulsions that do not

13. Sanouillet, *Dada à Paris*, p. 154.

need to be clear-cut or even readily identifiable, in order to make their influence felt.

However, being sensitive to that influence presents as much difficulty as giving it the credit it deserves. It is in the nature of the texts we are entitled to look upon as providing the theoretical basis of Dada and surrealist writing to shed insufficient light upon areas we may well feel to be most in need of illumination.

True enough, publication of André Breton's *Manifeste du Surréalisme* in 1924 marked an irrevocable break with Dada, not only for Breton himself, but also for those other former participants in Dada who agreed that Dada was now a thing of the past. It laid out relatively clear directives that may seem to have established a reliable basis upon which surrealist writing for the stage can be separated from Dada writing. But when we come to view the plays written in France during the twenties, we are not encouraged to believe that firm distinctions may be drawn with confidence. In one sense, the 1924 manifesto brought nothing that could conceivably challenge the continuity that made Dada a necessary prelude to surrealist activity upon the stage. It certainly did not set out unequivocal recommendations for the guidance of any surrealist eager or willing to write plays. Nor did it establish, either, how much benefit he might derive from what Dada had accomplished in the theatre, any more than it indicated how much he would have to discard as no longer pertinent, in Dada's legacy, to the aims that surrealism was dedicated to pursuing.

As things turned out, then, in the evolution of the theatre in surrealism the year 1924 was by no means as significant as might be expected; or at all events it was significant in a more restricted way than one might anticipate. Later on, of course, the independence of surrealism drama from Dada was not only an indisputable fact but also an undisputed one. The ultimate success of surrealism, in superimposing its requirements upon some of the experimental forms of theatre nurtured in Dada, was never in doubt. Our difficulty does not lie here. When, though, we begin to retrace the course taken by surrealism, in making its demands felt upon the stage, we do not take long to realize that 1924 makes its strongest claim upon our attention as we recognize the following. It simply confirmed certain tendencies noticeable in the French theatre of the early twenties. We cannot advance unless we appreciate that these tendencies reflect intuitions that Breton's first surrealist manifesto had the distinction of codifying into a theory of far-reaching and long-range effect.

The most we can ask of the *Manifesto of Surrealism*, therefore, is to help us detect, after the event, important divergences between Dada and surrealism at the very point, sometimes, where on the surface a parallelism seems to exist between their aims and methods in drama. For example, from their earliest haphazard experiments with playwriting, surrealists showed themselves content with letting their audience hear voices, instead of organizing verbalized feelings and responses in a dialogue meant to convey systematic thoughts and attitudes. But it would be naive to accept the function of surrealist dialogue as indistinguishable from that of dialogue as used in Dada plays like *La Première Aventure céleste de Monsieur Antipyrine* and *Le Serin muet*. Thus we need to ask where, why, and with what results surrealist practice on stage departs from Dada practice. We must determine how surrealists writing drama turn to account some of the liberative forces released by Dada and how needs peculiarly their own lead them to go further, imposing upon the theatre unprecedented demands having noteworthy consequences for the form and intent of drama. In this way only shall we be able to retrace the effects of a profoundly revolutionary spirit that, defying nineteenth-century standards, has left its mark upon the twentieth-century theatre.

Tristan Tzara was born in Romania. The authors of *Cérémonial pour . . . Sade*, Aelberts and Auquier, were born in Belgium; Radovan Ivsic in Yugoslavia. All the other writers whose works are examined here happen to be French. If it could be proved that ethnic diversity would ensure a more revealing variety of material, or would guarantee a more accurate impression of either Dada or surrealism on the stage, there would have been good reason to limit the number of French authors. But neither Dada nor surrealism encourages nationalist bias. Thus, while we might have included, for instance, either Aldo Pellegrini from Argentina, or Enrique Gómez-Correa from Chile,[14]

14. Aldo Pellegrini, *Teatro de la Inestable Realidad* (Buenos Aires: Ediciones del Carro de Tespis, 1964). Enrique Gómez-Correa, *Mandrágora rey de gitanos* (Santiago de Chile: Ediciones Mandrágora, 1954).

doing so would not have brought any significant modification to the image of drama projected by surrealism. Nor would it have affected the conclusions suggested by what we discover from consideration of the authors selected. Meanwhile, geographical distance and language differences tend to erect barriers, however small, between writers like these and contemporary surrealist activity at its focal point, France, as well as between them and the basic documents of surrealism. Except in the case of Ivsic, such barriers cannot be said to exist for those to whom preference goes here.

From Spain Pablo Picasso might have been chosen, and from Venezuela Edmundo Aray.[15] But these are, at most, parasurrealist writers. As such, they are granted no space below. Attention goes instead to authors whose undivided interest in Dada or surrealism is beyond question, during the period when they have felt the temptation of the stage. This means, naturally, excluding Jean Cocteau, considered to be a surrealist only by those who fail to understand why one of the founders of surrealism in France, Philippe Soupault, called him a "trickster."[16] It means, too, omitting Robert Desnos. Although Desnos' play *La Place de l'Etoile* was written in 1927, at the time when he actively participated in surrealism, the only version available is the one that was reworked in 1944 and published in 1945—years after his exclusion from the surrealist camp. For similar reasons, only the early works of Antonin Artaud and Roger Vitrac are pertinent to our discussion—precisely because these men are the two participants in the surrealist movement to whom the theatre meant most.

Readers seeking an analysis of surrealist elements in the early plays of Eugène Ionesco or Fernando Arrabal will have to look elsewhere since, so far as surrealism is concerned, each of these dramatists is a peripheral figure. There is no discussion here, either, of the affinities that may be said to exist between surrealism in the theatre and, for example, the drama of N. F. Simpson. Such matters may be properly said to belong to a study taking its place after this one, which concentrates in the interest of clarity upon the work of writers whose dedication to the aims of Dada or surrealism does not have to be weighed against inclinations or attractions of a diversionary nature. Every one of the

15. Pablo Picasso, *Le Désir attrapé par la Queue* [1941] (Gallimard, 1945). Edmundo Aray, *Twist presidencial* (Caracas: Ediciones del Techo de la Ballena, 1962).

16. See Jean-Marie Mabire, "Entretien avec Philippe Soupault," *Etudes cinématographiques*, No. 38–39 (1965), p. 31.

plays and dramatized texts selected for analysis here has been chosen so that, without distorting or limiting its scope, it may be treated exclusively in relation to the demands made upon the theatre by Dada or surrealism. As a result, in every instance precedence goes legitimately to those demands and to the results they produce. For, so far as they benefit the medium of drama, these texts do so incidentally to the pursuit of Dada or surrealist ends. It is, then, these ends that give significance to theatre in Dada and surrealism, whatever their consequences for drama.

Tristan Tzara

Nothing is more enjoyable
than baffling people.[1]

"Proportionately speaking," remarked Tristan Tzara, looking back to
Dada, "our attempts at renewal were placed on the moral level, poetic
or artistic research, in their close connection with the social order and
with daily comportment."[2] As he indicated on another occasion, Dada
"intended to make of poetry a manner of life much more than the accessory manifestation of intelligence and will." For Dada, "which advocates 'Dadaist spontaneity,' " art was, he said, "one of the forms,
common to all men, of that poetic activity whose deep roots become
one with the primitive structure of affective life."[3]

In the context of Dada the word "spontaneity" must be treated with
caution. It would be unwise to follow the lead Tzara appears to give
without noticing, first, that spontaneity was practiced in Dada only
within preestablished limits and with certain aims in view. "I am writing this manifesto," confessed Tzara in his *Manifeste Dada 1918*, "to
show that you can do opposing actions together, in one fresh breathing, I am against action; for contradiction alone, for affirmation too, I
am neither for nor against and I do not explain because I hate good
sense." Passing over the clumsiness of expression—in 1918 Tzara's command of French left something to be desired—one has no difficulty appreciating that he had definite goals in mind. "Perhaps you will under-

1. Tristan Tzara, "Conférence sur Dada," delivered in Weimar on September
23, 1922, and in Jena on September 25. This lecture was published in *Merz* (Han-
over) in January 1924. See his *Sept Manifestes Dada* (Jean-Jaques Pauvert, n. d.
[1963]), p. 137.
2. Tristan Tzara, *Le Surréalisme et l'Après-Guerre* (Nagel, 1948), p. 18.
3. Tristan Tzara, "L'Art océanien," quoted by René Lacôte in his *Tristan Tzara*
(Seghers, 1952), p. 68.

stand me better," he said in his 1922 lecture in Weimar and Jena, "when I tell you dada is a virgin microbe which penetrates with the insistence of air into all the space that reason has not been able to fill with words and conversations." Behind this colorful explanation lies a firm conviction, revealed during the interview Tzara granted Roger Vitrac in 1923: "There is a very subtle way [. . .] of destroying taste for literature. That is combating it with its own means and in its recipes."[4] The practice of literature serves to express the "will to destroy," which in Dada, Tzara pointed out, was "very much more of an aspiration toward purity and sincerity than the tendency toward a sort of sonant or plastic *inanity*, content with immobility and absence."[5]

Written about forty years after his first play, his last statement may seem to call for circumspect handling. In retrospect, does not Tzara attribute to Dada a higher degree of self-awareness than was present during the years of its most productive activity? Is there not reason to think that, during the fifties, he speaks of Dada as he would like it to have been, in a belated effort to dispel the very impression that, from 1916 onward, Dada had taken every opportunity to give? Limiting our attention to the theatre, should we not be fair in saying that, performance before an audience being an essential feature of Dada spectacle, performance really counted more than communication for Tzara and for those who shared his ideas?

Answers to these questions come soonest with appreciation of the following. During his years as a Dada activist, theatre seemed to Tzara to lend itself to development in two ways: "The theatre. Since it still remains attached to a romantic imitation of life, to an illogical fiction, let us give it all the natural vigor it had to begin with—let it be amusement or poetry."[6] To say that his first plays are, as a result of his preoccupation with poetry, theatre only by default is at best a half-truth. In reality they are extended poetic texts, delivery of which is entrusted to a number of voices so that the poetic monologue becomes, to take the example of *La Première Aventure céleste de Monsieur Antipyrine*, a double quatrologue.

At first sight, Jacques Baron's assessment seems negative: "The theatre of Tristan Tzara isn't theatre. It's anything you want. It's

4. Roger Vitrac, "Tristan Tzara va cultiver ses Vices," *Le Journal du Peuple*, April 14, 1923.
5. Tristan Tzara, introduction to Georges Hugnet, *L'Aventure Dada* (Galerie de l'Institut, 1957), p. 7.
6. Tristan Tzara, "Guillaume Apollinaire," *Dada*, No. 2, December 1917.

words, odd words . . . No it's not theatre, it's cabaret material."[7] One must remember, however, that Dada became articulate in Zurich at the Cabaret Voltaire, opened by Hugo Ball in February 1916, a month before he noted in his diary, "What we call Dada is a harlequinade made of nothingness in which all higher questions are involved, a gladiator's gesture, a play with shabby debris, an execution of postured morality and plenitude."[8] Just as Ball's words testify to the theatrical basis of Dada, so they intimate that theatre could never satisfy the demands of Dada as long as it aimed merely at amusing a cabaret audience. This is why we can look to Baron as a reliable guide, when approaching the Dada plays of Tzara. Quoting the latter's celebrated dictum, "Thought is made in the mouth," Baron declares apropos of his plays, "One can consider that the action, in this theatre you can't make head or tail of, is the 'drôle de drame' of giving birth to language: destruction and reconstruction of the word. That is what the spectator witnesses."

La Première Aventure céleste de Monsieur Antipyrine (The First Celestial Aventure of Mr. Antipyrine) appeared even before the first issue of the magazine entitled *Dada*, under the imprint "Collection Dada."[9] This means that the very first publication sponsored by Dada was a text Michel Sanouillet has described fairly as "a long dialogued piece by Tzara, performed by eight Dadaists, [. . .] so obscure that staging it was a wager."[10]

Those unfamiliar with Tzara's intentions might think he would have taken steps to ensure winning his wager when, four years after writing it, he staged *La Première Aventure* during a Dada demonstration in Paris on March 27, 1920. Yet the set and costumes, devised by Francis Picabia, did nothing to dispose spectators in the play's favor. On the contrary, the magazine *Comœdia* was able to report two days later, "The costumes are surprising, unexpected, ridiculous. They

7. Jacques Baron, *L'An 1 du Surréalisme* suivi de *L'An dernier* (Denoël, 1969), p. 141.
8. Hugo Ball, "Dada Fragments (1916–1917)," trans. Eugene Jolas. These fragments appeared originally in *transition* (Paris), No. 25, fall 1936. Taken from Ball's *Flucht aus der Zeit* (Munich and Leipsig: Dunker & Humblot, 1927), these notes are reproduced in Robert Motherwell, ed., *The Dada Painters and Poets* (New York: Wittenborn, Schultz, 1951). The sentences cited here come under the entry dated June 12, 1916 (p. 51 in Motherwell).
9. Tristan Tzara, *La Première Aventure céleste de Monsieur Antipyrine* avec des bois gravés et coloriés par Marcel Janco (Zurich: Imprimerie J. Heuberger, 1916), "Collection Dada."
10. Michel Sanouillet, *Dada à Paris* (Jean-Jaques Pauvert, 1965), p. 167.

clearly evoke the drawings imagined by madmen and correspond perfectly to the inconceivable text by Mr. Tristan Tzara." As for the set,
it consisted of the following, placed between the audience and the
actors: a bicycle wheel, a few ropes stretched across the stage, and
framed hermetic inscriptions like "Paralysis is the beginning of wis-
dom" and "You hold out your hands and your friends will cut them
off." One might well ask what relevance such a setting could have to
the celestial adventures of a man named after a headache remedy Tzara
used frequently. The author provided no answer within the play. The
only hints he seemed disposed to give were provided afterward, in his
1922 "Lecture on Dada": "What we want now is *spontaneity*. Not because it is more beautiful or better than anything else. But because
everything that comes from us freely, without the intervention of
speculative ideas, represents us. We must accelerate that quality of life
which is spent freely in every corner. Art is not the most precious
manifestation of life. Art does not have that celestial and general value
people are pleased to grant it." Characteristically, this approximate explanation takes a negative form instead of a positive one: Mr Antipyrine's adventures are celestial so far as Tzara's account of them is
anti-artistic.

Reviewing his experiences with *La Première Aventure*, Tzara was
to explain later still, "I invented on the occasion a diabolic machine
composed of a klaxon and 3 successive invisible echoes, for the purpose
of impressing on the minds of the audience certain phrases describing
the aims of Dada. The ones which created the most sensation were:
'Dada is against the high cost of living' and 'Dada is a virgin microbe.' "[11]
By no stretch of the imagination could information of this sort or the
manner in which it was conveyed be said to enlighten the public very
much. At most, Tzara made clear that in the theatre, information
rationally formulated and presented could not be expected of him.

The 1918 Dada manifesto does shed light on his methods, of course.
"Art," affirms the famous declaration that brought Dada to the notice
of André Breton and his friends in Paris, "is a private thing, the artist
makes it for himself; a comprehensible work is a product of journal-
ism." Logic, meanwhile, is "a complication" and "always false," drawing words and notions "toward illusory ends and centres." As it happens, these basic ideas in Tzara's best-known theoretical text simply

11. Tristan Tzara, "Memoirs of Dadaism," in Edmund Wilson, *Axel's Castle*
(New York: Scribners, 1932), p. 317.

reiterate some statements made in a "Manifeste de Monsieur Antipy-rine," published with his first play, two years earlier, after being read at the first Dada show in Zurich (Salle Waag) on July 14, 1916.

Tzara's 1916 manifesto informs us that Dada "remains within the European framework of weaknesses, but we want henceforth to shit in various colors to adorn the zoological garden of art with all the flags of the consulates." But noticeably missing throughout the text is some specific proposal for the theatre, or even a hint of an explanation for *La Première Aventure*. Delivered by Tzara himself in the course of the performance of his play in 1920, the "Manifeste de Monsieur Anti-pyrine" proceeded violently along a destructive course toward a final categorical assertion: "for art isn't serious, I assure you." Its author comes no closer, though, to commenting upon the conception of theatre illustrated in his first play than when stating inconclusively, "We are circus directors and whistle among the winds of fairgrounds, among the convents, prostitutions, theatres, realities, sentiments, restaurants, ohi, hoho, bang, bang."

The exclamatory sounds closing this statement are worth noticing. They echo a passage of totally incomprehensible dialogue in *La Première Aventure*. Occurring very early in the play, the following is typical of these:

> Mr Cricri
>
> Dschiloli Mgabati Baïlunda
>
> La Femme enceinte
>
> Toundi-a-voua
> Soco Bgaï Affahou
>
> Mr Bleubleu
>
> Farafangama Soco Bgaï Affahou[12]

Repetition by Mr Bleubleu (impersonated in 1920 by Philippe Soupault) of a phrase by the Pregnant Woman (played by Céline Arnauld) suggests an exchange from which the audience necessarily must feel excluded. Should a listener be inclined to console himself with the

12. Apparently Henri Béhar has in mind "words" of this kind, exchanged on this occasion between a pregnant woman and two men with outlandish names, when speaking of "the words of African sonority that give a rhythm to *The First Adventure*." Béhar sees them as indicative of Tzara's feeling for African art and of his belief that art is but a game to which its "primitive freedom" must be restored. See Henri Béhar, *Etude sur le Théâtre dada et surréaliste* (Gallimard, 1967), p. 153.

thought that he could hope to follow what they are saying if only acquainted with the language they use, he is soon disillusioned. Immediately after Mr Bleubleu's reply to La Femme enceinte, the following lines are recited by Paul Eluard, as Pipi. They confront us with the realization that Tzara eludes reason even when he avails himself of words for the most part French:

PIPI

amertume sans église allons allons charbon chameau
synthèse amertume sur l'église isise les rideaux
dodododo

As exemplified in *La Première Aventure*, the spontaneity characterizing Dada does not simply authorize articulation of meaningless sounds, to which a greater or lesser emotional value may be lent by the actor's mood as he declaims them. It entails also freeing words from logical sequence in such a manner as to divert attention from sense to sound. Thus *charbon* ("coal") elicits *chameau* ("camel"); a familiar word like *église* ("church") can engender *isise*, a neologism without traceable etymology; and the second syllable of *rideaux* ("curtains") sets off a repeated childish echo: *dodododo* > dodo, dodo ("bye-bye, bye-bye"). The absence of even a single verb or preposition (since we cannot understand *isise*, it is a matter of merely academic interest whether this might be either the one or the other) guarantees phonemes freedom of action. It also releases words from the necessity to respect any preimposed sense progression.

Verbal improvisation is encouraged by elimination of demands that rational sequence normally imposes upon the sentence. The same effect is to be observed in the "Manifeste de Monsieur Antipyrine." In English, Tzara's comments on art sound quite disconnected: "Art was a nut-brown game, children would assemble the words that have a ring at the end, then they would weep and cry the strophe, and put the dolls' booties on it and the strophe became a queen to die a little and the queen became a whale, the children would run until they became out of breath." In French, though, one can detect, toward the end at least, a connecting thread of sound, rather than of meaning.[13] Where

13. "L'art était un jeu noisette, les enfants assemblaient les mots qui ont une sonnerie à la fin, puis ils pleuraient et criaient la strophe, et lui mettaient les bottines des poupées et la strophe devint reine pour mourir un peu et la reine devint baleine, les enfants couraient à perdre haleine."

phonetics not semantics direct the verbal game, reason has no occasion to protest at puzzlement before the outcome.

Underlying the concept of "words in liberty" formulated by Tzara is the belief that, left to themselves, words will produce poetry. And so, where minimal concessions are made to syntactical structure in *La Première Aventure*, the author lets us see he has no confidence in its power to facilitate communication. Pipi's words are followed immediately by Mr Antipyrine's, recited in 1920 by André Breton:

> MR ANTIPYRINE
> Soco Bgaï Affahou
> Zoumbaï zoumbaï zoumbaï zoum
>
> MR CRICRI
> il n'y a pas d'humanité il y a les réverbères et les
> chiens
> dzïn aha dzïn aha bobabo Tyao oahiii hi hii hébooum
> iéha iéha
>
> MR BLEUBLEU
> incontestablement

If Mr Bleubleu gives his assent ("incontestably") to Mr Cricri's declaration that "there is no humanity there are street-lamps and dogs," he expresses no less approval of the nonsensical sounds emitted at the end of Cricri's pseudo-philosophical statement.

Herbert S. Gershman has remarked that Tzara's long poem *L'Homme approximatif* (1931), written during his period of association with surrealism, "presents a syntax and imagery not substantially different from that of *La première aventure céleste de M. Antipyrine* (1916)."[14] The surface impression—especially if one selects a passage from the latter carefully enough—is that nothing need be added to this evaluation. However, consideration of the *function* of syntax in *La Première Aventure* suggests that we ought to go a little further. We have to appreciate that, whereas in his later poetry Tzara will find some advantage in highlighting images by giving attention to syntax,

14. Herbert S. Gershman, "From Dada to Surrealism," *Books Abroad*, 43, 2 (spring 1969), p. 179. For a translation of the text in question see Tristan Tzara, *"Approximate Man" & Other Writings*, trans. Mary Ann Caws (Detroit, Mich.: Wayne State University Press, 1973). Also included in this volume are versions of the *Manifeste Dada 1918*, the *Manifeste de Monsieur Antipyrine*, La Deuxième *Aventure céleste de Monsieur Antipyrine*, and the ninth act of *Mouchoir de Nuages*.

he abides by syntactical usage in his first play only as long as it takes to incite listeners to seek in vain for a logical progression in feeling or thought.

"It was a matter of furnishing proof that poetry was a living form in all aspects, even anti-poetic ones, writing was only its occasional vehicle, by no means an indispensable one, and the expression of that spontaneity which for want of an appropriate qualifier we called Dadaist." Tzara's comment during a radio interview conducted by Georges Ribemont-Dessaignes in May 1950 aimed at giving a general idea of the poetic ambition of Dada.[15] It certainly did not purport to explain the poetic quality of *La Première Aventure céleste de Monsieur Antipyrine,* nor even to make clear why he had thought it worthwhile to cast his first play in dialogue rather than uninterrupted monologue form. Indeed what Tzara said in 1950 did more to relate his use of language—including the function it is made to serve in *La Première Aventure*—to Hugo Ball's ("We have developed the plasticity of the word to a point which can hardly be surpassed"[16] to Kurt Schwitters' in his *Sonata in Primeval Sounds,* [17] and to Ilia Zdanévitch's *zaoum* language.[18] Actually, there are no compelling reasons to believe dramatic arrangement would have appealed to Tzara as anything more than a convenience. Total indifference to character development, plot, and even unification of theme left little to be gained by dramatization, as this generally lends immediacy to a playwright's intentions. Talking of the time when *La Première Aventure* was written, Ribemont-Dessaignes observes pertinently, "General investigation at this moment tends toward recourse to incoherence, the dislocation of language" and speaks of the initiation of "a sort of technique of scandal."[19]

15. Cited in Lacôte, *Tristan Tzara,* p. 19.
16. See Ball, "Dada Fragments," entry dated June 18, 1916 (p. 52 in Motherwell).
17. Part of Schwitters' *Sonate in Urlauten* is reproduced in Kate Trauman Steinitz, *Kurt Schwitters: A Portrait from Life* (Berkeley and Los Angeles: University of California Press, 1968), p. 76.
18. According to Georges Ribemont-Dessaignes, prefacing Iliazd's *Ledentu le Phare, poème dramatique en Zaoum* (Editions du 41°, 1922), *zaoum* is "a language Russian in appearance, with words and onomatopoeia such that they allow of being the sense support for several words of neighboring sonorities [. . .]. In zaoum, each word carries, more or less emphasized, several meanings of differing order and planes, concrete or abstract, particular or general." For further information see Elizabeth Klosty Beaujour, "Zaum," *Dada/Surrealism,* 1972 (second issue, unnumbered), pp. 13–18.
19. Georges Ribemont-Dessaignes, *Déjà Jadis ou Du Mouvement dada à l'Espace abstrait* (Julliard, 1958), p. 56.

Having thrown in his lot with the surrealists, Tzara subsequently drew a distinction between the Cubist tendency to express "an immutable, static or eternal beauty," against which Dada reacted, and the trend Dada preferred to follow: to "bring out its *occasional* nature, due to *circumstances* and in which true merit lies in true integration into *present time*."[20] We learn from Tzara's 1931 essay that poetry was defined in Dada "as a reality that is not valid outside its becoming." Beneath this pretentious claim lay the belief that spontaneity, entailing freedom from all logical and reasonable restraint, eliminates in Dada the risk of producing a static form of beauty. Poetry *"tends to become* an activity of the spirit," argues Tzara. "It *tends to deny* poetry-means-of-expression." It can become solely an activity of the spirit "only by disengaging itself from language or from its form." True, as a footnote indicates, poetry as activity of the spirit embraces painting and sculpture and—Tzara is willing to admit by this time—even the surrealist objects projected by Breton and Dali, no less than written texts. All the same, his comments place the dramatized verbal experiments of *La Première Aventure* in an especially significant light. They bid us notice that "what touches on language was for Dada a problem and a constant concern."

Béhar sees *La Première Aventure* as "a striking example of poetry 'activity of the spirit' " (p. 151). Apparently without false modesty, Tzara expresses himself more cautiously. Dada, he explains, "seeks an issue in action and more especially in poetic action which often is identified with gratuitousness." He quotes as examples the announcement of a series of Dada visits to sites in Paris ironically selected for their lack of intrinsic interest (a trip to the church of Saint-Julien-le-Pauvre took place in 1921) and the announcement of ridiculous public events (members of the Dada circle once promised to have their heads shaved in public). Then he continues, "But another current, less demonstrative, came into being and developed rapidly. I have given only a sketchy idea of it in *The First Celestial Aventure of Mr. Antipyrine* (1916) and it was only later that we began in a consistent manner placing side by side words apparently having no meaning. These words being most often devoid of grammatical relationship (elliptical style), it was natural that a general tendency assumed outline in the form of an organized struggle with logic."

20. Tristan Tzara, "Essai sur la Situation de la Poésie," *Le Surréalisme au service de la Révolution,* No. 4, December 1931.

La Première Aventure is testimony to a conviction mentioned in Tzara's "Essai sur la Situation de la Poésie"; "I believed then that one could take away the meanings of words and that the latter could act in a poem simply by their evocative force." The experiment with language represented by his first play—examining "the consequences to be deduced from the capacity to flee the significance of words"—may well have seemed to him, as he reports, to become inoperative as soon as the poetic text had been reduced to a succession of words. Nevertheless, "If Dada was not to be able to give language the slip, it certainly established the unrest language caused and the shackles it placed upon the liberation of poetry."

Surely *La Première Aventure* can be viewed most productively in the perspective that Tzara's comments suggest we adopt. We should regard this play as having somewhat more to tell about its author's approach to language through Dada than about his general ideas on the theatre. At all events, treating *La Première Aventure* in any other way poses more problems than it solves.[21] As it is, Tzara still does not make it easy for anyone to trace meanings or preoccupations here, even where he seems to offer a few concessions in the form of grammatically consecutive statements.

For the most part, Mr Antipyrine's last speech is uninterrupted by phonic explosions:

> there is a great aureola where the worms move around in silence
> for the worms and other animals also have troubles
> pains and aspirations
> look at the windows that roll up like giraffes
> turn and multiply hexagons climb tortoises
> the moon swells marsupial and becomes a dog

It ends with the following words:

> a bad fellow is dead somewhere
> and we let the brains go on
> the mouse runs diagonally across the sky
> the mustard flows from an almost crushed brain
> we have become street-lamps

21. Thus, apparently unwilling to accept the consequences of his discovery that in Tzara's first play, "Words are produced freely, in defiance of all coherent organization, of logic and syntax," Béhar continues vaguely, "Although one can find in them a general meaning, or rather an order of preoccupations, here replies are not linked, do not respond to one another" (p. 151). One would be more impressed by such a reading if it specified a meaning, or at least elucidated some order of preoccupations.

"Street-lamps" is repeated nine times, before the play comes to a halt on Mr Antipyrine's laconic statement, "then they went away." In *La Première Aventure* Tzara does not undertake to trace a progression from the chaos of articulate sounds to the clarity of logical discourse. Instead, demonstrating in his closing section the breakdown of Mr. Antipyrine's supposed effort to communicate rationally, he practices the devaluation of conventional language. Grammar is not proof against poetry here, any more than poetry is circumscribed by grammatical form. We hear gibberish become a mode of communication between those performing before us. At the same time we witness the disintegration of language as we know it when, with every repetition, "des réverbères" loses more of its power to hold our respect as a linguistic sign and, little by little, is reduced in significance.

Comparing the Festival Dada held on May 26, 1920, and the Dada demonstration at the Maison de l'Œuvre the preceding March 27, Michel Sanouillet points out, among other things, that in the Festival the sketch *Vous m'oublierez* by Breton and Soupault corresponded to the same authors' *S'il vous plaît* and that Tzara's *La Deuxième Aventure céleste de Monsieur Antipyrine* "replaced" *La Première Aventure:* "Undeniably there was repetition," he asserts (p. 175). His observation puts us in mind of Breton's recollection: "Each time a Dada demonstration is foreseen—naturally by Tzara who doesn't tire of them—Picabia brings us together in his drawing room and *calls on* us, one after the other, to have some *ideas* for this demonstration. In the end the harvest isn't very abundant. The pièce de résistance will inevitably be the first or second . . . or n^{th} *Adventure of Mr Antipyrine* by Tzara interpreted by his friends eternally bundled up in tall cylinders of Bristolboard (when all else failed, that was his favorite 'idea,' Zurich must have been amused by it.)"[22] Unfortunately Breton's irony is prejudicial. It communicates the inaccurate impression that *La Première Aventure* had been performed in Zurich prior to presentation in Paris. More than this, it casts an unfavorable light on the second and last *Aventure*.

22. André Breton, *Entretiens 1913–1952* (Gallimard, 1952), p. 58. Breton's statement gives a hint of the acrimony that eventually sent him, Tzara, and Picabia their separate ways. Another clue is to be found in Picabia's remark, "I'd had enough of living among a gang who, having no ideas of their own, spent their time asking these of me" (cited in Ribemont-Dessaignes, *Déjà Jadis,* p. 100).

Whatever his opinion in the fifties, by the way, Breton did not object in 1920 to lending his impressive voice to the role of Oreille ("Ear") in *La Deuxième Aventure*. Nor is there any record of his having protested against participating in the following "conversation" with Ribemont-Dessaignes, impersonating Le Cerveau désintéressé ("The Disinterested Brain"):

THE DISINTERESTED BRAIN
sleep the general the heart carom
the grape tobacco the stomach nostrils with gray hair
the fresh pins
the testicular soap in the coffee
a rib of motor with nuts
and the frozen brain of the amorous aviator
> EAR
evacuate the cardiac roots of sickness eclipse and jewels
repertory
binoculars
anonymous ice
roseola
necktie of the streams and double assed zibeline[23]

Breton implies that *La Deuxième Aventure* prolongs the first and could easily be followed by a third or fourth episode. Clearly, though, he does not intend any allusion to plot continuity. While three of the actors beside Breton himself are the same in both plays, they all have different parts in the second. Eluard is now Mr Absorption; Aragon, not Breton, is Mr Antipyrine; and Ribemont-Dessaignes is no longer Mr Boumboum. In their new roles, they show no sign of recalling anything from *La Première Aventure*. There is no observable continuation of theme. The only constants are those that acquaintance with Tzara's approach to theatre teaches us to look out for: disinterest in character and plot development, disregard for logic, and pursuit of poetic effect beyond the range of reasonable, grammatical discourse. So far as making his position clear on these matters is still a fundamental concern, Tzara's second play necessarily marks no development beyond the first. When a writer's point of view is predominantly nega-

23. *La Deuxième Aventure céleste de Monsieur Antipyrine* was published in two parts: in *Littérature* (first series, No. 14, June 1920), and in Francis Picabia's magazine *391* (No. 14, November 1920). The complete text, running to only sixteen pages, was not published until 1938, in a printing of 125 copies, by the Editions des Réverbères.

tive, progress becomes incompatible with central aims. By the same token, he risks disappointing observers who anticipate seeing him "go further," even though they have no definite idea what direction he now could take. Presumably, this in part is why Henri Béhar finds *La Deuxième Aventure* inferior to *La Première Aventure* (p. 158).

Béhar contends that Tzara's second play "betrays a certain lassitude" (p. 159). One might argue, conversely, that fatigue inhibits expression less than the author's increased command of the French language, acquired between 1916 and 1920. At all events, even if we rule out the possibility that lack of familiarity with the mechanism of the French language helped Tzara find freedom in linking words, against custom and usage, when writing *The First Adventure*, we cannot but notice how much more supple is the language of *The Second Adventure*.

Between Tzara's first play and the following one, there is another small but noteworthy distinction. In the former, dialogue is restricted to exchanging statements that rarely bear visible relationship to one another. In *La Deuxième Aventure*, as the passage cited above testifies, one speaker may not only take up something another has said but actually complete his statement for him. The end result, however, is still confirmation of Tzara's negative attitude toward theatrical forms: increased linguistic flexibility only emphasizes his contempt for the conventional use of dialogue. When he simply distributes what has to be said among half a dozen characters, allocating his material haphazardly without perceptible purpose among a number of inconceivable figures, he makes his purpose abundantly clear.

The framework of dialogue is consistently used as a convenience, without acknowledgment of dramatic necessity. New verbs are tried out (Monsieur Absorption: "I already myself;" Oreille: "he alreadies himself;" [. . .] Monsieur Antipyrine: "I exportation"). Sounds are repeated with bewildering insistence: in reply to Mr Saturne's question "do you have frogs in your shoes?" Oreille repeats the letter *B* twenty-eight times in succession. Undismayed, Mr Absorption follows his own disjointed train of thought: "the horse tongs / of saturated ostrich sex organs." A few moments later Saturne is repeating the word "decidedly" nine times, prior to declaring "the uncovered forehead of the sun / naturally naturally." Later still, all six characters recite the word "tree" six times in unison. The barbaric sounds of *La Première Aventure* have virtually disappeared, though. Mr. Antipyrine unburdens himself of two rhythmic cryptic phrases: "tzaca tzac tzaca tzac tzaca

tzac tzaca tzac glisse" and "dadadi dadadi dadadi moumbinba dadadi."
But only one other character, The Disinterested Brain, resorts to even
one utterance of this type. After pedantically correcting Ear's pronun-
ciation of "feldspath" ("it's pronounced feeeeeeeldspaaaaaath"), The
Disinterested Brain gives vent to the exclamation, "badabà badabà
badabà gorille," which disturbs Mr Saturne no more than Ear's repetition of *B* distracts Mr Absorption.

As in *The First Adventure*, in *The Second* the important role of
humorous effects of this sort is to help discredit familiar language and
the conventional thought processes that language traditionally serves to
express. As a result it contributes to making wreckage of the convention of theatre and to directing attention away from established forms,
toward drama as amusement, as play.

Tzara's success in pursuing his subversive ends may be measured
fairly accurately from the response of his audience to *La Deuxième
Aventure*. Some reflection of that response is to be detected in a press
clipping, cited by Béhar (p. 159), dated June 6, 1920: "Phantasmal
beings dressed in black paper, with headgear of white cardboard cowls
line up on the platform. Their orchestra leader is better adorned: his
cowl is an expressive face on which are stuck a box of *Luculus* noodles
and a gray-gloved hand [. . .]. All the spectres begin to read their
parts [. . .] the listeners laugh, bark, thump walking sticks, stamp
their feet."

While the first *Aventure* had bemused its audience, the second
drew retaliation; as indeed did the whole Festival Dada, put on in an
eminently respectable concert hall, the Salle Gaveau. Perpetuated by
Breton and Ribemont-Dessaignes no less than by Tzara, tradition has it
that during the intermission certain members of the audience with-
drew to purchase steak for use as ammunition against those on stage.
Press notices do not confirm this, but there is evidence enough that a
sizeable number of spectators had had the foresight to arm themselves
with fruit and vegetables and saw the occasion as an opportunity to
practice catcalls and animal imitations. There are indisputable signs that
a significant percentage of those attending the Dada Festival came prepared to protest, regardless of the nature of the spectacle. Thus the
violence of their reaction is not to be attributed solely to the provocation given by the program of May 26 or by any part of that program,
either *La Deuxième Aventure* or *Vous m'oublierez*. It expressed, rather,
accumulated frustration with Dada's methods; that is, with methods

designed to induce frustration. In other words, to many of those watching and listening, *La Deuxième Aventure* appeared just what it was intended to be: further proof of the iconoclastic approach evidenced in *La Première Aventure*.

Opinions differ about Tzara's third play, *Le Cœur à Gaz* (*The Gas Heart*).[24] Recalling that this work was performed for the first time at the Galerie Montaigne in Paris, after the intermission during the first Soirée Dada (June 10, 1921), Sanouillet describes it as "termed 'Pièce de Théâtre' out of derision, and an excellent example indeed of Dadaist 'theatre' " (p. 283). In so doing, he comes close to appreciating how provocative was the statement made by Tzara, when presenting his play: "this is the only and the greatest three-act swindle of the century, it will bring luck only to industrialized imbeciles who believe in the existence of geniuses. The performers are asked to give the play the attention due a masterpiece of the force of Macbeth and Chantecler, but to treat the author, who is not a genius, with little respect and to take note of the lack of seriousness in the text which brings no innovation to the technique of the theatre."

For Jacques Baron, *Le Cœur à Gaz* is "nothing more or less than a poem by Tzara set in dialogue, and a perfectly dishevelled dialogue, if I may say so" (p. 145). Baron reports that Zdanévitch discovered coherent action in the play, "to the amazement of its author." Quoting the latter, Baron recalls, " 'It's extraordinary,' he used to say, 'when I hear Iliazd comment on my play, I have the impression I've written

24. *Le Cœur à Gaz* was originally published in the third issue of the magazine *Der Sturm* (Berlin) in March 1922 (pp. 33–42). A three-act play, it was published in France in May 1946, running to forty-four printed pages in the G.L.M. edition.
    Leonard Cabell Pronko dismisses *Le Cœur à Gaz* as " 'cute' " (*Avant-Garde: The Experimental Theater in France* [Berkeley and Los Angeles: University of California Press, 1962], p. 10), while Martin Esslin sees it as "a piece of 'pure theatre' that derives its impact almost entirely from the subtle rhythms of its otherwise nonsensical dialogue, which, in the use of the clichés of polite conversation, foreshadows Ionesco" (*The Theatre of the Absurd* [1961], rev. ed. [New York: Doubleday, Anchor, 1969], p. 320). Michael Benedikt inclines to agree with Pronko. Qualifying *Le Cœur à Gaz* as "a thoroughly innovative work," he nevertheless remarks that it "strikes us more with the force of pure visual and verbal spectacle than as what—even in the light of much later developments—can easily be considered theatre" (introduction to Michael Benedikt and George Wellwarth, *Modern French Theatre: The Avant-Garde, Dada, and Surrealism* [New York: Dutton, 1964], p. xxii).

Romeo and Juliet.' 'Perhaps,' Zdanévitch added, 'but there is something of *A Midsummer Night's Dream* too.'" On balance, though, there appears little reason to contest Sanouillet's evaluation of Tzara's third play as "something dashed off with no pretension other than to be aggressive and written in a few days entirely in Dadaist euphoria" (p. 383).

Putting on *Le Cœur à Gaz* in 1921, Tzara himself took the role of Sourcil ("Eyebrow"). Soupault was Oreille; Ribemont-Dessaignes, Bouche ("Mouth"); and Aragon, Œil ("Eye"). The cast was completed by Théodore Fraenkel as Nez ("Nose") and Benjamin Péret as Cou ("Neck"), both soon to be as active in the cause of surrealism as Aragon and Soupault.[25]

Tzara's prefatory announcement begins with some rudimentary but disconcerting stage directions: "NECK is above the stage, NOSE facing him above the public. All the other characters enter and leave *ad libitum.* The heart heated by gas chews slowly, much moving about, [. . .]."[26] From his vantage point, Nose can challenge those who come and go on stage: "A bit more life over there, on the stage," he exclaims at one point. But he provides a less than reliable link between audience and performers. When he asks where Ear is going, he receives a reply that, although nonsensical, still seems meant as a response. A moment later, though, to Nose's question about what he is eating, Ear replies irrelevantly, "More than 2 years have passed, alas, since I began the hunt. But you see one gets used to one's fatigue and as the dead man would be tempted to live, the death of the magnificent emperor proves it, the importance of things decreases—every day—a little . . ." Later still, Nose's cry, "Hey over there, sir," elicits nothing more from Ear than an echoing "hey," repeated thirteen times, while it apparently

25. Breton took no part in the Soirée. He had already begun to tire of Dada under Tzara's leadership. During a public attack upon Maurice Barrès, in the form of a mock trial held in May 1921, Breton as presiding judge had chided the witness Tzara for frivolity. "Question: 'Is the witness bent on seeming a perfect imbecile or is he trying to get himself confined?' Answer: 'Yes I am bent on passing myself off as an imbecile, but I don't try to escape from the asylum in which I spend my life.'"

26. "COU est au-dessus de la scène, NEZ vis-à-vis au-dessus du public. Tous les personnages entrent et sortent *ad libitum.* Le cœur chauffé au gaz mache [*sic*] lentement, grande circulation; [. . .]." As translated by Benedikt, in *Modern French Theatre,* these lines run: "Neck stands downstage, Nose opposite, confronting the audience. All the other characters enter and leave as they please. The gas heart walks slowly around, circulating widely; [. . .]." Apparently reading *marche* into Tzara's inaccurate spelling of *mâche,* Benedikt misses, among other things the word play based on the phrase *se mâcher le cœur,* to "eat one's heart out."

launches Neck upon the mock sentimental refrain that is his only contribution in the first act: "Mandarine et blanc d'Espagne / je me tue Madeleine Madeleine." Sometimes Nose's comments ridicule those of the Greek Chorus, as when he remarks time after time, "Oh, yes," regardless of the nonsense he has just heard, or when he greets someone else's lines with the similarly repeated "Yes I know." Addressing Eyebrow-Tzara, he observes, "It's charming, your play, but we don't understand anything in it," receiving the answer: "There's nothing to understand, everything is easy to do and take./The bottle-neck of thought from which will emerge the whip. The whip will be a myosotis./The myosotis a living ink-well. The ink-well will dress the doll."

The most striking feature of *Le Cœur à Gaz*, for Henri Béhar, is Tzara's use of repeated phrases. These are not exactly the "clichés of polite conversation" that abound here, as Esslin has noted. Nor are they phrases of the kind with which Eye opens the play: "Statues jewels grilled meat," repeated five times, succeeded very soon by "Cigar button nose," recited six times, as though a fitting introduction to the next statement: "he loved a stenographer." Béhar credits Tzara with innovation ("for himself and for the theatre in general") in systematically repeating commonplaces. He speaks too of "a sort of ritual" (p. 160), without acknowledging his debt to Benedikt, who has written, "While this ceremonial use of the banal is prophetic of the domestic verbal delirium employed by later writers especially for satiric purposes, the effect here is that of a concatenation of colliding chants, or of ritual" (p. xxii). Neither Béhar nor Benedikt, though, explains what is to be understood by ritual in the context of *Le Cœur à Gaz*.

Absent from the comments critics have made about the play is stress upon a fact that surely is not too elementary to notice. The action has hardly commenced when the following exceptionally rational exchange is heard:

> MOUTH
> The conversation is becoming boring, isn't it?
> EYE
> Yes, isn't it?
> MOUTH
> Very boring, isn't it?
> EYE
> Yes, isn't it?

MOUTH

Naturally, isn't it?

EYE

Evidently, isn't it?

MOUTH

Boring, isn't it?

This conversation is prolonged with only slight variations. And it recurs, practically word for word, as the climax to the first act, with Eye speaking Mouth's original lines, and Mouth repeating Eye's. Interrupting dialogue following the pattern of poetic irrationality laid down in the Antipyrine plays, Tzara speaks out clearly, but only to provoke his audience, to show he is fully aware that they will find incomprehensible a text in which "there's nothing to understand." So as to rule out misunderstanding, he entrusts discussion of how boring his drama is to Eye and Mouth, thus evaluating its anti-dramatic nature on the visual and auditory levels at the same time.

Nose, we see, is unable to draw meaning from what he hears:

MOUTH

We'll make of it a fine cloth for the crystal dress.

NOSE

You mean "despair gives you explanations of his exchange hearts."

MOUTH

No I don't mean anything. A long time ago I put what I had to say in a hatbox.

Nose's failure to impose sense upon what is said (even a sense that is his own form of nonsense) confirms that *Le Cœur à Gaz* was conceived as an act of defiance directed against the mode of communication theatre conventionally exemplifies. The value of Tzara's undertaking rests entirely upon his anticipation of opposition from the audience, who will find themselves faced with a play that, aiming to alienate, aggressively flaunts its purpose, to the greater displeasure of the spectators.

An essential feature of *Le Cœur à Gaz*, Nose's inability to mediate between the audience and those on stage, is indicative of the author's posture before his public. The play fulfills the function for which it was conceived when people watching it feel excluded, denied the chance to participate either intellectually or emotionally in what is happening before them. Everything hinges upon the author's contempt for the traditional theatre and upon the care he takes to insist that the effects obtained do not result simply from inexperience, ineptitude, or accident. This is to say that *Le Cœur à Gaz* was written for an unsympathetic, or even hostile audience, whom Tzara intended to antagonize, not placate.

To stage the play before an approving or even indulgent audience would seem to be inconsistent, therefore, inviting reactions in total contradiction with those it originally was supposed to provoke. A conversation such as the one reproduced above, between Eye and Mouth, loses its point once it is overheard by a public ready and willing to condone the use of dialogue of this nature. Apparently, though, Tzara saw nothing wrong with putting on *Le Cœur à Gaz* before spectators watching and listening in quite a different state of mind from that of persons who had seen it during the 1921 Soirée Dada. The prospectus of a program known as the *Soirée du Cœur à Barbe*, to be held on July 6 and 7, 1923, announced the following: music by Auric, Milhaud, Satie, and Stravinsky, to be performed for the first time; poems by Apollinaire, Baron, Cocteau, Eluard, and Tzara; a *zaoum* poem by Zdanévitch; dance by Lizica Codréano; new films by Man Ray, Hans Richter, and Charles Sheeler; an address ("Wipe your Nose") by Ribemont-Dessaignes. The presentation was to be completed by a performance of *Le Cœur à Gaz*, directed by Yssia Siderski, with sets by N. Granovsky, and costumes by Sonia Delaunay-Terck and Victor Barthe. None of the original cast was scheduled to take part. The role of Eyebrow was entrusted to a professional actor, while Jacqueline Chaumont of the Odéon Theatre was to play Mouth, and Saint-Jean, also of the Odéon, was to be Ear. Jacques Baron assumed the role of Neck; René Crevel, another future surrealist, was to be Eye. Pierre de Massot was assigned the part of Nose.

More noteworthy than the change of sex granted Mouth was the action Tzara took in availing himself of the services of professional actors and allowing his play to receive the attention of stage and costume designers. Sanouillet reports that the task of organizing the program for the *Soirée du Cœur à Barbe* fell "naturally" to Tzara (p. 380).[27] As early as the beginning of 1923, indeed, the latter started

27. Georges Hugnet presents the facts somewhat differently, suggesting that

looking for an auditorium "big enough to hold the crowd which, according to him," Sanouillet tells us, "the announcement of a Dada super-demonstration would not fail to attract." Tzara's connections with Zdanévitch made available the Théâtre Michel and the services of the Tchérez theatrical troupe. Recalling this, Sanouillet observes apropos of Le Cœur à Gaz, "To bring to its presentation more intentions than the author had when he conceived it was to mistake the meaning of the play. This however was the trap into which actors, decorators and stage director of the Tchérez company fell [. . .]" (p. 384).

It is not easy to accept the implication that, whether out of indifference or for some other reason, Tzara remained quite unaware of the manner in which Zdanévitch's friends were going about staging his play and so could be relieved of responsibility for the performance that took place on July 6. What really matters, however, is less whether Tzara really was accountable than this: Breton held him so, and therefore determined to protest. Details of Breton's intervention, no sooner had the play begun, are to be found in the eye-witness account supplied by Georges Hugnet. Climbing on the stage, Breton is said to have laid about him with a cane, reportedly breaking Pierre de Massot's arm.[28] After Breton and his active supporters Aragon and Péret had been roughly expelled, Eluard—who had already objected to inclusion of poems by Cocteau—disrupted activities until overcome by superior numbers; not, however, until he had qualified to receive a claim for damages subsequently brought, with complete success, by Tzara.[29]

Zdanévitch took the initiative in organizing a performance of Le Cœur à Gaz. See Hugnet, L'Aventure Dada, p. 97.

28. See Hugnet, L'Aventure Dada, p. 98. If this detail (included also in Maurice Nadeau's version of what occurred, Histoire du Surréalisme [Editions du Seuil, 1945], p. 54) is true, then one can only marvel at Pierre de Massot's dedication, continuing as he did in his role of Nose after order had been restored. De Massot, by the way, was to write a warm tribute to Breton after the surrealist leader's death, remarking of Breton's commitment to Dada, "He was to give himself to it entirely until the day when Dada, cutting a dogmatic figure, was in danger of becoming what always horrified him: a literary school" (André Breton le Septembrisseur [Eric Losfeld, 1967], no pagination).

29. Benedikt's version of the incident is fictitious: "At its [The Gas Heart's] première with professional actors, in 1923, the poet Paul Eluard, representing Tzara's literary camp, came to blows on the stage with André Breton, the leader of a new rival literary group which was soon to become, under his leadership, the Surrealist movement" (p. xxii). Sanouillet appeals to our sense of righteous indignation when inviting condemnation of Eluard (p. 384). He passes over

Reviewing the incident, Ribemont-Dessaignes asks in *Déjà Jadis*, "But was Dada in question? It hardly seems so. One must rather accuse the excesses of human nature, the animal counterbalancing the angel! A circus spectacle rather than a tragedy" (p. 105). Beyond doubt, growing out of causes that need not concern us here, personal antagonism did influence both the form of Breton's protest and the violence which greeted it. But, as was usually the case with Breton, a matter of principle was involved, so important as to give the *Soirée du Cœur à Barbe* historical significance far more than mere anecdotal interest.

The *Soirée du Cœur à Barbe* differed from previous Dada demonstrations in being an organized spectacle. It was in fact conceived for presentation before a passive or at least consenting audience. Repeating *Le Cœur à Gaz* within two years of its original performance, Tzara could hardly have counted on taking the public off guard the second time. Hence its 1923 revival betrayed the cause in which the play had been written. Moreover, when, to say the very least, Dada antitheatre became semiprofessional theatre, staged before spectators even a little predisposed in its favor, it changed disturbingly in character. From Breton's standpoint, it now appeared, instead of using the theatre to achieve Dada aims, Tzara was serving the theatre and accepting the compromises entailed in doing so.

Alluding to these compromises, on August 4, 1923, Roger Vitrac wrote an important article for *Les Hommes du Jour*, calling it "Guet-Apens" ("Snare"): "It is advisedly that we use this title, for the battle of the Michel Theatre was no accident and not born of fortuitous circumstances, but was perfectly and fully premeditated." Remarking that *Le Cœur à Gaz* had been written "in a few minutes" for the Galerie Montaigne demonstration, Vitrac went on, "That is to say, this play was not one." Recalling the absence of costumes and stage sets when the play was put on the first time, he referred to Aragon, Eluard, and Péret, who took part in it: "These men at the time considered *The Gas Heart* not as a poetic or theatrical work, but as a part of the demonstration fit simply to make the public mad." In addition he pointed out:

> If Mr Tristan Tzara felt obligated to dress this play with costumes by Mme Delaunay and Cubist stage sets, if he wanted to

Tzara's actions of calling the police and instituting legal proceedings against Eluard —something for which Breton never forgave Tzara.

present it to the public in a pot-pourri of works by so-called "modern" celebrities, it was with an indisputable artistic purpose to which his former friends could not be party. They had only one means at their disposal: not only to sabotage the performance but to make their dissent public and irremediable. The best way was to put Dada in the auditorium and to provoke the author and actors systematically. This is what they did.

After what happened with *Le Cœur à Gaz* on July 6, the management of the Théâtre Michel deemed it wise to cancel the second and final performance, scheduled for the following day. But if Breton and his associates hoped they had taught Tzara a lesson, they did not have to wait long to be disabused. On May 17, 1924, a new Tzara play was staged at the Théâtre de la Cigale, during one of Count Etienne de Beaumont's Soirées de Paris. Called *Mouchoir de Nuages* (*Handkerchief of Clouds*), it was to be published the following November, just after Breton's *Manifeste du Surréalisme,* and at a time when, historically, Dada was definitely a thing of the past.[30]

Sanouillet praises *Mouchoir de Nuages* as being "fairly surprising in tone and scenic conception, full of fancy and Dadaist humor" (p. 389). Béhar faithfully echoes his comment: "The interest of this tragedy is not so much in the subject as in the scenic conception and in the Dadaist humor with which it is stamped" (p. 164). True enough, examination of the text reveals that Tzara's fourth play warrants mention under the heading of formal inventiveness. In its printed version, *Mouchoir de Nuages* is preceded by a prefatory note. Here, after a flattering word for Beaumont (who evidently bore, among other expenses, that of having the actresses dressed by Lanvin), Tzara's note offers these instructions for staging the play:

> The scene is a closed space, like a box, from which no actor can get out. All 5 surfaces are of the same color. At the rear, at a certain height, a screen that indicates the place of the action, midstage enlarged reproductions of illustrated postcards, on rollers that a stagehand unrolls as the acts proceed, without hiding himself from the spectators.
>
> In the middle of the stage a platform. To left and right chairs, dressing-tables for making up, the properties and costumes for the

---

30. Tristan Tzara, *Mouchoir de Nuages,* Antwerp: Editions Sélection (reprinted from the magazine *Sélection*), 1924, subsequently published in Paris by Editions de la Galerie Simon in April 1925.

actors. The actors are in sight throughout the play. When they are not performing, they turn their backs on the public, dress or talk among themselves.

The acts are played out on the platform, the commentaries off the platform. At the end of each act, the light changes suddenly so as to shine only on the commentators; the actors are no longer in their roles and leave the platform. The light changes suddenly also at the end of each commentary and the spotlights above and at the side shine only on the platform. The electricians and lights are on the stage.

Two assistants place the properties on the platform or remove them.

Since Tzara's concept, though interesting, is hardly of startling originality, it comes as quite a surprise to hear Louis Aragon give it the highest praise: "I have already said elsewhere and I insist on repeating that this play is, after *Ubu Roi* and *Les Mamelles de Tirésias,* the most remarkable image of drama in modern art."[31] To place *Mouchoir de Nuages* beside the works for which Alfred Jarry and Guillaume Apollinaire are remembered as having made an indispensable contribution to the avant-garde theatre of the twentieth century is a bold gesture on Aragon's part. It is also a somewhat misleading one, since its author does not go on to vindicate his claim that Tzara's play is especially important for modern drama. Instead, Aragon concentrates upon a feature of *Mouchoir de Nuages* that does not manifest itself before the eleventh act.

According to Tzara's own description, his play is an "ironic tragedy or a tragic farce in fifteen short acts, separated by fifteen commentaries." Its action "belongs to the realm of the serialized story and the novel."[32] At the beginning of Act XI the following conversation takes place between four of the commentators:

> A
>
> Excuse me, here we don't understand at all what our heroes are doing in the Avenue de l'Opéra.
>
> E
>
> Oh yes you do, I've already told you, they are going to the theatre.

31. Louis Aragon, "Petite Note sur les Collages chez Tristan Tzara et ce qui s'en suit," in his *Les Collages* (Hermann, 1965), p. 144.
32. Tristan Tzara, "Le Secret de *Mouchoir de Nuages,*" *Integral* (Bucharest), No. 2 (April 1, 1925), p. 7.

D

It isn't absolutely necessary for them to go along the Avenue de l'Opéra.

C

After all, that's right, this scene could have been left out.

It transpires that "our heroes" are going to watch a performance of *Hamlet,* represented by three abridged scenes transcribed in Act XII, apparently from the slightly modified version of Jean-François-Victor Hugo's nineteenth-century translation.

Incorporation of Shakespeare's text constitutes something Aragon calls the technique of collage in Tzara's play. It is to this that Aragon wants to direct attention. Collage excites his admiration because it functions in *Mouchoir de Nuages* not merely as a verbal borrowing, but also to affect subsequent plot development. After the audience has been permitted to hear material taken from *Hamlet,* one of the commentators speaks of the Poet whose adventures give *Mouchoir de Nuages* a measure of focus, explaining in Act XII, "What did he want? He wanted, this way, the hook of his lie to catch the carp of truth. He brought the Banker and his wife to the theatre to catch them in the trap."[33] All the same, whether or not we incline to share Aragon's admiration for what Tzara accomplishes by his use of collage, we can hardly say that the playwright's achievement has much meaning in the context of Dada.

Béhar is accurate enough when declaring *Mouchoir de Nuages* to be "one of the rare cases in Dada and surrealist theatre" in which staging is treated "with care and competence by the author" (p. 164). Where he is remiss is in omitting to stress, or even to mention, that care and competence are at variance with the aims pursued in the theatre by Dada as much as by surrealism. The sophisticated use of stage lighting in Tzara's play, to take an example, is inconsistent with Dada, to the extent that it is a theatrical trick. Whatever Tzara manages to do, his play marks the surrender of Dada to the requirements of the theatre, not the conquest of the theatre by Dada. The compromise to which the author submitted when allowing *Le Cœur à Gaz* to be produced at the Théâtre Michel was as nothing beside the compromise evidenced in the text of *Mouchoir de Nuages*. Or, to put it another way, the in-

33. Aragon's text reproduces Tzara's inaccurately. Where the latter speaks of "la carpe de la vérité," the former has "la coupe de la vérité."

crease in theatrical skill observable in the later play must be credited less to the demands of Dada than to Tzara's infidelity to these. One notices the results particularly when scrutinizing the commentaries. These clearly derive from remarks in his earlier dialogued texts, like those of Nose in *Le Cœur à Gaz*, but reveal a marked change in outlook.

During a discussion between commentators placed in the fifth act, we hear what follows:

A

Do you think that Herrand is travelling too because he was bored with Andrée?

D

Personally, I couldn't say.

E

Nor could I.

C

This is why this play is badly constructed. Although we are the commentators, that is, the subconscious of this drama, we are not permitted to know why the poet does not love Andrée.

B

The fact that you are playing the role of Andrée's friend on the platform doesn't give you the right to believe you are her friend in reality.

A

But she could very well be, outside the action, off stage, in true reality, at home, what do *you* know?

C

Oh! this is boring, always the same discussion on the difference between theatre and reality.

Indeed it is boring, and in quite a different way from the repetition of the affirmation of boredom in *Le Cœur à Gaz*. Tzara is tedious here because he covers well-worn ground and turns up nothing new. Hence the lines transcribed above would not deserve citation if they did not indicate a revealing shift of emphasis in his writing for the stage. He now talks on the level of ideas, of concepts—arguing the conflict between theatre and reality. He has become a self-conscious artisan of drama, with Pirandellian pretensions.

More than this, as betrayed in the use he makes of commentary, his intentions have altered radically. In *Mouchoir de Nuages*, the commentators' task is to interpret and therefore to justify the playwright's technique; as in Act VI, for instance:

C
Let's go back in time now.
D
As in the cinema.
A
What was Andrée doing when the poet left?
C
We shall see.
B
Lower the tulle curtain!
E
The curtain of memory!
The tulle curtain comes down.
D
The scene is Andrée's apartment.
A
The impression of shapes isn't that of dreams. It merely indicates that the scene doesn't take its normal place in the chain of time, in the logical linking of the acts.

When the sixth act is over, B demands that the curtain of memory be raised, while A orders, "Let's return now to the other reality, to true reality, to the reality of Handkerchief of Clouds." When, noting that the play has reached its halfway mark, D suggests an intermission, C is firm: "No, the author does not want an intermission. He says that it was the intermission that killed the theatre." Dutifully, A summons the actors: "On stage for eight . . ."

Perhaps what we have just heard is a reminder of how the intermission during the Festival Dada at the Salle Gaveau gave the audience time to organize its protest against *La Deuxième Aventure céleste de Monsieur Antipyrine*. But if it is in dialogue of this sort that Béhar joins Sanouillet in saluting Dada humor—neither cites examples, so one is not sure—we can only protest against identification of archness and artificiality with the humor generated by Dada's iconoclastic principles, with a form of humor totally absent from *Mouchoir de Nuages*. The author who followed the adventures of Mr Antipyrine is obviously not the man who allows A to comment on the poet's conduct in

Mouchoir de Nuages: "Put yourself in his place, he *needs* to take poetry for reality and reality for mirage." Nor is he the man who permits B to reply: "For my part, if I didn't know in advance what direction the author has given his play, I'd not hesitate for a second to proclaim that poetry is a negligible product of latent madness, and that it isn't the least bit necessary to the upward march of civilization and progress." One sees well enough that stressing illusion and contrivance undermines the idea that drama should be convincing imitation of reality. But Tzara goes on—at the expense of spontaneity, by the way— to exploit ambiguity in *Mouchoir de Nuages.* And he does so in a fashion that incites his audience to concentrate upon the play as a literary entity, no longer a vehicle for destructive anti-artistic attitudes.

Fancy is indubitably present. But it rests upon an appeal to complicity and even collusion, unprecedented in the earlier plays of Tzara. This is an appeal that replaces the challenge by which, in the latter, the public had been required to divest themselves of respect for drama and for the contract into which playwrights are assumed to enter with their audiences. The day has gone when Tzara would delight in joking at the public's expense. In *Mouchoir de Nuages,* whatever jokes we encounter are meant to be enjoyed by everyone. Earlier, Tzara's purpose was clearly to test how much his audience could tolerate, to find the breaking point of tolerance and then push beyond it. It was in exceeding the limits of theatre that the Antipyrine plays and *Le Cœur à Gaz* found their *raison d'être* as expressions of Dada. In using commentary to enter into a dialogue with its public, *Mouchoir de Nuages* testified to Tzara's defection from Dada, showing that he had succumbed, at last, to literature.

Georges Ribemont-Dessaignes

What I write my reasoning does not direct.
It comes all on its own, almost without me,
at least without supervision.[1]

IN THE COURSE OF radio interviews taking place in 1952, published under the title *Entretiens*, André Breton spoke of Tristan Tzara, Francis Picabia, and Georges Ribemont-Dessaignes as "the only true Dadas" (pp. 64–65). Having authored no plays, Picabia does not require discussion in the present context. All the same, Breton's mention of his name reminds us that Picabia and Tzara began corresponding in 1918, after the former had aroused the latter's interest with his *Poèmes et Dessins de la Fille née sans Mère*, which came out that year. Writing from Paris on May 21, 1919, to express regret that the Romanian had not yet been able to come to the French capital, Picabia added, "Fortunately, I have my friend Ribemont-Dessaignes: he is working a lot at the moment and what he does is really what I like best—his works have incomparable value, his own slip-stream and the richness of sunshine— . . ."[2] Not long after, a lengthy letter from Breton to Tzara, dated January 14, 1920, alluded so abruptly to Ribemont-Dessaignes that we can only conclude Breton to be answering a question of Tzara's: "I don't yet know Ribemont-Dessaignes well enough."[3] However, by the time *Comœdia* conducted a survey among its subscribers later the same year, asking them to name their five favorite plays, Breton's acquaintance with Ribemont-Dessaignes's activities had at least reached the

1. From the autobiographical notes supplied by Georges Ribemont-Dessaignes for *Le Bulletin bimensuel du Groupe libre de Bruxelles*, December 20, 1926 (hereafter cited as *Le Bulletin bimensuel*).
2. Cited in Michel Sanouillet, *Dada à Paris* (Jean-Jaques Pauvert, 1965), p. 487.
3. *Ibid.*, p. 455.

point where, beside Jarry's *Ubu Roi*, Marivaux's *Le Jeu de l'Amour et du Hasard*, and Synge's *The Playboy of the Western World*, he was able to cite both *L'Empereur de Chine* and *Le Serin muet*, due for publication together in Paris in early 1921, under the imprint Au Sans Pareil and in the "Collection Dada."

1921 was to have seen the appearance of an international Dada anthology, *Dadaglobe*, conceived by Tzara the year before. Although the collection never came out and was not even completed, certain notes survive, over Tzara's signature. These include a biographical sketch of Ribemont-Dessaignes, ending with, "He is a man of his time, pamphleteer and dramatist of the Dada movement."[4]

Defenders of Roger Vitrac's reputation may wish to dispute Michel Corvin's claim that Ribemont-Dessaignes was "by far the most productive dramatist in the Dada and surrealist groups."[5] But there is no denying Ribemont-Dessaignes's special interest in drama, evidenced in an unpublished play, *R. S. des Chiens de Chasse*, which its author dates from 1924–25, in his projected *Où est le Singe*, mentioned in 1926, and in the dramatic works *Le Bourreau du Pérou* (performed in November 1926), *Larmes de Couteau* (staged in December 1926), and *Sanatorium* (put on in November 1930). As for *L'Empereur de Chine*, Ribemont-Dessaignes dates its composition from the beginning of 1916.[6] He insists in *Déjà Jadis*, "While Dada was preparing in Switzerland, being as completely unknown to me as Tristan Tzara, *The Emperor of China* was one of the first pieces of evidence from before Dada to be an integral part of Dada" (pp. 51–52).

After such a statement, supported by proof of enthusiasm on the part of Tzara, Picabia, and Breton, there appears little reason to pause over Sanouillet's evaluation of the historical significance of *L'Empereur de Chine* as "not only the first Dadaist theatrical work, but also the first authentically Dadaist manifestation (before the fact) conceived in France, beyond all foreign influence" (p. 116). Still, something needs to be said that will take us in a different direction from Sanouillet, who seems intent on persuading his readers to believe that Dada in the theatre originated in France. Tzara's salute to Ribemont-Dessaignes is clear indication of Dada's freedom from confining

4. See Michel Sanouillet, "Le Dossier de 'Dadaglobe,'" *Cahiers Dada Surréalisme*, No. 1 (1966), p. 121.
5. Michel Corvin, "Georges Ribemont-Dessaignes et le Laboratoire 'Art et Action,'" *Cahiers Dada Surréalisme*, No. 1 (1966), p. 160.
6. Ribemont-Dessaignes, autobiographical notes in *Le Bulletin bimensuel*.

theories about the ideal nature of theatre. Leading theoretician of Dada, Tzara unhesitatingly acknowledged the contribution of a writer whose first play, arranged in three acts, was so traditionally structured as to contrast sharply with his own Antipyrine texts—a play in free verse, incidentally, from which poetry of the kind he himself practiced was entirely absent.

It took until early in December of 1925 for *L'Empereur de Chine* to be performed. Even then, it was not put on within the framework of a *manifestation*—long since a thing of the past—with the author's friends as actors, as had been usual in Dada. It was staged by the Laboratoire de Théâtre Art et Action, founded by Edouard Autant and Louise Lara as early as March 1919, "for the affirmation and defense of modern works." In all probability, of course, the length of *L'Empereur de Chine* had precluded its presentation earlier, within some Dada spectacle. All the same, the play's relative conventionality of form and its success with the critics[7] raise questions regarding the promptness with which it was admitted to the Dada canon. The circumstances of its composition help answer these questions and set *L'Empereur de Chine* in perspective.

Déjà Jadis reports that Ribemont-Dessaignes wrote his first play while serving in the Family Information Service, which had its offices in the Ecole Militaire building of the Ecole de Guerre. Drafted in 1915, after escaping military service earlier, for the first time he was brought into contact with the Army, finding himself responsible for writing official responses to inquiries about men missing in action. Recalling that intellectuals predominated among his office mates, *Déjà Jadis* informs us that they were generally of a defeatist turn of mind. It was among these men, who included the writer André Billy, that Ribemont-Dessaignes wrote his play "on green file paper and Ministry of War letterhead" (p. 51).

The play opens with a supervisor in a busy typist pool distributing letters of the alphabet, by the dozen. The alphabet constitutes the "raw

7. See Ribemont-Dessaignes's autobiographical notes in *Le Bulletin bimensuel:* "*The Emperor of China* has the unexpected luck to meet with a success in the press usually unknown in Dadaism. Henri de Régnier, Henri Bidou, Paul Souday, to cite only the most important, each gave it a laudatory review."

material" from which he invites his staff to make their "merchandise"
—"Lyric poetry. / Cantata, epithalamium." Immediately after, stagehands exchange unrelated words that, in a while, fall into some sort
of order:

> FIRST STAGEHAND
> He is rolling in a barrel from the top of the hill.
> SECOND STAGEHAND
> Who will stop him then?
> THIRD STAGEHAND
> He is obeying gravity.
> FOURTH STAGEHAND
> Poor man, he is going to kill himself.
> FIFTH STAGEHAND
> He is fat, he will rebound.
> FIRST STAGEHAND
> He will get up late tomorrow.

Quite casually, a theme seems to emerge from the chaos of disconnected words, through reference to a man who remains unidentified,
engaged in an activity for which no explanation is forthcoming. One
thing therefore becomes clear without delay. Ribemont-Dessaignes
appears totally indifferent to his obligation, as author, to account for
the presence of the characters he brings on stage. Furthermore, he does
not bother to justify assembling them before us.

An old man puts matters this way: "It's not a question of judging, /
but of being a witness" (I, 5). However, there is reason to believe that
Henri Béhar goes too far when speaking of "a deliberate will to baffle
the spectator" in Ribemont-Dessaignes's first play.[8] To follow Béhar,
we should have to disregard a warning issued among the playwright's
autobiographical notes:

> The author's judgment on himself: he who knows himself well,
> enjoys bad health. The more one weighs oneself, the less one
> knows oneself. Above all because gravity changes from day to
> day. Clothes deceive less than nudity, even in the eyes of women.
> Anyway, all that matters little. I am a bald man who isn't bald, a
> general who isn't a general, a seducer who isn't a seducer. In the
> middle of the cable linking me with reality, I find a little relay.
> But I am not skeptical, or anti-skeptical, for nothing is as fine as

8. Henri Béhar, *Etude sur le Théâtre dada et surréaliste* (Gallimard, 1967), p. 113.

an illness. I prefer the illness of the trombone to that of rage, for example, to that of the violin. But I should like not to die or to smash everything up afterward.

In a word, I speak no differently in reality and in dreams.[9]

It is unwise, this statement suggests, to accept Béhar's assertion that Espher, Emperor of China, commits suicide at the end of the first act out of "love of the Absolute" (p. 115). Too much in what the playwright has just told us warns against believing he would directly solicit such an interpretation of his character's actions. What is more, looking at the play itself, we find evidence that necessarily arouses suspicions about Béhar's hypothesis.

When we meet Espher at the beginning of the opening act, he is not emperor but chief of government in China. He himself insists, "We must distinguish" (I, 2). He finally accedes to his daughter's wishes in becoming emperor; not, though, before she has attempted parricide, before he has raped her, or before he has had four old men stabbed and beheaded at a meal to which he invited them. The act ends abruptly with a soliloquy (I, 8), revealing Espher's conviction that it is time to leave this world. Espher, placing a noose around his neck, mounts his throne. "And when they come to salute Espher," he comments, "they will prostrate themselves before / The Emperor of China." After inscribing his name and title on a placard, he strangles himself.

In isolation, Espher's final violent gesture is so ambiguous as to border on gratuitousness. To be given full meaning, it has to be placed in context and considered against what happens before and after.

In the fifth scene we meet some old men, one of whom remarks, "The threads of heaven have broken the link that bound them to heaven." Although we are not sure to whom or to what he refers, an allusion to gravity is clear enough, recalling the reference to gravitational force in the very first scene. When a second old man points out, "The people are seeking their head," a third declares that their need can be filled only by Espher. The latter, who thought he knew who he was, while still no more than governor, dies on an incomplete inquiry into his own identity when, emperor at last, he takes his own life.

There is a curious echo of the opening scene, here, audible to any-

9. See *Le Bulletin bimensuel*. The beginning of the extract cited here is ironically modelled on the phrase *Qui se pèse bien se connaît*, "to know one's weight is to know oneself," and variations upon it, well known to users of public weighing machines in France.

one who has read *Le Bourreau du Pérou*, where the Peruvian Executioner is served by a typist who remarks to the Minister of Justice:

> Excuse me, sir. A thing isn't definitive until it has been pronounced by my typewriter.
> A man isn't dead, even if his head has rolled under the influence of gravity into the bran basket, until I myself have written: Dead. (I, 3)

But there is more involved than establishing why Ribemont-Dessaignes begins *L'Empereur de Chine* as he does. Espher's inability to define himself, at the moment when life is leaving his body, calls for examination in relation to the following conversation between him and his daughter:

> ONANE
> Be emperor.
> It is the clothing that you have to change.
> Why do you hesitate?
> ESPHER
> Gold is heavier than lead.
> ONANE
> Why do you speak of lead?
> ESPHER
> Is that not the best means of preserving the
> body, in its heavy darkness? (I, 4)

Returning to Espher's soliloquy, we notice it begins with an affirmation of confidence in his power to resist gravity: "I shall be the point at the upper limit, insensitive to the pull of the earth." He ends up dead, nevertheless. At first sight, then, Espher's fate does not seem to have much to do with Onane's confession to a midwife she visits during her pregnancy: "A force compelled me, which I resisted / So that it would be stronger" (II, 5). Understanding that there is indeed a significant connection here demands consideration of Onane's behavior when, incensed by contradictory answers given by priests whom she consults on the meaning of death, she screams:

> Let them be hanged to teach them the meaning of top and bottom,
> No, burn all three of them together.
> They shall know what it is to die outside the body. (II, 4)

Onane's rage takes on meaning when we appreciate that concepts of right and wrong, reward and punishment, and so on are excluded from *L'Empereur de Chine,* as they will be later from *Le Bourreau du Pérou.* In the latter, the Executioner's typist, ironically named Amour, affirms that "The just and the unjust are not discernible. Everything a judge does is just," adding without delay, "When a man is unjust, he is not a judge. Anyway judges are idiots" (I, 3).

During the second act of *L'Empereur de Chine* a woman turns to a friar for help, but finds no reassurance. On the contrary, he asserts:

> This is what God says
> And the Emperor repeats:
> Eat and drink, and do your business,
> And if you have a pain in the belly
> cry as much as you want.

When the poor woman who has sought spiritual guidance, "red with shame, flees in tears, pursued by laughter," the friar calls her back to give her two enormous loaves of bread:

> Hey woman,
> Here is your burden, may it be a
> heavy one! (II, 3)

Like the second, the third act of *L'Empereur de Chine* is characterized by violence that goes unabated, despite Espher's death in the last scene of the first act. War brings with it senseless ferocity now. In anticipation of the assault, in *Le Bourreau du Pérou,* upon the idea that innocence guarantees safety, in *L'Empereur de Chine* (III, 8) a child's throat is cut. When a woman refuses to drink the boy's blood, she is kicked in the stomach until she falls to the ground, transfixed by a sword. Throughout, gravitational pull takes grotesquely horrible forms. After threatening to take a blind girl's lover from her (II, 6), for example, Onane tears out one of the young woman's glass eyes. Exclaiming, "It is heavy. / How quickly it would fall to the ground if I dropped it," Onane throws the eye away, leaving her victim to fumble about on all fours.

If the first act is Emperor Espher's and the second Princess Onane's, the third belongs to Prince Verdict. His relationship to Espher and Onane is not specified. However, the effort made by the old men to enlist his support in persuading Espher to become emperor suggests that Verdict is Onane's brother. Given the relationship between the young woman and her father, this seems to be confirmed by Onane's attempt to seduce Verdict (II, 8), after she has provoked three other men to attempt raping her all at the same time. Defecting to the enemy in the final act, Verdict displays a remarkable talent for heartlessness and brutality. A final confrontation scene lets us watch him grasping Onane by the hair. A disjointed exchange, during which Onane's words "Lightness / Air in the air" are answered by his cry "Weight at the end of its fall," is terminated when Verdict, whose exclamation "Me" recurs insistently, cuts Onane's throat.

The closing scene of the play (III, 10) shows Onane's head, attached by the hair, swinging from a long line. As predicted by Verdict, standing before it, the head's pendulum swing will follow a diminishing arc until it finally hangs vertical. Hence the end of *L'Empereur de Chine* leaves us anticipating the final conquest of gravitational pull. Onane's severed head has become that plumb line which, only three scenes earlier, just before news reached her of the defeat of her forces by Verdict's, she spoke of having to hand so as to be "more sure of the vertical."

In the course of a soliloquy ending with the announcement that he will change to Minister of War, the Minister of Peace refers explicitly to gravity—"the primary force of the earth" (III, 1). War is evidently an expression of that force; hence its ineluctable nature:

> There are virtue and vice, good and evil.
> Bottom and top.
> We fight because trees grow vertically.
> And because men have the earth under their feet. (I, 4)

Indeed, the Minister contends, peace has continued for the past fifteen years simply because he has managed to maintain it "solely by a subtle seesaw play," permitting him to "impose hard penal restraints upon all who venture to have an irrational / weight." Like the pendulum swing of a plumb line not yet hanging true, the maintenance of equilibrium by seesaw motion represents denial of gravity. Of necessity, this can be only temporary in nature, since too much tempts man to "break the equilibrium," to borrow the significanct phrase used by Onane at the moment when she is about to stab her sleeping father (I, 6).

Espher's life is not spared because Onane relents, but because, waking up, he overpowers his daughter. The important thing is that Onane's conduct is no more subject to analysis as a case history in aberrant sexuality than is her father's. Rather, both Espher and she succumb to the temptation to destroy an equilibrium that temporarily resists gravity: to rape Onane, her father throws her to the ground. The end of the second act of *L'Empereur de Chine* bears out what we have come to suspect. Entering Espher's bedchamber, Onane allows us to understand that she is in love with her dead father, commenting pertinently: "An avowal which no possibility will be able to efface again. / Upset equilibrium. / My father" (II, 9).

But what has all this to do with the suicide of Espher? Obviously, Espher has something in common with the Peruvian Executioner, Mr Victor, who hangs himself after observing, in *Le Bourreau du Pérou*, "Power, power, Pftt! An empty barrel. Death. My old hands have knotty fingers from strangling. But no paradise opens up any more. [. . .] I know what remains for me to do." A more direct answer comes from an article of Ribemont-Dessaignes's, "Civilisation." Published in the third issue of Picabia's magazine *391* on March 1, 1917, "Civilisation" spoke of "Fatal submission to the laws of gravity."

Ribemont-Dessaignes expanded his statement in the eleventh number of the same magazine, dated February 1920, under the heading "Non—seul Plaisir":

> What is more, according to historical experience the quality of heroes increases with the uselessness of heroic gestures. The heroism of the last war, eminently utilitarian, is of low police quality. The policemen from the east threw themselves on the policemen from the west. They massacred one another, the latter being ruffians to the former, and vice versa. There is no specific difference between a detective and a thief. However, it must be recognized that the bandit attains pure heroism much more naturally.
>
> One can have the Illiad and the Odyssey printed in gold braid on one's sleeve, and a south-Oranese palm-grove planted on one's chest, and still rape little girls, sleep with women for money, steal one's neighbor's gold and seek election to the Chamber of Deputies. This is simply a sign of a fine temperament.

Reviling those who see in Art "a body of religious aesthetic rites" and "derive laws of harmony and balance from the autumnal wind ruffling their hair, or their sex organs in a mirror," Ribemont-Dessaignes nevertheless remarked that people with "rancid marmalade" for brains will "outlive us."

L'Empereur de Chine, its author tells us,[10] brings together a number

10. Ribemont-Dessaignes, *Le Bulletin bimensuel*.

of ideas scattered throughout the poems he was writing around 1916. It "constitutes an anti-philosophy." Regarding the latter, his comment presents no surprise, after what we have discovered in his play: "this anti-philosophy is still properly speaking a philosophy of gravity."

Gravity, for Georges Ribemont-Dessaignes, has nothing to do with seriousness. It is simply the opposite of weightlessness, the downward pull that admits of no resistance. Fostered to a considerable extent, it would seem, by the environment in which *L'Empereur de Chine* came to be written, pessimism shows plainly through "Non—seul Plaisir," underlying the negative aspects of its author's anti-philosophy. In *L'Empereur de Chine*, in other words, Ribemont-Dessaignes's is an *anti*-philosophy in the sense that the playwright's purpose is not to illustrate or promote a constructive program. His play reflects the ineluctable breakdown of order and system. The characters it brings together are not prompted to actions for which their creator claims or —more important—even admits responsibility. Thus, whether as spectators or as readers, we are made keenly aware of the absence of a controlling intelligence carefully marshalling evidence for which our reason calls in vain. To Ribemont-Dessaignes, nihilism is something that is neither to be argued nor presented persuasively. It merely pervades *L'Empereur de Chine*, as a self-evident truth that it would be inconsistent for him to set about demonstrating with any degree of formality. Independent of deliberate intent, impulses find expression, being, so to speak, the raw material of the anti-philosophy that the author instinctively denies artistically-polished presentation.

It is not that the playwright makes a conscious effort to be discreet, either. He does not refuse to speak out clearly. Instead, it is a matter of permitting us to witness the unsupervised communication of feelings that evidence an attitude adopted nonreflectively. In consequence, there is nothing surprising in the discovery that a marked discrepancy exists between Ribemont-Dessaignes's reading of his own text (in his autobiographical notes, as in *Déjà Jadis*) and in its assessment at the hands of some of his critics. The latter's views are useful, in fact, only so far as they permit us to appreciate how distorted an impression the author is content to permit his play to give its public.[11]

11. One example will suffice. Condescendingly disposing of *La Deuxième Aventure céleste de Monsieur Antipyrine*, *Le Cœur à Gaz*, and *Vous m'oublierez*, Martin Esslin finds *L'Empereur de Chine* and *Le Bourreau du Pérou* "more substantial works" that "really try to create a poetic universe with validity on the stage" (*The Theatre of the Absurd* [1961], rev. ed. [New York: Doubleday,

Speaking of the conception of Dada he came to share with Tzara and Picabia, Ribemont-Dessaignes remarks in *Déjà Jadis*, "Above all, people had to be taken by imbecility much more than by the novelty of distinguished poultry chaud-froid in philosophical papier-mâché" (p. 80). And as early as 1926, evidently looking back to the recent activities of Dada, in an article declaring "We are in a time of bankruptcy," he spoke of "the burning pleasure of destruction" that he and his associates had enjoyed.[12] The concluding sentence of "Non—seul Plaisir" faithfully reflects the mood of the time, as caught in Ribemont-Dessaignes's writings:

> There is no remedy. The remedy would be a sheet of flaming gasoline. The civilized and those who lay claim to civilization under pure consumption by fire. The trade-winds would have their chance with the dust afterward. This is utopian.
>
> There is a means to remedy the absence of a remedy. It is to incite the masses to destructive fanaticism, to savagery, to incomprehension of all that is "noble." When the artist can no longer go out without having his cheek covered in spittle and losing an eye, that will be the beginning of a fresh and happy era. For men will never have had purer and more enormous pleasures. And never will our "art" have been more lively and more vigorous.

Anchor, 1969], p. 321). It might seem that the odd phrasing used by Esslin signifies a wish to give full credit to the freedom with which uncensored feelings are voiced in Ribemont-Dessaignes's theatre. But we are disabused soon enough when Esslin defines Onane as "a wilful and cruel sex-kitten" and her father as "a sadistic tyrant." Hastening to assign Ribemont-Dessaignes's first play to the place it suits him to reserve for it, Esslin hopes to achieve his end at the price of unacceptable generalizations: "*L'Empereur de Chine* is a powerful play that combines the elements of nonsense and violence which characterize the Theatre of the Absurd. Its weakness lies in the insufficient blending of its elements into an organic whole, and in the length of its somewhat rambling design" (p. 322).

Even if his last phrase were less jumbled, Esslin would still be bending the play to his own requirements. More reluctant than he first appears to be to acknowledge the powerful expression of subconscious drives in *L'Empereur de Chine*, he apparently blames the playwright for not submitting his dream to a design calculated to bring out some philosophical pattern. Yet nothing could have been more foreign to the mood in which Ribemont-Dessaignes wrote. From what we know of the origins of his first play, it appears that the author did not feel constrained to sketch characters in *L'Empereur de Chine* with such firm outline as one would infer from Esslin's description of Onane and Espher. Nor did he feel it necessary to place his main protagonists in situations by any means as heavy with philosophical implications as Esslin would consider essential to dramatic success. In other words, the man who wrote *L'Empereur de Chine* cannot be described accurately as possessed by a desire to communicate a message of the kind that students of philosophical drama are trained to detect.

12. Georges Ribemont-Dessaignes, "Les Hommes," *Marie* (Brussels), Nos. 2–3, July 1926.

Measuring the distance separating *L'Empereur de Chine* from theatre erected upon philosophical pretensions means, at the very least, considering the conduct of Espher and Onane.

In the context of Dada, to which its author gladly assigns it, less importance attaches to features of *L'Empereur de Chine* bearing the telltale signs of amateurishness than to the following. Characterization requires less than customary development here, because the question of psychological motivation is irrelevant.

The circumstances under which four old men are summarily executed upon Espher's orders (I, 5) remind us more of the impulsive ferocity of Jarry's Ubu than of the cruelty that externalizes the hero's sense of the absurd in Camus's *Caligula*. Espher's actions neither follow nor announce tortuous self-examination of the kind offered by Camus so as to make us regard Caligula's behavior as an anguished commentary on the human situation. Like Onane, Espher is ultimately controlled by forces he cannot resist. His fate gives emphasis to the warning issued by the President in *Le Bourreau du Pérou*: "Don't forget that the sky overtops you. The earth is an enemy which holds you by the feet" (I, 1). In situations such as Ribemont-Dessaignes prefers, psychological motivation becomes superfluous. This, then, is what Espher's suicide dramatizes. Succumbing to the delusion of undisputed power, the emperor actually does no more than surrender to the force of gravity that, eventually, will immobilize his daughter's oscillating head.

In an article written in 1929, Georges Ribemont-Dessaignes points out, "People come back periodically to the subject of human destiny. That is a concern as sterile as one presiding over a search for the point in space toward which the sun and its system are heading."[13] The nihilism underlying this statement is just as visible in a remark by Mr Victor, in *Le Bourreau du Pérou*: "Ah, ah, what could I do? All this is ridiculous in the extreme. People search, people search, as if there were something to find!" (III, 3). Moreover, it is expressed with characteristic violence when Mr Victor's sense of futility does not save a young madwoman from strangulation at his hands.

Before immolating the innocent young woman, the Peruvian Executioner has his two assistants tear out her eyes, to be added to a collection he is making. This bizarre collection is for use in a camera of his own invention, utilizing eyes as lenses. Explaining how it works, he

13. Georges Ribemont-Dessaignes, "Politique," *Le Grand Jeu*, No. 2, 1929.

talks of "The eyes of victims who pay the penalty, lenses which establish the mystery of knowledge and of God" (I, 6). These words immediately elicit from Amour the response, "You have become a philosopher, a great philosopher." One can doubt Amour's ironic intent only so long as one ignores the crime for which three innocent men are subsequently thrown to their death in a cesspool (II, 7)—"excess of intellectuality opposed to the good sense of the State."

Le Bourreau du Pérou strengthens our conviction that Ribemont-Dessaignes's aim in *L'Empereur de Chine* is not to provide representative emotions or lucid scrutiny of significant states of mind. Instead, he returns obsessively to the dominant theme of irresistible gravitational attraction, which engenders significant motifs. Of these not the least important is the motif of the clock that has ceased to tell time. Its pendulum hangs vertical, releasing the action of the play from temporal flow, without liberating us from the anxiety of time:

> If this clock indicated the time progressively,
> Who could say if it is not fast or slow?
> When the moment comes, it goes as it pleases
> And plays time like an accordion that dispenses to the ears
> A tune of which the least one knows is that it is
> Definite. (II, 2)

At the end of this scene, someone gives the time, with blatant contradiction, as both three minutes past nine and twelve twenty.

Ribemont-Dessaignes behaves characteristically when he leaves his audience to resolve the enigma of time. It is no less characteristic of him that, after a dialogue constructed of non sequiturs, in the last scene of *L'Empereur de Chine*, he should bring his play enigmatically to a close with a statement stressing realism, in contrast with what precedes it: "An old woman died of hunger yesterday in Saint-Denis." Apparently unrelated to all that goes before—and introduced with an aggressive abruptness that gives the impression, at first, that the author has allowed himself an extraneous comment, from outside the context of his drama—the last line establishes a disturbing link between the imaginary action of *L'Empereur de Chine* and the sad realities of human existence. One last time, Ribemont-Dessaignes reminds us of the existence of an infallible law. Gravity, he lets us see, operates off stage as well as on, and no less cruelly.

Describing the manner in which Art et Action staged *L'Empereur de Chine*, Michel Corvin has remarked that the company followed its usual custom. This means that the designer attempted to reduce the play to an idea that could be communicated visually, by means of stylization in sets and costumes. In addition, it entailed on this occasion using life-size silhouettes, designed to synthesize essential attributes. For example, the silhouette of the Minister of Peace who changes to Minister of War was divided vertically, formal wear on one half of the body contrasting with sword-belt and arms made of cannon barrels, on the other. The actors delivered their lines from behind or beside the silhouettes representing them.

Even though a letter from Ribemont-Dessaignes to Louise Lara, dated April 30, 1926, speaks politely of "the charming and so intelligent manner" in which his play had been put on, an earlier letter to Edouard Autant reveals that charm and intelligence were by no means qualities that accorded with the author's own preferences:

> I have thought over your proposal that I explain the philosophical meaning of *The Emperor of China*. I thank you for this proposal but—there is a but: here it is—
>
> There are several levels in this play, of course. That is to say at least the level of drama, the level of feeling, the philosophical level . . . (There might perhaps be many more! but all this is so long from the critical point of view, and when writing I thought of less things, at least I didn't itemize. The unconscious looked out for the conscious, if you like.)
>
> So, since it's a matter of theatre, I think precedence should be given to drama, with a struggle between lyricism and irony.
>
> The rest must only be suggested!

After expressing confidence in his correspondent and in Mme Lara, Ribemont-Dessaignes continues:

> I think that under these conditions, it is preferable to give no advance philosophical explanation. Bewilderment? That matters little, for it cannot be avoided; and it is better that people be mistaken than misled from the beginning by a statement of ideas which at once takes on a dogmatic air.

Noting that to give firm shape to ideas already distant from him in time would be prejudicial—something to which he was opposed—the playwright advises the actors to think of the action, stressing that "The little they know of the rest will suffice."[14]

The tenor of Ribemont-Dessaignes's letter is characteristic. It helps show that, at the moment of composition, he concerned himself little, if at all, with formulating unambiguous statements in his plays. Thus, wondering about his right to kill an innocent woman in *Le Bourreau du Pérou*, Mr Victor offers a comment that some people watching the first act must find singular: "It's quite comical." Out of context, this phrase may not seem worth stressing. None the less, when the time came to turn his text over to Mme Lara, the playwright made a confession that gives it weight: "I don't at all know if you will be able to make something of *The Peruvian Executioner:* I myself don't know if it is comic or tragic: I think all the same we must opt for the comic: the abundance of corpses in it takes away the idea of tragedy! The tragic would come on its own in certain scenes."[15] The indecisiveness betrayed in this letter to Mme Lara proves how little the tone of his plays held Ribemont-Dessaignes's attention, while he was writing. Far from working within prescribed theatrical modes, he did not bother to ask himself how this or that play was to be classified until the time came to have it produced. Even then, he remained unwilling to impose upon the public a message of his own fabrication. What is more, he continued to be just as reluctant to see a message brought out by the director, even when the passage of time had helped the author recognize that certain impulses must have influenced his writing, without his being fully aware of their existence.

Written between *L'Empereur de Chine* and *Le Bourreau du Pérou*, Ribemont-Dessaignes's *Le Serin muet* (*The Mute Canary*) evidently was composed in the same spirit and with the same indifference to preconceived plan and purpose. First performed during the Dada demonstration at the Théâtre de l'Œuvre on March 27, 1920 (with *La Première Aventure céleste de Monsieur Antipyrine*, then, and *S'il vous plaît*), *Le Serin muet* had been written the previous year, to pass the time while Ribemont-Dessaignes was recovering from influenza.[16] In

14. Both these letters are reproduced in Corvin's article (see note 5 above), the one to Mme Lara on p. 169, the one to her husband on p. 168.
15. Letter dated August 24, 1926, reproduced in Corvin, "Georges Ribemont-Dessaignes," pp. 170–71.
16. Ribemont-Dessaignes, *Le Bulletin bimensuel*.

Déjà Jadis the author insists that his short dramatic text was not composed for the occasion, with Dada propaganda in mind (p. 71).

With characteristic discretion, Ribemont-Dessaignes tells us in his memoirs what his play was not intended to do. He supplies no information, however, about what he wished to accomplish in *Le Serin muet*, or even about what he now thinks he achieved. All one can be sure of, to begin with, is this: He was spared the limitations that necessarily go with writing a *pièce de circonstance*. Thus he was able to retain a spontaneity without which *Le Serin muet* would have been, decidedly, subject to closer supervision of a polemical—and therefore reasonable—kind than *L'Empereur de Chine*. All the same, it is unlikely that in 1919 he continued to be as ignorant as in 1916 of the activities of Tristan Tzara, whose ideas Picabia's enthusiasm must surely have led him to share with Ribemont-Dessaignes.

In the circumstances, it is curious to hear Béhar argue that *L'Empereur de Chine* is closer to Dada than is *Le Serin muet*, "a work of great clarity which has recourse to no Dada artifice." Béhar maintains that one could even say the latter is "not at all Dadaist," were it not for the play's theme, which he finds common to Dada and surrealism: "the channels of noncommunication" (p. 125). The theme of noncommunication in twentieth-century literature can hardly be considered a Dada patent, duly exploited (profitably or not) by surrealism. Therefore, dealing with *Le Serin muet*, Béhar finds himself in an odd situation, having to question his own earlier assertion that Ribemont-Dessaignes is "the most fruitful dramatist of Dadaism, unjustly misunderstood and forgotten" (p. 110). This seems to result from his attributing the "great clarity" of *Le Serin muet* to the playwright's use of symbols.

Hesitating not a moment, when opening his discussion of the setting of this play (a bare stage on which stands a ladder), Béhar asserts, "We understand that this ladder symbolizes the universe in which men move about on different levels, without ever meeting on the same plane" (p. 126). From this moment on, his reading of *Le Serin muet* credits Ribemont-Dessaignes with wishing his audience to appreciate that the ladder "is the key to the play, the symbol of our human condition" and with asking the rhetorical question phrased on his behalf by Henri Béhar: "Are we not all prey to our own dreaming?" (p. 127).

Even if Ribemont-Dessaignes's aversion to symbols were not a logical consequence of his refusal to preach to his audience, there would be evidence enough within *Le Serin muet* to discourage over-simplification of this kind. Indeed, the evidence suggests that the play-wright may well have set a trap for spectators and critics devoted to the idea that, in the theatre, obscurity necessarily denotes the conceal-ment of deep and far-reaching meaning. When Riquet picks up the cage containing the mute canary, he absurdly takes the bird for some-thing it patently is not: a hydra. Ocre takes himself for the composer Gounod, despite the fact that he is black, by the way. Barate thinks herself Messalina and is quite willing to call Ocre Gounod, provided he will satisfy her sexual needs ("I love you, Gounod, I have an enor-mous amount of temperament"). Ocre wonders whether Barate is not Saint Cecilia, finally declaring, "You don't know it, but you must be Marguerite."

Perhaps things are not what they seem here. But changing their identity makes it no easier to explain them. And the same is true of people. What Barate says of Riquet, after he has withdrawn to the top of his ladder—to go hunting, incidentally—is as true of Ocre or of Barate herself: "My husband has gone out. Gone out of himself, pris-oner of something else." Nevertheless, Ribemont-Dessaignes draws the line at explaining the nature of the imprisonment to which his three characters have fallen victim, and which makes Barate *certain* she is Messalina while persuading Riquet that he has "consciousness of all values" and is "archiepiscope of the whole earth."

In Armand Salacrou's philosophical drama *La Terre est ronde*, a parrot brought back from the New World typifies the unrelenting changelessness of human life, when it is discovered to be capable only of repeating words that Europeans have taught it. In Ribemont-Des-saignes's *Le Bourreau du Pérou*, the President's parrot has been brought back from Europe, since Peruvian parrots "learn to speak well only in Europe." However, when the President's parrot asks what time it is, the Minister of the Interior hastens to explain, "That means 'Good morning, gentlemen.' One only needs to know this" (I, 1). But since "What time is it?" is the only phrase the parrot utters, one needs to know how to interpret what it says in a multitude of ways: "How many things there are in this 'What time is it?'," the Minister exclaims with ludicrous pride. As for the mute canary who lends his name to Ribemont-Dessaignes's one-act play, it is said to know all Gounod's tunes by heart. Challenging Ocre's claim that this is so, Barate asks, "If he is mute, how do you know he knows them by heart, since he can't repeat them?" Ocre's reply is uncompromising: "That's the way it is. He is mute and I know that he now knows all my music." Logical discussion is inadmissible—even a discussion based on the premise that, not being Gounod, Ocre has written no music, thus making it perfectly easy for the canary to have committed all his music to memory. The fact is, we are assured by the President in *Le Bourreau du Pérou*, "With animals you never know where you stand."

Naturally, Ribemont-Dessaignes places us under no obligation to respect the President's opinion, giving us no reason to believe that the character speaks for his creator, on the subject of the animal kingdom or about anything else. Nevertheless, the President's words introduce an element of doubt that weakens our faith in the reliability of birds as symbols in Ribemont-Dessaignes's dramatic universe. Surely, Amour's comment is not to be ignored: "It is tiring always to know."

Reminiscing about the first performance of *Le Serin muet*, in which Barate was played by Annette Valère, Ocre by Soupault, and Riquet by Breton, the author recalls in *Déjà Jadis*, "I remember that André Breton, who is always conscious of the value of his person and carries himself with great dignity, was quite dissatisfied to figure thus in a play of which he was not the author, perched on the steps of a ladder" (p. 71). As we would expect, Ribemont-Dessaignes's casual remark about Breton leaves more questions unresolved than it answers. How were actors selected for Dada theatrical presentations? And why, in this case, did Breton accept a part in which he reportedly felt ridiculous? Any reply to the latter question, especially, must be speculative. Seeking an answer would contribute little to a general discussion of the attitude Ribemont-Dessaignes brought to the practice of Dada in the theatre, but for one small detail.

Stage directions are anything but intrusive in *Le Serin muet*. But by use of adverbs they meticulously indicate how actions are to be carried out. Referring to Riquet, the following is no exception: "He climbs majestically toward the top of the ladder and sits on the last step." Nothing here or anywhere else proves that Ribemont-Dessaignes had Breton in mind for Riquet, when he wrote his play. All the same, if mere accident led the organizers of the Théâtre de l'Œuvre demonstration to entrust to Breton the role of pompous Riquet, there is reason to think that Ribemont-Dessaignes saw no cause to protest.

No purpose would be served at this stage by touching upon personal antagonisms unless they pointed to divergence of opinion that sheds light upon the conception of Dada defended by Ribemont-Dessaignes. The possibility that he may have had Breton in mind when creating Riquet is worth entertaining for one reason only. It would be an early sign of differences soon to become so pronounced as to alienate them, when Dada gave way to surrealism.

In 1929 Breton, who had been directing surrealist activities for half a decade, received a critical letter from Ribemont-Dessaignes. Dated March 12, it complained, "You seem, underneath personal considerations, to have a concern to construct. Well, any wish to act constructively seems to me to be literature. You run from it, but it has a grip on you, and all the motives that guide you and what comes from it continue to be what you belch forth all the same, *literature*." Bitterly, Ribemont-Dessaignes continued: "You are incapable of adopting and of maintaining at the very least the negative point of view to which I remain faithful."[17]

In Ribemont-Dessaignes's work, the dominant motivating force is nihilism. This remains as true of his writings after the collapse of Dada as it was before. Hence his skepticism about Breton's proposals for reconstruction and redirection, once surrealism had replaced Dada. Symptomatic of all that separated him from Breton is his article entitled "Politique." This text grew out of a crisis within the surrealist camp. Yet, while one cannot rigidly impose the framework of Ribemont-Dessaignes's thinking in 1929 upon plays written by him several years earlier, "Politique" reflects several significant attitudes. These may be viewed without distortion as representative of a state of mind unchanged since the time when he was writing *L'Empereur de Chine*, even though his essay is colored by his recent quarrel with Breton and by his new alignment with the Grand Jeu group.

"Searching for happiness seems to me an imbecile preoccupation," declares Ribemont-Dessaignes. Thus, for him, revolt is not a sign of aspiration born of hope for better things. It is a necessary response to the conditions imposed by society. Yet it cannot presume to carry the promise of improvement. In "Politique" we read that "the revolt of individuals against social tyranny operates a revolution that does not cease so long as contraction has not reduced collective security to

17. Ribemont-Dessaignes's letter is reproduced in an article by Louis Aragon and André Breton, "À Suivre: Petite Contribution au Dossier du certains Intellectuels à Tendances révolutionnaires (Paris 1929)," in *Variété* (Brussels), 'Le Surréalisme en 1929' (June 1929), p. xxx.

peril; then comes a tyranny much more strict than the one preceding it, but it is accepted by the individuals, who, in these circumstances, have been only the preservative glands of society and have fulfilled their external functions only to mark their endocrine functions and to favor hormones."

As Ribemont-Dessaignes sees it, "Man hates man. Hate is the strongest link between men: it is the individual's revenge against the bonds of collectivity. However much it liberates, it still binds to the same point as love." The incestuous passion depicted in *L'Empereur de Chine* calls down no moral condemnation from the playwright, any more than the marital squabbling that brings Riquet and Barate to blows in *Le Serin muet*. It earns no more approval, either, since one form of love is no more or less reprehensible than another. "We know what aim love pursues," Ribemont-Dessaignes comments in "Politique," "It becomes one with the aim of hate, and, in the final analysis, turns out in the end to be only destruction. Whether we speak of the collectivity or of the individual, and whether one thinks one is freeing oneself for the other person, love and hate arrange things so that they create a vacuum, or, if you prefer, empty a cesspool."

True, Breton was no less convinced of the baleful effects of society. He would gladly have set his signature to the following statement in "Politique": "But revolt remains the only possibility of escape and of liberation; and, in advance, the mere possibility of accepting social laws, whatever they may be, fills me with disgust. Given the obscurity of its fatality, society gradually becomes one with God. Accepting the demands of the former becomes submission to God. The only resource remaining to us is to manifest our existence in revolt against this chameleon-faced personage." Where Breton would differ profoundly from Ribemont-Dessaignes is not only in his faith in love as a redemptive, liberating agent, but also in his refusal to regard revolt as a merely despairing gesture, inevitably futile. The contrast is marked between his outlook and that of Ribemont-Dessaignes who argues in "Politique" that "it is pointless to move away from a negative position, since we can deduce nothing that we did not conceive in the first place."

From what we have just read it is clear that Ribemont-Dessaignes was not deluding himself when he spoke of the anti-philosophy of *L'Empereur de Chine*. There is no reason to doubt that he was fully aware of the paradox of his situation as a writer for whom denying a philosophy means affirming one. In "Politique" he recognizes that "whatever the attitude one adopts, however negative it may be, one comes up against the positive, at the exit." However, his definition of the positive merely reiterates his conviction that progress is an illusion: "earthquakes, volcanic eruptions, plague and other occurrences of the same nature we have to reckon with and against which the negative is inoperative."

Against the background of Ribemont-Dessaignes's essay in *Le Grand Jeu*, the shallowness of pseudo-philosophical pronouncements like Riquet's "Ah! life is dull like an old tooth," with unenlightening variations like "Barate, life is dull like a toenail," take on strictly ironical value. In the world of *Le Serin muet* the only certainties rest upon the sort of delusion that makes Barate believe herself to be Messalina, while the mute canary thinks of himself, Ocre assures us, as Juliet's nightingale. Irony testifies to the author's determination not to be his own dupe as he mocks Riquet, who prides himself on being "nourished upon realities," yet still delivers the following lines: "But in any case one has a certainty. It is that outside oneself/There is nothing." Contradiction and self-contradiction offer no surprises, as they become the key effect in the play. In *Le Serin muet*, the author of *L'Empereur de Chine* has Riquet declare, "To be free is nothing. But liberty is everything." He has Barate and Ocre shot dead, not because they are designated victims in a *crime passionnel*, but because the woman's husband, from the top of his ladder, has mistaken them for panthers. And he has a mute canary sing Gounod, inaudibly.

Louis Aragon

Scandal for scandal's sake.[1]

IN ONE FORM OR ANOTHER, Dada preached and practiced negativity. For this reason it held immense appeal for several young men in Paris, once they had discovered that surviving the 1914–18 war meant they could no longer expect to pick up the threads of a literary career some of them had hoped to lead in the days before they were conscripted. Among these, one of the most gifted, possessing a remarkable facility with words, was Louis Aragon. Born in 1897, Aragon was one of the first in Paris to feel curious about Dada activities in Zurich. He soon came to see in Tzara's writings—poems, criticism, and manifestoes—a declaration of war and in Tzara himself a new Rimbaud.[2] Soon closely associated with two men of his own age, Breton and Soupault, who both shared his enthusiasms, he co-edited with them an anti-literary review ironically titled *Littérature*, fully agreeing with the evolving editorial policy that was shortly to bring the magazine into conformity with the anti-aesthetic program of Dada.

In his own writings, Aragon was never to show any particular attraction to the theatre. His poems and especially his polemical texts (*Traité du Style*, 1928) and brilliant imaginative prose (*Le Paysan de Paris*, 1926) constitute his most significant contribution during the years of his friendship with Breton, terminated when he finally gave up surrealism for communism. But although his two plays, written before he was thirty, reflect secondary concerns, they are no less interesting to us for doing so.

Written as early as 1917, "Alcide" is an early text of Aragon's that

1. Louis Aragon, preface to *Le Libertinage* (Editions de la Nouvelle Revue Française, 1924), pp. 18 and 19.
2. See Roger Garaudy, *L'Itinéraire d'Aragon* (Gallimard, 1961), p. 82.

he has related to both his plays, *L'Armoire à Glace un beau Soir* (*The Mirror-Wardrobe One Fine Evening*) and *Au Pied du Mur* (*Backs to the Wall*). In it we find a statement that helps cast light on each of them:

> But can we today not despise the facile tragedy that is born of the impact of feelings, desires, and destiny? It would be too convenient, really, to move us by suspending death over the heads of puppets for three or five acts. There is however before us an everyday tragedy, that of the grotesque, the preposterous, that of the terrible laugh which empties the soul like a shell of its nut and which shakes the body like a sensual pleasure too strong to leave behind only the bitterness of dissipated intoxication. [. . .] To be truly lyrical one must dignify the very things men despise, but without deforming them, starting with a jeering laugh to make it into a magnificent laugh.[3]

"Alcide" intimates that innovatory ambitions underlie *L'Armoire à Glace*, so making it easier to see where this play complements *Au Pied du Mur*.

In the prologue to the latter, a woodcutter's attempt to report what is in the newspapers is interrupted so often by comments from five other woodsmen that he loses his desire to share whatever information he has. When he and his friends have finally left the stage, they are replaced by someone called the Speaker, nude except for collar and tie, top hat and boots. The Speaker promises, "we shall reveal ourselves to be sentimental rather than boilers, swallows rather than Shakespearean." Talking of love, he draws aside the curtain and holds out his hand to a young woman whom he introduces as "Madame Tosini, in the role of Olympe, a young coquette married to the banker Silas Randau." As soon as Olympe has read aloud a letter from her lover ("You will never see Frédéric again"), the stage goes dark. The Speaker is now heard supervising what the orchestra is to play and also what the lighting technicians have to do—bring up the lights on a room at an inn. Here a young man answering to the name of Pierre is writing at a table.

For a short while it seems as though the action of *Au Pied du Mur* is going to take a realistic turn. Pierre—who is really Frédéric—informs Mélanie, a servant at the inn, of his intention to leave in the morning,

3. Louis Aragon, "Alcide ou De l'Esthétique du Saugrenu," reproduced in the preface to Louis Aragon and Elsa Triolet, *Œuvres romanesques croisées* (Laffont, 1964), p. 2.

then invites her to spend the night with him. But no sooner has the stage darkened once again than an absurd conversation takes place on the proscenium between a salesman for Lido suspenders and an electric arc. Realistic action appears to resume as we see Pierre-Frédéric in his room, inducing Mélanie to drink poison as proof or her attachment to him. But Frédéric's ironical comments puts us on our guard: "A sensational turn of events," he remarks, "or the pity of it, no no." Mélanie's appeal for the antidote, after she has put the poison to her lips, makes him exclaim, "Well, false sweetheart, ho ho what a good play." When, to prove her love, Mélanie proceeds to spill the antidote on the floor, Pierre, contrary to the usages of melodrama, tells her he does not return her love and throws her out to die.

Yvette Gindine's summary of *Au Pied du Mur* might persuade many of her readers to believe that nothing more happens in this play than we have already noted. She places it "in the tradition of an exacerbated romanticism à la Musset," commenting, "Its hero lyrical and sadistic at the same time takes dreadful revenge for disappointment in love upon a servant at an inn whose passion he tests by making her drink poison. The plot is cut across by comic scenes in which Aragon mingles light-hearted fancy of the *Comédies et Proverbes* type and surrealist humor."[4] Martin Esslin takes the same line. Calling the main plot "romantic to the point of ridiculousness," he goes on to declare, "The appearance of fairies and Parisian workmen in overalls cannot disguise the fact that basically this is a romantic play in the vein of Musset or Victor Hugo, revealing, through its modernistic trappings, Aragon's essential traditionalism, which later emerged in his beautiful wartime poetry and his monumental social novels."[5] The truth is that traditionalism of the kind marking Aragon's poetry in the forties—severely criticized by Benjamin Péret in the name of surrealism, incidentally[6]—is no more present in *Au Pied du Mur* than in *L'Armoire à Glace*. What counts in both plays is the personal manner in which Aragon chooses to present material that is traditional on the surface only. To begin with, it is surely worth noticing that the Speaker asks whether the scene between Frédéric and Mélanie is a dream and that

4. Yvette Gindine, *Aragon: Prosateur surréaliste* (Geneva: Droz, 1966), p. 53.
5. Martin Esslin, *The Theatre of the Absurd* [1961], rev. ed. (New York: Doubleday, Anchor, 1969), p. 331.
6. See Benjamin Péret, *Le Déshonneur des Poètes* (Mexico: Poésie et Révolution, 1943).

Aragon withholds his own answer to this question. When the Speaker proposes to decide the matter by simply flipping a coin, the coin falls in the dark, where no one can see it.

If, instead of following Esslin and Miss Gindine, we turn to Roger Vitrac's account—as reported by Jacques Baron—of the performance of *Au Pied du Mur* at the Vieux-Colombier Theatre in June 1925, we come upon a detail that leaves us thinking that Aragon may well have meant the Speaker's question to sound superfluous. While Frédéric is provoking Mélanie to drink the poison, one phrase recurs in what he says to her: "Je parle en général" ("I am speaking in general"). At first its use strikes us as a sign of Pierre's cunning, denoting how skilfully he will bring Mélanie to suicide. But repetition weakens this impression and stimulates aggravation in its place. On its fourth occurrence at the Vieux-Colombier, one exasperated spectator, choosing to understand the phrase as meaning "I am speaking as a general," cried out, "Then get on a horse."[7] The loud applause that Vitrac told Breton greeted this feeble witticism confirms that Aragon had reason to congratulate himself. He had made his play something quite different from a pale imitation of romantic theatre. *Au Pied du Mur* was, and still is, an act of provocation.

An *entr'acte* brings together Madame Tosini, dressed in Olympe's clothes, naturally, and Mademoiselle Aumuse. The latter admits that, while playing her part as Mélanie, she felt an irresistible urge. Had her scene with Frédéric gone on longer, she confesses, she would have shouted out irrelevantly the nonsensical rhyme, "Petit rat, petit riz, c'est le roseau qui l'a pris." Unperturbed, Madame Tosini remembers that they have an apologue to deliver. Both actresses now dutifully face the audience, only to begin at once examining some invisible object under a magnifying glass. This object, we are led to believe, is a child so small he can be held in the palm of a hand. Monsieur Tontaine, who plays the innkeeper, Trapèze, appears, announcing that he is to be the prompter in "this comedy," as he calls it. When Monsieur Givre, who impersonates Frédéric, comes along too, we are given a demonstration of his inability to count up to thirty-three.

So far as the ensuing conversation between the four persons on stage makes any sense at all, it does so as a succession of unrelated advertising slogans—none of them, as it happens, for Lido suspenders.

7. See Jacques Baron, *L'An 1 du Surréalisme* suivi de *L'An dernier* (Denoël, 1969), p. 140.

Finally Tontaine advises Mademoiselle Aumuse to throw her baby out with the garbage. Madame Tosini faints, but is quickly revived when the other woman tickles her. All four leave the stage together, grimacing and twisting their bodies to musical accompaniment.

The *entr'acte* in *Au Pied du Mur* neither explains what has preceded it nor prepares for what will follow in the second act. Now we see Frédéric in the mountains, dressed for climbing, and the Speaker, wearing identical clothes. For the first time, we are to notice how alike the two are: they can be told apart only by the broom carried as an alpenstock by the Speaker. The latter tries to persuade Frédéric that he loves himself, not Olympe. When, shortly afterward, the young lady comes on the scene, accompanied by her maid, she admits to having no idea how she came to be in a part of the world for which she is not suitably attired. A passage of broad farce follows, as Olympe and Betsy become involved with a goat-herd, three naked fairies, and three workmen. Next Trapèze makes his entry, no better able to explain his presence in the mountains than anyone else.

As if all this were not disconcerting enough, far from making an effort to persuade us to take the incidents he presents seriously, Aragon stresses how ludicrous they are. He uses understatement, having the maid remark, when the fairies have finished throwing her wig about like a ball, "You can say what you like, what is happening to me isn't ordinary." He employs also frank admission, when Olympe's question to the goat-herd, "My friend, am I really on a glacier?" is succeeded by her exclamation, "That's hard to believe." And he shows he is not averse to provocation, letting Trapèze say, "I ask you now, there's no rhyme or reason to this."

Evidently it is not sufficient to relegate all we are permitted to see and hear in the second act of *Au Pied du Mur* to the realm of fanciful dreams. If this is indeed a dream, then it is one in which all the people familiar to us on stage share together, and where each of them is quick to see in those he encounters mere figments of his own imagination. It is at the same time a dream in which each of them simultaneously perceives the same apparition—Mélanie—who exerts in this play, Béhar justly observes, "an inexplicable attraction" at the center of "a magnetic field."[8]

When Frédéric arrives, he recognizes Mélanie without hesitation

8. Henri Béhar, *Etude sur le Théâtre dada et surréaliste* (Gallimard, 1967), pp. 221–22.

and strikes her with his piolet: "You will no longer leave the limbo into which I precipitated you . . ." Mélanie falls from the rock where she stood, leaving him alone until the Speaker enters with a lantern: "There you are alone with yourself, Frédéric. Now or never's the time to have a little picnic." Ignoring this advice, Frédéric loses himself in reflections upon human experience as "the power to deceive oneself," commenting that our imagination "makes us suffer great hardships."

In his own estimation, Frédéric is "a steadfast truth between two lies." Supposedly seeking to rid himself of the memory of Olympe, who is promiscuous, and Mélanie, who may have been the goat-herd's mistress (are they not "the two sweethearts who lied" whom he mentions?), he cries, "Kill, Frédéric, kill. Forget those dead branches that clung to your clothes." Turning now to his alter ego, whom he berates ("Ostentatious self, papier mâché, shooting-gallery figure"), he exclaims, "Will you clear out of this?" The Speaker seeks to defend himself, hinting that the alternative to self-centered communion with the self (the picnic) is "the carnival of the exterior world." However, Frédéric reveals his unwillingness to accept either alternative: "Their masks or your dismal face, toad? Neither your cancer nor their pox, shadow." The Speaker's riposte that he cannot be dismissed provokes Frédéric to immediate violence. Shouting, "Disappear, phantasmagoria of myself," he throws his piolet at the Speaker, extinguishing the lantern. At the same moment the spotlight on Frédéric goes out.

Reviewing all that has taken place, we recall that the prologue let us see a man who had information to share but who gave up his attempt to communicate it. During the second act, we watched a man observing another search for something on the ground and then asking what was missing. The only reward his solicitude earned him, we remember, was a slap in the face. Is there a lesson to be learned from this? Of course, the spectator is guaranteed immunity from physical violence by the footlights. But he cannot avoid the blow aimed at his curiosity, the very kind of curiosity usually satisfied in the theatre. Using a plot that at very best can be described as disjointed, presenting sequences in which dream and reality shade off into one another, Aragon betrays no interest in beguiling or persuading anyone. On the contrary, he seems intent upon fostering and sustaining the audience's sense of disorientation and dislocation. Thus the Speaker, in whom we felt entitled to see a reliable guide through the scenes following his first appearance, turns out to be no more than a projection of the self that Frédéric finally rejects. Consequently, once he has been discredited as authoritative commentator upon the action of *Au Pied du Mur,* the play no longer appears to have a center of gravity. It simply backs us against the wall, leaving us to make whatever we can of the incidents it brings together, supplementing conclusions that reason adduces with those that imagination proposes. After Frédéric has put out the Speaker's lantern, from the darkened stage the hero's voice is heard saying, "A lone man crossing the set," while a shooting star points the way to the exit.

L'Armoire à Glace un beau Soir is a somewhat shorter and apparently more cohesive piece dedicated to Roger Vitrac, whom Aragon used to meet almost daily at the time when the play was on the stocks, between the autumn of 1922 and April 1923, while its author occupied an administrative position at the Théâtre des Champs-Elysées. The opening is eye-catching, if nothing else. Before the closed curtain, a young French soldier meets a woman and engages her in desultory conversation:

> THE SOLDIER
> What's wrong, little lady? You look all out of sorts.
> THE WOMAN
> It's the times we live in, I tell you: there's no place for us any longer. One feels constricted even in one's dreams, you know.

Words like these present no special novelty in the theatre, naturally. They have an unusual ring, here, because they contribute to the development of no dramatic situation. Nor do they do anything to explain why the woman is nude, wears a flowered hat, and has a baby carriage perched on her shoulders.

Other characters visible on the proscenium at this point include Siamese twins, the President of the Republic, and a man fifty years old whose nose stretches to his chest. When the soldier embraces the nude woman, the President asks, "Well, Sir, what do you think of those people?" Lifting his nose with one hand, the man replies, "I don't concern myself with those people, I ask nothing of you. I have my own affairs. There is a time for everything in life." Then he pedals off stage on his tricycle.

Also present is one of Aragon's friends, Théodore Fraenkel, accompanied by a stylishly dressed woman, with a hennin on her head. Fraenkel introduces her as "naturally a fairy." So, naturally, the President asks why she is a fairy:

> THEODORE FRAENKEL
> She is a fairy because she is with me.
> THE PRESIDENT
> Is she mute?
> THEODORE FRAENKEL
> Naturally, since she is with me.
> THE PRESIDENT
> And what have you come to these deserted regions for?
> THEODORE FRAENKEL
> We have come to tell you that the play is going to begin and that you are boring everyone with your wailing. Off you go!

As two men appear, carrying a mirror-wardrobe, Fraenkel tells all those on stage that they are in the way and orders them to leave. Only when the wardrobe is in place and everyone has gone does the curtain rise.

Looking for reasonably identifiable connections, dramatically viable, that would authorize speaking of all we have just seen as a prologue to the following action, leads to disappointment. Without delay we find that Aragon wishes to do everything he can to bring about the change predicted in the section of the preface to *Le Libertinage* subtitled "Down with limpid French genius": "Sooner or later will come the bankruptcy of intelligence, community property, poverty of spirit" (p. 27). The only conceivable relationship to be detected here has little or nothing to do with dramatic necessity, then. The introductory section to *L'Armoire à Glace* leaves us demanding an explanation that the playwright never supplies. Meanwhile the main body of the play takes direction and vitality from mystery and from hints at the existence of a solution that, in the end, is denied us also. So far as the prologue and all that comes after are linked, this would appear to be by an underlying principle of negativity. The former simply refuses to satisfy our curiosity. The succeeding action exploits conventional elements of mystery in such a fashion as to demonstrate that the author has no respect for the mystery as a theatrical mode. To emphasize his indifference to his responsibilities before his audience, Aragon who warns, when prefacing *Le Libertinage*, "Get this into your heads, I don't want the laughers on my side," brings back the prologue characters at the end of his play, in circumstances that ridicule the spectator's hope of seeing an acceptable solution provided.

True, to someone watching for the first time a break does seem to occur between the unrealistic happenings in front of the curtain and the action commencing, once the curtain goes up, against a setting laconically described in the stage directions as "a vulgarly furnished room." Before long, though, it is clear that in *L'Armoire à Glace* Aragon makes a wager he is justifiably confident of winning. He borrows typical features of melodrama, situating the action of his play against a middle-class background. But he does so, apparently, with the primary aim of invalidating the conventions upon which both the social and the melodramatic theatre rest. Inconsequential elements soon liberate his text from the realistic tradition, undermining any claim it might be thought to have to the kind of recognition and respect that at first, he seemed intent upon soliciting.

Yvette Gindine speaks of *L'Armoire à Glace* as exemplifying a "disconcerting aesthetic," but has no further observation to offer (p. 52). Henri Béhar affirms that in this play "everything can be explained scenically" (p. 221), regrettably supporting this contention with not a single explanatory comment. Michael Benedikt displays greater sensitivity when noting a "tension between the daringly old-fashioned structure of the play proper and the irrationality of the actions of its characters" (p. xxv). This, incidentally, seems to him to "bring fresh dimensions to both Surrealist theatre and domestic melodrama." Benedikt's hypothesis is that the use of "a common plot" in *L'Armoire à Glace* represents "an effort to keep the play in an actable form—to weight it, as it were, to the stage."[9] It is more likely, however, that Aragon wants to take advantage of contrasting the well-worn situations he utilizes for his own purposes with the development he chooses to give those situations. In *L'Armoire à Glace*, certainly, we find a contrast that takes on significance in the light of his conviction that "the beautiful is the unexpected."[10] "The traditional idea of beauty and good," insists the preface to *Le Libertinage*, "we shall oppose with our own, however infernal it appears" (p. 16).

L'Armoire à Glace uses ingredients of mystery (what does the

9. Michael Benedikt and George Wellwarth, *Modern French Theatre: The Avant-Garde, Dada, and Surrealism* (New York: Dutton, 1964), p. xxv.
10. Aragon, "Alcide," p. 29.

wardrobe contain?) and bedroom farce (is it the wife's lover?) as well as well-tried related dramatic techniques like suspense (will Jules open the wardrobe?) and overtones of horror (Jules's uneasiness when Lénore unaccountably incites him to open the wardrobe door). But speculation (why did Jules go out to buy a hammer?) meets no positive response, while false leads (does the strange disappearance of Mme Léon's husband give away the identity of Lénore's supposed lover?) only confuse us. What holds our attention most of all is Aragon's lack of concern to make sure we will be convinced by what his characters say and do. This is only to be expected, we must agree, from a man who comments, when prefacing *Le Libertinage*, "What escape me are the merits of those psychological dialogues on which a whole literature has fed and in which the partners monologue all the way through about love" (p. 12). Anguish and premonition are expertly communicated in *L'Armoire à Glace*. But they lose their force when exaggeration leads to patently ridiculous postures and dialogue, which serve to emphasize Aragon's contempt for French classical tragedy: "Accepting to be at best only the author of *Phèdre* escapes me," the preface to *Le Libertinage* makes clear (p. 21).

Esslin, who equates surrealism with the exclusive practice of automatic writing, described in Breton's first manifesto, calls Aragon's play "a fairly conventional drama interrupted by surrealist interludes" (p. 331). It would be more accurate to say that the discrepancy between what Lénore says and Jules replies gives the spectator the strange feeling that he is watching two plays at once. Lénore seems to belong in a parodic version of nineteenth-century melodrama. Jules, on the other hand, appears to have come out of a pedestrian bourgeois drama, scrupulously drained of dramatic intensity. As a result, Aragon's play is distinguished by a kind of emotional oscillation that throws audience response off balance.

In this strangely off-key drama, ambiguity finds expression through disturbing tonal variations, as when Lénore's fantasies about violent treatment at her husband's hands alternate with platitudinous aphorisms like Jules's "The shortest jokes are the best." Indeed, ambiguity is so effectively maintained throughout *L'Armoire à Glace* that it is difficult to follow Béhar when he assures us that Jules "understands the situation very well" and "prefers to enjoy the superiority of his *position*" (p. 211). Missing from this interpretation is some inkling of the predicament in which Aragon places his audience when leaving them to decide for themselves how much of all they hear and see is meant to be taken seriously. Missing also is some sign that Béhar has reflected upon the following statement in the preface to *Le Libertinage*, "By the magic sign of ink I limit my thought in its consequences. There is no longer much chance that it will exceed itself, forget itself. It ought to be forbidden to plant milestones on roads in this way: land-surveyors have a slim notion of the infinite" (p. 20).

Resisting the limitations of language, when writing *L'Armoire à Glace* Aragon allows his audience to suspect that Lénore may be engaged in a game, no less than Jules. We have the impression that the couple has played the same game before. Yet it looks as though the husband is in no mood to participate this fine evening. While Jules tells her to prepare dinner, Aragon grants Lénore the convenience of an aside so that, as theatrical convention permits, she can enlighten those watching. She takes her chance to deliver an unequivocal prediction: "Sooner or later, whether the wind howls or drops, he will want to open the wardrobe."

Even if we are witnessing one of those dramas that, as Jules confides, he and Lénore play from time to time, we gather that the action of *L'Armoire à Glace* is not to be dismissed lightly. These dramas "take on too much the face of life," the husband tells us, "A beautiful face of truth." Admitting to Lénore that he has given her a taste for "these fictions," Jules points out at the same time, "There you are, caught in the trap." His words may be taken literally, since Lénore is momentarily imprisoned in his arms. However, the spectator has so little opportunity to feel certain of anything in this play that he may well think he is entitled to believe the game has become more dangerous for Lénore than she expected. In any case, as time passes the atmosphere of *L'Armoire à Glace* becomes increasingly serious. This is particularly the impression we receive when Lénore starts urging Jules to open the door of the wardrobe she previously wished kept shut (so that her lover will not suffocate?), while Jules wants her to continue forbidding him to do so (in order that his rival will be eliminated?). The "charade," as Jules calls it, goes on too long to leave us comfortable in the thought that it is no more than a charade, the mere "comedy" of which Jules speaks. Irony disturbs our preconceptions when he exclaims, "A good play" and "This is an extraordinary show, it's not a banal spectacle." One of his remarks now strikes us as especially pertinent: "All this is more than the imagination can take." In consequence, we fall back on reason for assistance. We find ourselves seeking rational explanations for the motives that have prompted those on stage to change tactics radically.

Searching for external clues and hints, we may recall at this point the following declaration in Aragon's *Le Con d'Irène:* "The erotic idea is the worst mirror. What one glimpses of oneself in it makes one shudder."[11] Or we may be reminded of these lines from his *Traité du Style:* "Not to mention the fact that a mirror-wardrobe just so happens to be all that everyone finds to say when they don't understand, and that a mirror-wardrobe, it so happens, could be the perfect definition of humor."[12] Unfortunately for those only at ease with simplified solutions, Aragon proceeds at once to dispose of the lead he has just given: "Not for me, since I know."

The rebuff administered in this last remark compels us to recognize that rationalization offers no sure guarantee of release from the confusion one feels before the conflicting emotions and actions assembled in *L'Armoire à Glace.* Everywhere our need to know—about the significance of Jules's gesture in shattering the mirror on the wardrobe, for example—is frustrated and receives scant satisfaction. Everything seems to point to the mystery of the wardrobe's contents as the key to the puzzle, "the key to the mystery," as Jules calls it, when pleading with Lénore to forbid him to open it because doing so will send him mad. If, before the end, we can discover who or what is inside, it is reasonable to expect to have discovered the true motives for Jules's conduct and for Lénore's. Hence we look forward to the moment when Jules fulfills Lénore's prediction as we would to the dénouement of a conventional drama. Yet when he does finally open the door, "We see all the characters of the prologue come out of the wardrobe. Holding hands, they advance to the proscenium while it gets darker and the curtain falls." These characters, who now dance a jig before sitting down, are the ones reason advised us earlier to dismiss from mind as irrelevant to the main action of the play and whose return at this juncture common sense is reluctant to condone.

It is interesting to notice that one critic at least can account for the

11. *Le Con d'Irène,* p. 24. This rare erotic work, originally published without date and publisher's name in 1928, has appeared over the name of Albert de Routisie in an English translation by Lowel Blair: *Irene* (New York: Grove Press, 1969).

12. Louis Aragon, *Traité du Style* (Editions de la Nouvelle Revue Française, 1928), p. 134.

reappearance of the prologue characters only by the stratagem of disregarding Aragon's text. Summarizing the prologue, Henri Béhar tells us, in direct contradiction with the stage directions, that the stagehands who bring on the mirror-wardrobe make everyone disappear inside it (p. 211). In other words, he wants us to believe that, ignoring Théodore Fraenkel's orders to clear the stage, the "incongruous people" featured in the prologue submissively enter the wardrobe (something we do not see them do, of course), so that their presence there will be rationally explicable when the time comes for Jules to open the door. Béhar would have us think that Aragon prepares the surprise ending of his play so carefully and so obviously that it will come as no surprise at all. Yet Aragon could not have done such a thing without knowingly contradicting himself, thus encouraging the very impression that the introductory comments prefacing Le Libertinage show him determined to destroy. Speaking of the fact that people used to call him skeptical, Aragon remarks:

> I bore this epithet with fairly light heart at first. It troubled me hardly at all that they misunderstood a fury I felt. Years went by, and I understood that little by little my thought was being travestied. Everything dictated by one or other of my passions they turned into a sally, a manner of speaking. In France everything ends up in flowers of rhetoric. They selected in me the least unusual, and I was going to please the very people who could not have talked with me for five minutes without getting angry. [. . .] Well no: I shall not allow the masquerade any longer. No one shall be able to make me take the deep indignation I feel for the ridiculous amplification of a smile. (pp. 7–8)

The promise made at the end of this statement explains why, from the moment when the wardrobe is brought on stage, while the prologue characters are sent off, it never leaves our sight. At the end of L'Armoire à Glace emergence from inside the same wardrobe of everyone we met before Jules and Lénore came on the scene is a direct challenge to reason, just like the stage magician's illusion of the vanishing lady. In fact, it is even more disturbing. For whereas we expect an illusionist to trick us, we are unprepared for what takes place at the end of Aragon's drama. The playwright who has hinted at psychological motivation in characters set against an insistently realistic background cheats us, finally, of the consistent explanations he has encouraged us to anticipate. His behavior gives point to an observation made

in the preface to *Le Libertinage:* "Thus is explained for me my inso-
lence and my life: *you* cannot do anything against the shadow to which
my realm extends" (p. 14).

"What makes the theatre as dead as we are, Anicet used to say,"
one reads in Aragon's *Anicet ou le Panorama* (1921), "is no doubt that
its sole material is morality, the rule of all action: our period can
hardly take any interest in morality." Confronting us with material we
can make neither head nor tail of, in *L'Armoire à Glace* just as in *Au
Pied du Mur,* Aragon declines to draw any moral. Instead, he has
Fraenkel get to his feet and announce, "Now or never's the time to talk
politics," before leading the President of the Republic to the prompter's box. The President breaks into a song having no bearing either on
politics or on what the audience has just witnessed. When the lights
come up again, the stage is bare. The orchestra begins playing a military march.

In the theatre, a willing suspension of disbelief is a sign of the audience's confidence in the playwright. Specifically, it denotes faith in his
ability to provide a spectacle from which they will derive pleasure, or
profit, or even both. A dramatist who, after inviting such an act of
confidence, breaks the contract into which he has entered by doing so,
repudiates the fundamental characteristic of the theatre as an expression
of social exchange. The act of suspending disbelief has to be an unusually conscious and deliberate one, a token of especially good will,
when we are viewing *L'Armoire à Glace,* where gestures (Lénore's
crucifixion pose in front of the wardrobe, for instance) as well as
words are singularly exaggerated. It is therefore particularly vexatious
to the spectator to have to face the discovery that the trust he has
shown was apparently unwarranted.

Our well-intentioned effort to seek excuses for features of the play
we may have generously attributed to the author's inexperience has
been wasted, it now appears. Meanwhile it has become evident that,
counting on our cooperation, he has taken advantage of it, and of us.
Even as we sit wondering whether anything is going to happen on
stage after the orchestra has finished *Sambre-et-Meuse,* our first reaction is to feel that we are victims of a pointless hoax. However, if
tempted to infer only that it is just as well to cut our losses, promising
to be more wary in future, we miss the contribution Aragon has to
make to our understanding of the place of theatre in Dada and surrealism. In *L'Armoire à Glace* he lures us into defending the respectability

of established dramatic forms before demonstrating his own contempt for them. Here old structures of conventional drama become no more than the substructure upon which the playwright attempts to erect something quite different from what past experience has persuaded his audience to expect. Before he has finished with us, we have come to appreciate that, to him, banality and inconsequence in the prologue offer no more—and no less—reliable channels of communication than does the language of melodrama overlaying the erotic violence that the remainder of his play appeared designed to bring to our notice. Reintroducing the disparate collection of characters haphazardly assembled in the prologue, Aragon makes us face the fact that all is equally untrue. Everything, we find, is an illusion, an act of prestidigitation, when Aragon decides to invite us to accompany him as he moves through a conventional theatrical mode on a Snark hunt all his own.[13]

When Aragon's two plays were staged, Dada was no longer active in Paris. *Au Pied du Mur* was first put on at the Collège de France in June 1925, just before its production at the Vieux-Colombier Theatre. *L'Armoire à Glace* was presented at the Grenier jaune, Rue Lepic in Paris, on March 27, 1926. By the mid-twenties surrealism had replaced Dada and already had found in Louis Aragon one of its most brilliant exponents.

Le Libertinage, published on March 31, 1924, appeared more than six months in advance of Breton's *Manifeste du Surréalisme*, preceded by a prefactory text that internal evidence allows us to date from 1923. This preface makes one important thing clear. While Aragon was certain that Dada was now a thing of the past, he was by no means sure what would replace it. He speaks significantly of "an absolutely new state of mind that we were pleased to name the nebulous movement" (pp. 24–25). He states further that the *mouvement flou* to which he refers was identified by Breton, himself, and four or five friends as succeeding the collapse of Dada, which he confined to the years 1918–21. Moreover he explains, "I am justifying the nebulous, not compromise. It is a matter of rendering several exits impassible."

13. Aragon translated Lewis Carroll's *The Hunting of the Snark* into French. His version appeared in Chapelle-Réanville-Eure in 1929 with The Hours Press.

To the extent that it expresses his concern with *le flou,* everything in *Le Libertinage, Au Pied du Mur* and *L'Armoire à Glace* included, represents for its author a reaction against Dada. But this is not to say that, by merely taking thought, Aragon could or even imagined he could succeed in casting off characteristics that had enabled him to make a valued contribution to the cause of Dada. On the contrary, his preface shows quite plainly that he continued to regard these characteristics as expressive of his deepest needs. Therefore one cannot ignore one significant fact. The most uncompromising advocate of Dada principles would have applauded the rhetorical question formulated in the preface to *Le Libertinage:* "Is there an idea worth pausing over?" He would have approved no less Aragon's declaration: "I should like everything passing through my head to stay so briefly that I myself will never again find the memory of my thought" (p. 22).

Without displaying any awareness of self-contradiction, Aragon expresses in the introductory section to *Le Libertinage* both an impulse to break new ground and continued trust in instincts he is by no means prepared to stifle, when leaving Dada for something he hopes will be more in keeping with his current desires: "It is not just from today onward that I know myself to be a champion of disorder," he insists. On the question of continuity in Aragon's thought, the preface to *Le Libertinage* leaves no doubt at all. "I have never sought anything else but scandal," Aragon declares, "and I have sought it for itself."

From his standpoint in 1923, literature, poetry, and art are worth defending against the destructive program of Dada, in the measure that Aragon is reluctant to abandon the "convenient method of provoking scandal," which they seem to him to provide (p. 18). In fact, his preface lists for over half a page (pp. 14–15) the various occasions—including the recent war and Dada itself—for scandal of which he has already taken advantage. As Aragon pictures himself on this page, "with lips of defiance and a little dynamite in his fob pocket," he naturally comes to the defense of the inexplicable against the reasonable, in the two plays he deemed worthy of a place in *Le Libertinage:* "The inexplicable exists, whatever snobs have said about it. I am and shall remain against the partisans of foolishness and those of intelligence. I take sides with mystery and the unjustifiable" (p. 24). Hence, as expressed through *L'Armoire à Glace* and *Au Pied du Mur,* love of scandal does not confine Aragon's creative impulse to the iconoclasm preached in Dada. It opens the door upon other perspectives. These are, time will show, perspectives that surrealism invests with relevance. "May every movement of my mind be a step forward, and not a mark left behind" is Louis Aragon's prayer in *Le Libertinage*, which testifies to his preparedness to advance from Dada to surrealism.

André Breton and
Philippe Soupault

We must undoubtedly establish another order.[1]

IN A LETTER TO TRISTAN TZARA written on January 22, 1919, André Breton reported, "What I loved most in the world has just departed; my friend Jacques Vaché is dead," adding, "It is toward you that all my glances turn today." On July 29 following, Breton insisted, "I think of you as I have never thought before . . . except of Jacques Vaché; I have said so (that is, before acting I almost always come to an agreement with you)."[2] Subsequently, Breton voiced his respect for Tzara in *Littérature*, publicly avowing that Tzara now exerted over his imagination somewhat the same fascination as that anti-intellectual, anti-artistic marginal figure, Vaché, had done.[3] Much later, citing in *Entretiens* a statement by Tzara—"I am not a writer by profession and I have no literary ambitions. I would have been an adventurer on the grand scale [. . .] if I had had the physical strength and nervous resistance to see this one exploit through: not getting bored"—Breton was to comment, "It is evident that such an attitude brought him very close to Jacques Vaché, which will lead me to transfer to him a good share of the confidence and hopes I placed in Vaché" (p. 53).

Writing to Tzara on April 4, 1919, Breton observed, "I tend as you

1. André Breton and Philippe Soupault, "Barrières," *Les Champs magnétiques* [1920] suivi de *Vous m'oublierez* et de *S'il vous plaît* (Gallimard, 1967), p. 69.
2. Letters cited in Michel Sanouillet, *Dada à Paris* (Jean-Jaques Pauvert, 1965), pp. 440 and 446.
3. See "Clairement": "I admit to having transferred to Tzara some of the hopes that Vaché, if lyricism had not been his element, would never have disappointed." "Clairement" is reprinted in Breton's *Les Pas perdus* (Editions de la N.R.F., 1924). The sentence cited here occurs on p. 134.

do only to divest myself of artistic prejudices, the only ones I still have."[4]
"To kill art," he continued, seemed to him, just as to his correspondent,
"most urgent." This is why in a letter to Francis Picabia on January 5,
1920, he expressed pride in the fact that he pronounced the word "demoralization" as often as Tzara did. Breton added, "It is to this demoralization that we apply ourselves, Soupault and I, in *Littérature*."
Soupault, incidentally, had written to Tzara soliciting material for the
magazine on February 7, 1919.[5]

The weight of evidence seems convincing enough. All the same,
what we have heard Breton say does call for comment. To begin with,
the first sentence of the declaration attributed to Tzara in *Entretiens*
runs together two separate remarks. These occur some distance apart
in a letter from the Dada leader dated September 21, 1919, some eight
months after reading the 1918 Dada manifesto had led Breton to express confidence in its author. Moreover, while Breton evidently did
look to Tzara to replace Vaché, he soon came to fear in his Zurich
correspondent the consequences of the very negativism that had attracted him originally. June 12, 1919, found him enumerating "several
ways of succumbing": death (Lautréamont and Vaché, naturally); involuntary senile decay of the kind displayed by Barrès, Gide, and
Picasso when they began taking themselves too seriously; and voluntary senile decay like that of Rimbaud, giving up poetry for commerce,
or Jarry, seeking escape through drugs. Then Breton asked urgently:
"But you, my dear friend, how will you get out? Answer me, for
goodness' sake, do you see another window?" Sooner or later, the
future promoter of surrealism foresaw, Tzara was in danger of "dis-
qualifying" himself.[6]

This letter highlights one fact overlooked by many who recognize
without difficulty that, after idealizing Tzara from afar, Breton was
bound to feel some disappointment when they met, upon the former's
arrival in Paris at the beginning of 1920. Even before the Romanian
left Zurich, Breton was starting to have significant misgivings about the
Dada program, as outlined by Tzara. "Another little objection," he
wrote on October 7, 1919, "which fixes my attitude a bit more in relation to yours: The absence of system, you say, is still a system, but the
more attractive one; *I* find it [neither] more attractive nor more un-

4. Cited in Sanouillet, *Dada à Paris*, p. 443.
5. Ibid., pp. 505 and 568.
6. Ibid., p. 445.

attractive."[7] The characteristic of Dada termed in Breton's January 5, 1920, letter to Picabia "un *réflexe de défense*" was the one appealing most to the young Frenchman, as a necessary feature of a process of liberation to which he felt drawn. Even so, reservations began to form in his mind as soon as he realized that, for Tzara, demoralization was an end, not a means. Hence, to Breton, assertion of independence for his own views and needs, destined to find expression in surrealism as an autonomous entity no longer linked with Dada, meant resolving the conflict engendered within him by an impulse to revolt and the negative forces released by the same impulse.

There is some hint of that conflict in his letter to Tzara of April 20, 1919: "I am writing little at the moment, thinking out a project that must convulse several worlds. Don't think this is childishness or delirium. But the preparation of the *coup d'état* can take a few years." It would be wishful thinking, of course, to read into this remark a precise allusion to the project ultimately given a name in the *Manifeste du Surréalisme* of 1924. But that matters little. More to the point is noticing how Breton continues: "I am burning with the wish to inform you of this but after all I do not know you well enough. If I have a crazy confidence in you, this is because you remind me of my friend, my best friend Jacques Vaché. But perhaps I must not place too much faith in this resemblance."[8]

As a first step, it is essential to distinguish the direction that the future surrealist leader feels impelled to take out of Dada, when attempting to escape the penalty of disqualification that Tzara was soon to reveal himself quite content to accept. Dealing with Breton, we have to consider in which ways, although written in close proximity to Dada, certain of his early works—those collaborative ones in theatrical form, specifically—evade the limitations that Dada necessarily imposed.

Tzara was shortly to leave Zurich when Breton informed him on Friday, December 26, 1919, "I have just finished with Soupault a play in four acts."[9] A couple of weeks later, this first announcement was elaborated on Wednesday, January 14, 1920—only three days before

7. Ibid., p. 451.
8. Ibid., p. 444.
9. Ibid., p. 454.

Tzara's arrival in Paris: "I have just finished a play in collaboration with Soupault: 'If You Please' a drama in 4 acts. We are trying to get it staged next spring."[10]

Three things merit notice before we go any further. First, Breton and Soupault did not have to wait until Tzara had joined them before feeling the urge to write their first play or even before thinking of having it staged. Second, they had previously worked side by side on a significant series of texts that time would justify acknowledging as a landmark in the history of the emergence of the surrealist spirit. These texts, *Les Champs magnétiques* (*The Magnetic Fields*), were written in the summer of 1919, serialized in *Littérature,* and published in book form at the end of May 1920.[11] It is advisable therefore to examine the first Breton-Soupault play, written so soon afterward, for possible signs of tendencies that finally will divert the theatre from the track to which Dada had committed it, setting it upon another, which will be given direction by surrealist principles. Third, the comments that critics and literary historians have made on *S'il vous plaît* (*If You Please*) are, generally speaking, unreliable. Henri Béhar, it is true, avoids serious distortion by taking refuge in vagueness. He situates the play "on the border of dadaism."[12] Martin Esslin, though, dismisses it summarily as "bizarre and largely improvised,"[13] while Sanouillet inaccurately dates it from January 1920 (p. 315).

Sanouillet notes correctly that *S'il vous plaît* was performed at the Salle Berlioz on March 27, 1920, beside *La Première Aventure céleste de Monsieur Antipyrine* and *Le Serin muet.* He points out that Breton and Soupault both took part, as did Mlle L. Moyon, Paul and Gala Eluard, Théodore Fraenkel, Henry Cliquennois, and Georges Ribemont-Dessaignes. Béhar lists the same participants. However, the distri-

10. Ibid., p. 455.
11. On July 29, 1919, in a letter to Tzara, Breton excused himself for sending a copy of his *Mont de Piété* (1919). He insisted, "Wait, please, before you judge me, for the appearance in September of *The Magnetic Fields* [. . .] or only the publication in book form of J. V.'s letters, for the introduction I have done." On September 21, Tzara wrote to Breton of awaiting his book impatiently (see Sanouillet, *Dada à Paris,* p. 448). *Les Champs magnétiques* is dedicated to Jacques Vaché, whose *Lettres de Guerre* appeared in 1920. See *Lettres de Guerre de Jacques Vaché* (K. éditeur, 1949). See also the pages devoted to Vaché in Breton's *Anthologie de l'Humour noir* [1940] (Jean-Jacques Pauvert, 1966), pp. 493–503.
12. Henri Béhar, *Etude sur le Théâtre dada et surréaliste* (Gallimard, 1967), p. 186.
13. Martin Esslin, *The Theatre of the Absurd* [1961], rev. ed. (New York: Doubleday, Anchor, 1969), pp. 319–20.

bution of roles provided by Béhar (p. 338) gives the impression that only the second act of *S'il vous plaît* was staged, no character being mentioned in his list who appears in any of the other acts. Tristan Tzara, for his part, has claimed that only the first act was performed, accompanying this statement with a wildly inaccurate version of the content of Act Two.[14]

Trying to explain the fact that "the literary style of the piece varies widely," Michael Benedikt falls into confusion when he comments, "perhaps less because of its collaborative origin than because of the desire of its authors to flaunt [*sic*] the usual literary goals of homogeneity of style."[15] One comes closer to the mark when remembering the following. Simply stated, the purpose underlying this drama appears to be to demonstrate the ineffectuality of conventional theatrical forms in two acts that, rationally speaking, lead nowhere, before traditional modes are combated more vigorously in an innovative third act. The fourth and final act makes no attempt to render Act Three palatable to any spectator who may not have found it to his taste.

Act One opens as though its authors have every intention of abiding by the usages of bourgeois drama. Hinting broadly at the existence of a love triangle, the first scene lets us hear Paul ("40 years old, moustache in the American style") speaking passionately to a young woman. Scene Two brings on Valentine's husband, François, who announces his intention of leaving Paris on a trip to Geneva that his wife has urged him to take. At this stage, Breton and Soupault seem content to borrow stock situation and predictable effect. With unconscious irony, François says to his wife, "I hope you are not going to be bored," and tells Paul, "Try to keep her amused. I'm counting on you, old friend." A similar use of conventional material can be observed in Robert Desnos' film script *Midi à quatorze heures*.[16] As is the case with Desnos' use of cinematographic clichés, conventionality at first lulls our suspicions in *S'il vous plaît*. In *Midi à quatorze heures*, conventional beginnings lead to unaccountable mysterious developments. In the play by Breton and Soupault, psychological motivation is totally disregarded, thus offering no acceptable explanation for the violent gesture bringing the opening act to an end.

14. See Tristan Tzara, *Le Surréalisme et l'Après-Guerre* (Nagel, 1948), p. 20.
15. Michael Benedikt and George Wellwarth, *Modern French Theatre: The Avant-Garde, Dada, and Surrealism* (New York: Dutton, 1964), p. xxiv.
16. See J. H. Matthews, *Surrealism and Film* (Ann Arbor: University of Michigan Press, 1971), pp. 57–58.

As in *Midi à quatorze heures*, in *S'il vous plaît* outworn situation initially seems to function as a shortcut to apprehension of the authors' meaning. Spectators are deluded into thinking themselves on familiar ground, and so entitled to adopt their accustomed posture vis-à-vis the drama being enacted before them. Eventually, however, they discover that the elements of the spectacle in which they have come to place confidence are the least capable of justifying what takes place in the end. With François safely out of the house, Paul can take advantage of his friend's absence. But he does not make love to Valentine, as his amorous language earlier led us to anticipate that he would. In direct contradiction with the pompous commonplace he delivered at the start of the third scene ("A door closes and our life begins"), he murders her with a revolver carried in his pocket.

It is reasonable to assume that the second act of *S'il vous plaît* is going to help elucidate the first. However, instead of meeting expectations, Act Two develops quite independently of Act One. Set in a business office run by Létoile ("40 years old, clean shaven, Legion of Honor, tortoise-shell glasses"), it presents a mysterious figure—played by Breton—engaged in a bewildering variety of activities, some of them rather exotic.

Létoile "enjoys the same faculties as God," observes a man who asks him to help recover stolen jewelry—only to be referred to the police. In every situation that would appear to have been designed to illustrate his powers and uncover his motivation, Létoile's actions are just as paradoxical. When two ladies come to appeal for funds "in a good cause," he generously gives them a large sum. Then he promptly has the police summoned to arrest them for stealing. Learning now that they have a license for what they are doing, he reclaims his money and calmly burns it before their eyes. Next, when a veiled lady consults him on her marital difficulties, this supposed marriage counselor seems far more disposed than she to insist upon divorce. After her departure, Létoile proceeds to dictate a notice of reward for information about the whereabouts of two women (the fund raisers?) whom he accuses of stealing the jewelry we heard him decline to recover. Then, as marriage broker, he follows truisms on the joys of conjugal life with an order to two policemen to arrest his latest client "for the murder of his mistress, Madame Valentine Saint-Cervan." Is this, at last, the connection between Act Two and Act One? If it is, then why is the man

Létoile accuses visibly younger than Paul, and why does he have a curly blond moustache?

A delegation of employees arrives to present grievances. "It's hard to give wallets back," they point out. Also, "The other day we disguised ourselves separately upon your orders, and you had us follow one another." Létoile is firm, however: "I owe no explanation. If you are not satisfied, I'll not detain you." Arrival of a police inspector who talks of charges that remain unspecified (he is impersonated by Ribemont-Dessaignes) leaves Létoile unperturbed as the act comes to an end:

THE INSPECTOR
You are charged . . .
LETOILE
What difference do you think that makes to me?[17]

Observing that *S'il vous plaît* is composed of "a series of playlets constructed according to the best rules of dramatic art but perfectly incoherent" (pp. 166–67), Michel Sanouillet gives Breton and Soupault less than their due. Carefully put together according to established dramatic methods, the individual sections making up the first two acts of this play do not achieve total incoherence, and are not intended to do so. This, in fact, is what frustrates the spectator whom the application of familiar techniques has persuaded to believe he is witnessing theatre of a kind he knows well: like Act One, Act Two almost succeeds in making sense to him. Apparently, though, as a result of some lapse that he finds unaccountable, each time the playwrights fall just short of accomplishing something he thought they wished to do.

In both of the first two acts, the degree of technical competence displayed is far from negligible. Thus to give full credit to the experiment carried out in *S'il vous plaît* one must start by admitting that its authors had enough skill, should they have cared to do this, to make sure of erecting the second act upon the foundation laid in the first. Intention, not incompetence, therefore underlies the incoherent plot structure of the first half of their four-act drama. In aggressive fashion, Breton and Soupault demonstrate how proven ingredients can be arranged in a manner that shakes the stability of dramatic convention. Outward respect for form merely conceals, temporarily, their lack of respect for the unity from which formal considerations traditionally draw both purpose and value. Being deprived of purpose, form guar-

17. *Les Champs magnétiques*, etc., 1967 ed., p. 179.

antees nothing in *S'il vous plaît*. Thus it loses significance, so increasing the audience's exasperation as time goes by, instead of alleviating it. To anyone inclined to leave his seat, after the second act, the playwrights have nothing to add to the words used by Létoile, when declining to detain those looking to him for an explanation of his conduct.

But what of those spectators—or readers—who persevere? It should come as no surprise to them to find the third act, set in a café where two men are playing cards at three in the afternoon, without any observable connection with what it follows. However, this new sequence does more than confirm that *S'il vous plaît* is wilfully discontinuous. Focusing attention on a young man about thirty and a prostitute, it lets us in on a strange conversation. Beside this one, the amorous dialogue involving Paul and Valentine earlier appears a model of clarity. Act Three contrasts even more sharply with the second act. And of course it sounds nothing at all like a conventionally realistic conversation between a streetwalker and a prospective client.

Although interrupted here and there by commonplaces, the words exchanged between Maxime and Gilda represent a violent challenge to theatrical language in the naturalistic vein. True, their conversation closes with a direct attack upon idealism (Gilda: "Don't insist, my dear. You'd regret it. I have the pox"). Yet for the most part it is pitched at a level that sets the third act quite apart from the rest of *S'il vous plaît:*

GILDA
The instinct to please resembles a well. Believe me, rings are nothing. There is in Paris on the big boulevards such a slight incline that almost no one has managed to avoid slipping on it.

MAXIME
The most touching maps of the world are the silvered globes in which the café waiter from time to time puts a serviette away. Caged birds like these little shining spheres. It all comes down to the same thing, singing with the street, or the sewing machine.

GILDA
I know liberty through certain finer attachments.

MAXIME
The kingdom of heaven is peopled with assassins. There is a swing awaiting you higher up. Do not lift your head yet. (pp. 182–83)

No explanation comes from any of the Dada writings of Tzara for such dialogue as we have just sampled. Nor does any statement, inspired by Dada principles, coming from some other writer, help account for it. Not until Breton's *Manifeste du Surréalisme* appears in 1924 does one encounter comments offering guidance to an understanding of why Maxime and Gilda talk as they do.

Declaring that the forms of surrealist language are best adapted to dialogue, Breton notes in his first surrealist manifesto that, in dialogue, two thoughts confront one another, the one reacting to the other. The important factor here is the nature of that reaction, he believes: "My attention, prey to a solicitation it cannot decently reject, treats the opposing thought as an enemy." Hence when one talks to someone, he can turn the other person's thought "to account" in a reply that "distorts" it, or, more exactly (Breton employs the verb *dénaturer*) "changes its nature" (p. 49). Emphasizing this point with the assistance of examples furnished by pathological states of mind, "in which sensorial disturbances takes the patient's complete attention," Breton asserts that something of this disorder passes into every conversation, despite our effort to be sociable. The important thing is that, in the examples of echolalia ("How old are you?"—"You.") and Gasner syndrome ("What is your name?"—"Forty-five houses.") offered in *Le Manifeste du Surréalisme*, the patient has the advantage, because "he imposes himself through his replies upon the examining doctor's attention—and is not the person asking questions" (p. 50).

Breton's 1924 text goes on to explain that, to date, poetic surrealism has applied itself to establishing dialogue "in absolute truth" once again, by "freeing both interlocutors from the obligations of politeness." As a consequence, each one simply pursues his own soliloquy, "without seeking to derive any special dialectical pleasure from it or to impose in the least upon his neighbor." Statements uttered under these conditions do not serve to present a thesis, nor even to develop a consecutive theme. As for the replies they bring forth, these, "theoretically," have nothing to do with the vanity of the speaker. "Words and images offer themselves as springboards to the mind of the listener," Breton explains: "This is how, in *Les Champs magnétiques*, the first purely surrealist work, those pages grouped under the title *Barrières* must present themselves. There Soupault and I show ourselves to be those impartial inter-locutors" (p. 51).

Glancing down a page of "Barrières," we have the impression that Breton and Soupault respect logical progression in arranging statements we anticipate finding rationally acceptable. However, an attempt to read the page, which one would expect to confirm this impression, denies it validity. Instead, we find grammatical structure—generally most carefully respected in surrealist writing—to be a trap.

Our habitual responsiveness to a familiar grammatical sequence evidences inculcated prejudice in favor of a rational order that surrealists seek to overthrow. Thus in the extract below, stress falls upon things seen, against common sense and in no reasonably perceptible order. What we are made to see is brought to our attention in a manner that reproves the principle of cause and effect, which, incidentally, makes grammatical structure seem authoritative:

> "The rivers are not mirrors, much better ones have been made in the past ten years. With a stone I can break all the mirrors in the city where we live and insects smaller than the cries of infants voluptuously burrow into the foundations of skyscrapers."
>
> "No doubt, and yet we are not witnessing central pillaging. You are wrong in thinking that our voices serve to fill spaces that signify. We were not born very long ago."
>
> "Alas! A friend of the family gave me an octopus and, so that this respectable animal should not know hunger, a green liqueur that contained liquid metal polish. The invertebrate wasted away before our eyes and when, two days after its death, we cleaned out the bowl, we had the joy of discovering a mauve shell which was called chalcedony."
>
> "That's happened before. I myself could tell you of an embellishment which followed the visit by the President of the Republic. From a bunch of keys he had placed under glass was born an official clock that struck the hour of restorations." (p. 59)

We need read no further to appreciate how the confidence engendered by the reassuringly logical succession of introductory phrases ("No doubt," "Alas!," "That's happened before"), identifiable when the page is merely scanned, collapses upon close examination of the text.

In the dialogued passage entitled "Barrières," each response is less of a reply to what goes before than a new departure. The underlying idea, Breton has explained, was to "Take to the highest point the misunderstanding of conversation. This is what results. One of the interlocutors writes a few phrases very quickly. The other reads them very quickly without really getting to know them. He continues in the same way."[18] Thus to varying degrees each response finds impetus in the statement preceding it. Yet in no case is development reasonably controlled by what came first. As a consequence, the reader is made aware of gathering imaginative momentum, while at the same time becoming increasingly conscious of the speakers' disrespect for logical sequence. Indeed, where one is most aware of a consecutive order, the imaginative content seems to have been diluted, as when mention of "a magnificent doorway" elicits the pedestrian response: "The most magnificent doorways are those behind which one reads 'Open in the name of the law!' " (p. 64). This means that "Barrières" impresses most when it lends substance to the assertion that Breton boldly makes in his first surrealist manifesto: "Surrealism does not permit those who devote themselves to it to forsake it when they please. There is every reason to believe it acts upon the mind in the manner of narcotics; like these it creates a certain state of need and can impel man to terrible revolts" (p. 51).

The elements giving "Barrières" its characteristic quality are the very ones that we find to be present in the dialogue between Gilda and Maxime. It is worth noticing, therefore, that Alain Jouffroy has reported, when presenting a reprint of *Les Champs magnétiques*, "It was André Breton himself who wished, at the time when he gave his approval for a reprinting of the original surrealist text, that these two plays [*S'il vous plaît* and *Vous m'oublierez*] be included [. . .]" (p. 8). Clearly, toward the end of his life Breton was eager to direct attention to features that those plays had in common with *Les Champs magnétiques*. Although the *Manifeste du Surréalisme* does not cite *S'il vous plaît* as an example of poetic surrealism, it is possible—thanks to *Les Champs magnétiques*—to grasp an essential fact, evidenced as early as the first play that Breton and Soupault wrote together. At a time when he was still dedicated to the cause of Dada, Breton already had begun to look out of "a new window." It was a window he had had to find for himself, Tzara having proved incapable of directing him to its location.

18. See *Change*, special number on *Les Champs magnétiques*, No. 7 (1970), p. 19.

To talk of *Les Champs magnétiques* is to open the question of automatic writing and its role in surrealism. This, in turn, means discussing the relationship of surrealism to Dada. Those, led by Michel Sanouillet, who seek at all cost to minimize the individuality of surrealist aspiration and who claim for Dada the paternity of the most publicized methods by which surrealists have pursued their aims argue that the best-known of these methods, automatism, is a purely Dada discovery. However, Anna Balakian has challenged their claims, through her examination of Breton's debt to Dr Pierre Janet.

It is Miss Balakian's contention that surrealist automatic writing should be viewed in a "strictly scientific context." She insists that it was thanks to his medical studies, not to Dada, that Breton became acquainted with the phenomenon of automatic writing, and argues that he tried to practice it as a scientific device:

> In Janet's teachings, and in Breton's adoption of them, psychic automatism becomes a breach in the wall that had previously shut off some of the most fundamental areas of man's knowledge of self. It is a means to an end; it foretells the gradual lifting of *le grand interdit*. It is part of the process of making man divine, as it gives him access to the sub rosa functioning of his mind without outside aids or provocations; it is a gate to self-observation and therefore to insight, to an enlargement of the magnetic field of his reality; it can lead to the eventual abolition of the man-made frontiers between material and spiritual existence.[19]

In automatism practiced within a scientific context, Miss Balakian comments elsewhere, what is irrational is "the effect produced on the observer when the mind is, in the process, unburdened of the overwhelming armor of patterns which are called 'rational' because of collective, social agreement."[20]

One senses that Miss Balakian gives more attention to Breton's interpretation of Janet's *L'Automatisme psychique* and *De l'Angoisse à l'Extase* than to their author's intentions in publishing these works. But in so doing she performs the useful service of indicating how different is the role of automatism to the surrealist leader from the role reserved

19. Anna Balakian, *André Breton: Magus of Surrealism* (New York: Oxford University Press, 1971), pp. 30–31.
20. Anna Balakian, "Dada–Surrealism: Fundamental Differences," *Proceedings of the Comparative Literature Symposium*, III, 'From Surrealism to the Absurd' (Lubbock: Texas Tech University, 1970), 22.

for it in Dada. Whether justifiably or not, from the medical standpoint, inspiration from Janet did contribute to helping Breton make of automatic writing, as Miss Balakian goes on to say, "not a device for the vilification of the human image, or the satirical representation of man's linguistic inefficacies, but rather a resource for the release of the latent powers of words" (p. 23).

We shall return to this question shortly. For the time being, we may readily forgive a reader of *Littérature*'s September–October 1920 number (in which the first three acts of *S'il vous plaît* were published) for being quite insensitive to the differences Miss Balakian helps us identify between automatic writing in Dada and automatism as practiced during the composition of the third act of the Breton-Soupault play. A note informed him abruptly, "The authors of IF YOU PLEASE wish the text of the fourth act not to be published," so leaving him to speculate about its content and to wonder whether Act Four might have furnished the all-embracing explanation he was now denied. Benedikt's deduction—made, as it happens, in ignorance of what takes place in the fourth act—is that the note after Act Three (and which he translates incorrectly, by the way) is one of "many outward signs of the then contemporary movement, Dada" (p. xxiv). No doubt those acquainted with as much of *S'il vous plaît* as *Littérature* made accessible would have concurred in this judgment. What is more, consultation with someone who had seen the play performed would surely have strengthened their impression.

During the final act, the house lights are lowered but not extinguished entirely. On stage, two "insignificant characters" stop in a street by a doorway. Consulting his watch, X says he is leaving. Y remains, walking up and down, looking upward, brushing off his sleeve, blowing his nose. From the auditorium comes the question, "That's all?" On stage, Y looks surprised, but says nothing. A second member of the audience intervenes, despite efforts to silence him: "I don't understand anything. It's stupid." Presumably encouraged by another spectator who cries "If only it were amusing!" Spectator No 2 stands on his seat and delivers the following speech, to the accompaniment of applause:

> I repeat that I don't understand anything. It's probable that I'm not the only one. For some time now, on the pretext of originality and independence, our fine art has been sabotaged by a

gang, increasing in number every day, who are, for the most part, only agitators, lazy fellows or practical jokers.

The curtain comes down. Undeterred, Spectator No 2 goes on:

> It is easier to get yourself talked about in this fashion than to attain real glory at the cost of hard work. Are we going to put up with the most contradictory ideas and aesthetic theories, the beautiful and the ugly, talent and force without style, being placed on the same footing, from now on? I appeal to our traditional good sense. It shall not be said that the sons of Montaigne, Voltaire, Renan . . . (pp. 188–89)

At this moment yet another spectator, one who earlier questioned No 2's right to say what he thought ("You have the right to leave"), interrupts: "Throw him out. Continue." The fourth act now begins once again, causing No 2 to lose patience altogether. He and his wife leave, but not before he has exclaimed, "It's shameful," shaking his fist at the stage. In the ensuing hubbub the cries "*Vive la France*" and "Continue" can be distinguished. The call "Author" brings on two actors, in place of Breton and Soupault, and the curtain comes down for good.

Only hindsight can offer clarification where it would have been difficult, around 1920, for Breton and his friends to see clearly all that their efforts implied. It is plain, today, that the argument put forward by Ribemont-Dessaignes in *Déjà Jadis* uses inadmissible simplification of facts so as to cast Breton in the role of unsavory opportunist. "The truth is," declares Ribemont-Dessaignes, "that Breton no doubt never had anything of the dadaist about him and that he used Dada to draw the vague idea he had of Surrealism with difficulty from its matrix, and to appear afterward as the chief of a conscious and organized group" (p. 90). It is quite unjust to suggest, as Ribemont-Dessaignes does, that, in allowing *S'il vous plaît* and *Vous m'oublierez* (*You Will Forget Me*) to be presented within the framework of Dada spectacles, Breton and Soupault were knowingly guilty of passing surrealism off as Dada. Indeed the former has confessed in his *Entretiens*, "Soupault and I, for instance, got no little satisfaction from the fact that a sketch of ours [*Vous m'oublierez*], at the Salle Gaveau, earned us a bombardment of eggs, tomatoes, and beefsteak that the spectators precipitately went out for during the intermission. What the public thought of us we thought in return, a hundredfold" (p. 58). The end of *S'il vous plaît* ridicules the kind of objections voiced during and after Dada demonstrations. Nothing in the text of the fourth act, printed for the first time in 1967 from a copy Breton had retained, gives us to understand that, when bringing their drama to a close, the playwrights wished to appear in any guise other than that of Dada activists.

In the long run, though, the point at issue is not whether Breton and Soupault could be accused of being surrealists masquerading as dedicated members of the Dada movement. The negative aspects of their theatre were unquestionable and unquestioned credentials for admission to the Dada circle. But this does not alter the fact that, in retrospect, the most striking feature of their first play, written while they were in contact with Dada, emerges better when it is considered in the perspective appropriate to surrealism. What matters, really, is that, already alarmed at seeing Dada "fighting the Battle of *Hernani* every month" and complacently using "the same stereotyped tactics," Breton and Soupault, however little they realized this, were advancing through Dada scandal toward something more positive, in which Tzara clearly had no interest.

When *S'il vous plaît* and *Vous m'oublierez* are examined in conjunction, the parallel observable between the language used in the third act of the former and the dialogued section of *Les Champs magnétiques* takes on particular significance for anyone concerned with the early manifestation of the surrealist spirit in the theatre.[21] Considered side by side, these plays certainly merit a better fate than the one reserved for them by Anna Balakian, who writes them off as "dramatic fragments which today are of no more than documentary interest" (p. 64).

All the same, what Sanouillet has to tell us of *Vous m'oublierez*, when commenting on the Festival Dada that saw its performance, invites us to give it scant attention. Preoccupied with proving that Dada "was getting out of breath already," rather than with giving *Vous m'oublierez* its due, Sanouillet mentions the second Breton-Soupault

21. It is not without significance that Anna Balakian has reported, with regard to *Les Champs magnétiques*, "When the work was finished, neither poet made any attempt to identify publicly which part belonged to him, and the impression of continuity is expertly maintained. However, in discovering on a marked copy who wrote what in the collaboration, I was able to observe the dialogue character of much of it, which makes the automatism appear like a game of ping-pong" (*André Breton*, p. 63).

play after the first as proof of repetitiveness in Dada ideas (p. 174). Another critic adopts a less sympathetic attitude. Citing Breton's complaint in *Entretiens* about the monotony of Dada tactics and his slighting references to "the nth *Celestial Adventure of Monsieur Antipyrine*," Béhar remarks, "one could say as much of the plays of Breton and Soupault, acted by their friends. Between *S'il vous plaît* and *Vous m'oublierez* there is very little difference, and the latter sketch could be added to the preceding play, as fourth act, without its being apparent, so much does the dislocation of rules of composition authorize additions or cuts" (p. 191). Reluctant to entertain the idea that Breton and Soupault may have been even the slightest bit more inventive than Tzara, neither Béhar nor Sanouillet considers the possibility that the authors of *Vous m'oublierez* might have taken a step forward, for which writing *S'il vous plaît* had prepared them.

Sanouillet affirms that *Vous m'oublierez* "has real theatrical value" (p. 177), but without specifying whether this quality guarantees or denies the text value as an expression of Dada. Whatever he wishes us to conclude, his remark bears little relationship to the significance that *Vous m'oublierez* assumes in the light of surrealism.

From where the surrealists stand, there seems no reason at all why, as theatre, this play should demonstrate any improvement over its predecessor. Technical competence has no bearing upon the standards by which surrealists evaluate writing for the stage. Recognition of this fact promotes responsiveness to the second play authored by Breton and Soupault as, from the surrealist viewpoint, complementary to the drama it followed. To these playwrights it seemed less important to break new ground than to continue in the direction they had begun exploring in the third act of their first stage play.

It is not difficult to detect in *S'il vous plaît*'s third act an armature of consecutive dialogue, beneath apparently inconsequential language denoting a striking departure from familiar theatrical usage. *Vous m'oublierez*, however, dispenses with a rational substructure of this sort, which becomes redundant in a sketch that brings together Robe de Chambre ("Dressing Gown," played by Philippe Soupault), Parapluie ("Umbrella," impersonated by André Breton), Machine à Coudre ("Sewing Machine," acted by Paul Eluard even though it is a female role), and an unknown man (Théodore Fraenkel).[22] Pursuing ends

22. Two scenes from the play were published in the first number of the maga-

peculiarly their own, the authors are willing now to relax dramatic structure totally. In fact the vestiges of conventional drama that do survive in *Vous m'oublierez* are reduced to such ridiculously restricted proportions that their presence can have no function other than an ironic one. At one point, for example, a remark by Sewing Machine seems intended to introduce a theme of proven theatrical vitality: "You know Flag, don't you? You know he does not forgive. If I fall into his claws I am lost" (Scene 2). But neither Umbrella nor Dressing Gown pays serious attention. On the contrary, by a process typical of this sketch, conversational links are soon severed. Before long Sewing Machine is crying, "Umbrella, listen to me, I have nothing to tell you!"

Sustained and consecutive dialogue has no place in a play that allows Umbrella to take time to write up a ludicrous multiplication sum on a blackboard and to offer a description of Paris straight out of a guide book. No attempt is made, meanwhile, to interest the audience in what the grotesquely named people on stage do, or in their relations with one another. On the contrary, discontinuity is the governing principle throughout. Umbrella whispers in Sewing Machine's ear, "The virgin is ready? Not everything can be sung to the tune of impatient stamping feet, if the yellow daisies whirl around, lottery flowers, in the place of closing eyes" (Scene 2). Sewing Machine's reply shows that she admits no obligation to *respond*, in the accepted sense of the word. Rather, she claims the same privilege to follow her own thoughts as was granted the unidentified speakers in "Barrières": "Do you want string or oranges? My fine boss made me a present of a pair of suspenders and that is not all. Department store elephants, come running with your dark lanterns. The sun has not set. Dressing Gown! Are you there, dear?"

Between the composition of the first Breton-Soupault play and that of the second, the authors' conception of the nature of communication has evolved. Instead of rehearsing the familiar, language is now called upon to pioneer more boldly exploration of the unknown in the direction at which Anna Balakian has hinted. Increasingly, logical incoherence opens the door on poetry.

Two points call for stress, here, to dispel confusion regarding

zine *Cannibale* on April 25, 1920. The complete text, dated May 1920, appeared subsequently in *Littérature* (Nouvelle Série, No. 4, September 1, 1922), which had also published Lautréamont's *Poésies* (transcribed by Breton from the only known copy in the National Library, Paris) between March and June 1919.

poetry as surrealists speak of it, and poetry of the kind advocated by Tzara and those whose ambitions were circumscribed, like his, by Dada principles. The emphasis upon impeccable grammatical structure so noticeable in *Les Champs magnétiques* shows well enough that, as co-founders of surrealism, Breton and Soupault were by no means inclined to agree with Tzara over the poetic virtue of "words in liberty." Meanwhile, comparison of *Vous m'oublierez* with Ribemont-Dessaignes's *Le Serin muet* highlights in the former another fundamental departure from Dada practice.

It is by no means true that, as Béhar affirms when discussing Riquet's conversations with Barate, in *Le Serin muet* "each of the two characters pursues his own monologue, without attending to the other's words" (p. 128). Each listens, albeit with no more attention than is necessary to make it possible for him to try diverting the other's monologue to a direction more congenial to himself. In *Vous m'oublierez* we face something more complex. To explain it, we have to be aware of influences upon Breton and Soupault to which Tzara and Ribemont-Dessaignes were quite impervious.

Béhar seems to believe he has caught Breton and Soupault out, as though he had detected some unconfessed crime. He talks accusingly of "aesthetic preoccupations" as being "all too evident" in their *Vous m'oublierez*. Apparently, he has not noticed that in *Entretiens* (pp. 58–59), with no sign at all of reluctance, Breton's recollections of his period of association with Dada give prominence to a sense of tradition that, we are told, was important to "at least two or three" of those who participated in Dada activities. Being a literary tradition that extended back into the nineteenth century, it could hold little appeal for a Tristan Tzara. All the same, it exerted a strong enough attraction over Breton and Soupault, at the time they were writing their second play, to make *Vous m'oublierez* less than fully comprehensible unless we realize how fervently it pays tribute to Lautréamont.

In *Entretiens* also we find Breton speaking openly of the violence of certain "imperatives" to which, around 1920, Lautréamont's *Les Chants de Maldoror* submitted him and a few close friends (p. 42). In this connection, he comments upon the preoccupation they all shared with "the *lyrical* phenomenon in poetry," explaining his understanding of lyricism in these terms: "that which constitutes going in some sort of spasmodic way beyond controlled expression" (p. 43). The best definition of lyricism as he saw it then, he recalls, is the fourth *Chant,*

with its remarkable comparisons, of which the most celebrated in surrealist circles is, "Beautiful as the chance encounter, on a dissecting
table, of a sewing machine and an umbrella." What clearer indication
could one have than the presence on stage of Machine à Coudre and
Parapluie that, writing *Vous m'oublierez*, Breton and Soupault had
Lautréamont in mind?

To estimate how deep was the loyalty that Breton and his friends
came to feel for Lautréamont, one has only to open *Entretiens*, which
reproduces a statement by Soupault that Breton says he would gladly
have countersigned: "It is not my place, or anyone else's (do you hear,
Gentlemen, who wishes to receive my seconds?) to judge the Count.
One does not judge M. de Lautréamont. One recognizes him as he
passes and one bows to the ground. I will give my life to the person,
man or woman, who will ever make me forget him" (p. 42). What is
important is that the surrealist attitude with regard to Lautréamont
was, from the first, fiercely defensive and strongly proprietory in nature. This is why in *Vous m'oublierez* the general public's ignorance
about his work was not merely anticipated but actually turned to account in keeping the audience at a distance. When Sewing Machine
pleads, "Explain to me, Umbrella, and I will leave," Dressing Gown
replies sharply, "No explanations" (Scene 2).

Presentation of *Vous m'oublierez* in the course of a Dada show
has had the consequence of encouraging everyone to assess this play
exclusively in relation to Dada. Thus attention has gone naturally to
aspects of the Breton-Soupault text that seem typical of the iconoclastic approach favored in Dada. These include Sewing Machine's
question to Umbrella, which presents no novelty to those who have sat
through certain other Dada plays before hearing *Vous m'oublierez*: "Is
this comedy going to come to an end?" (Scene 2). They include too
conversations like the following, in which Umbrella's interpretation of
Sewing Machine's word *temps* as "weather," not "time," disrupts logical sequence in a manner that, apparently, does not trouble Sewing
Machine at all:

> SEWING MACHINE
> Umbrella, for pity's sake, answer me, where do we stand with
> time?
>
> UMBRELLA
> Variable. (*Correcting himself*) Set fair.

SEWING MACHINE
You love me.   (Scene 2)

Better acquaintance with the writings of Lautréamont might have redressed the balance, making it possible for public and commentators alike to appreciate that Breton and Soupault were not content with merely engaging in Dada provocation. They were reaching out for something that lay beyond Dada and would have long-range consequences of the most profound significance for surrealism.

That both Breton and Soupault were in the process of turning away from Dada is evident once we consider the structure and function of dialogue in their second theatrical experiment.

Whereas the Dada dialogue of Tzara shocked by its disjunctive nature, by the anti-rational juxtaposition of words, the language of surrealism would aim at seducing reason, at persuading the imagination to surrender before the enticing images of the marvelous. In the course of explaining why he had taken over the direction of the magazine *La Révolution surréaliste*, Breton wrote in its fourth number (July 15, 1925) of "the conviction we all share here, that is to say, that we are living in the very midst of modern society on such a serious compromise that it justifies every audacity on our part." He continued, "Who speaks of having us at his disposal, of making us contribute to the abominable comfort of this world? We want, we will have the beyond in our time. All we need for that is to listen to our impatience and to remain, without any reticence at all, at the disposal of the marvelous."

Occupying an intermediary position between Dada and surrealism, *Vous m'oublierez* offers pertinent evidence that Anna Balakian might well have included when presenting her thesis that Dada "had proved only to be a cry of freedom *from* certain stilted conventions of living and communication," while Breton "stressed freedom *for*."[23] In its typical form, the Dada playwright's sense of responsibility—and this is as true of Ribemont-Dessaignes as it is of Tzara—had consisted in declining to accept the obligation to meet his audience on their ground. For the surrealist, *Vous m'oublierez* warned, responsibility would lie,

23. Balakian, "Dada–Surrealism: Fundamental Differences," pp. 17 and 18.

rather, in luring spectators into magnetic fields (*champs magnétiques*) where they would no longer be able to find customary bearings.

The theatre inspired exclusively by Dada aims at challenging the audience to protest by refusing to provide what the public felt entitled to expect of a play. Its practitioner could congratulate himself when he had turned the tables on his audience. Recalling the Salle Gaveau demonstration, Tzara exclaimed with pride in *Le Surréalisme et l'Après-Guerre*, "The spectacle was in the auditorium, we were assembled on stage and watched the public unleashed" (p. 20). But while negation was the mainspring of Dada, it was to be for the surrealists a key to effects in which their convictions led them to see positive value. Hence, in the perspective soon to be formally adopted by those listed as advocates of surrealism in the *Manifeste du Surréalisme* of 1924, it was less important to worry over the literary air that *Vous m'oublierez* had, next to *La Deuxième Aventure céleste de Monsieur Antipyrine*, than to recognize what prospect of release it offered from the impasse of Dada.

Vous m'oublierez begins on an interrogative note. It closes without having provided rationally acceptable answers to the questions it has raised, either among the characters on stage or in the minds of the audience. Although posed three times, Robe de Chambre's query elicits no response, even when he opens a window to shout it to the world— "Tell me: what then is that tree, that young leopard which I caressed the other day when I came home?" (Scene 1). As for the answer supplied by Parapluie to a question he himself has asked—"a dead animal under a piece of furniture"—it makes no more sense whether we read the question "*Qu'est-ce que l'acacia?*" as "What is acacia?" or as "What is gum arabic?" (Scene 2). In *Vous m'oublierez* we are denied the right to protest in the name of reason, when hearing Robe de Chambre give the very same answer to two questions that he in turn raises: "What is honor?" and "What is the future?" (Scene 2). Robe de Chambre could evidently say, "My role is to establish nothing," just as Parapluie does before remarking, "I am twenty-four years old and wear glasses" (Scene 2). To the authors of this play, stating the obvious (Breton, who wore spectacles, was twenty-four at the time *Vous m'oublierez* was staged) establishes nothing. They prefer therefore to challenge our reluctance to be guided by anything but reason, which, in the world of pedestrian reality, presides despotically over the ordering of verifiable facts.

The question-and-answer technique as employed in *Vous m'ou-blierez* is a means of confronting the public with the inadequacies of reason. It betokens an inclination that later works for the stage will show to be characteristic of surrealism, expressive of an abiding impulse to divert the theatre from dramatic to poetic ends, as surrealists define and pursue these. Needless to say, then, poetry as surrealists speak of it is not compatible with theatre, as it is in the case of the plays of Maeterlinck, but at variance with theatrical usage. Thus, in contrast with the informative style of pointless guide-book descriptions of Paris to be found in *Vous m'oublierez*, remarks like the following, by Machine à Coudre, stand out sharply defined: "My hair leans over the river and my lips are long venomous fish" (Scene 2).

Recurrently in *Vous m'oublierez* statements of this nature are isolated at the expense of dialogue continuity. Their poetic appeal is thus set off by their gratuitousness, which undermines theatrical unity. Remarks like Parapluie's—"I told you so: a bowl of camomile-colored sky has a less sweet taste than your little niece's glance" (Scene 1)— have that "fairly bizarre quality" that held Breton's attention, one evening just before he fell asleep, in a phrase that presented itself to his consciousness without his being able to explain its origin. In the Breton-Soupault play we come across a significant number of remarks of this kind, reminiscent of the spontaneously generated phrase that prompted Breton to investigate automatic writing in the hope of accumulating statements no less disturbing to reason than the first one to have impressed him: "There is a man cut in two by the window." Speaking of the products of automatism in his first surrealist manifesto, Breton declared, "Poetically speaking, they strike us thanks to a very high degree of *immediate absurdity*, the characteristic of this absurdity being, upon closer scrutiny, to give way to everything that is admissible, legitimate in the world: the disclosure of a certain number of properties and facts no less objective, in the final analysis, than the others" (p. 38).

This explains why, in *Vous m'oublierez*, the right to question what others say is forfeited by everyone present:

SEWING MACHINE
Pretty white days, necklace of nights, distant clouds, flowers of boredom.
DRESSING GOWN
What?

SEWING MACHINE
Nothing, rattle-mechanism.
        Silence. (Scene 2)

The role of dialogue in surrealism is anything but the reconciliation of poetry, as surrealists refer to it, with reason. The principle underlying its use favors extending to the maximum the distance between question and answer, statement and response. As a result, dialogue presents significant analogies with the process of image-making described in the *Manifeste du Surréalisme:* "It is false, in my opinion, to claim that 'the mind has grasped the relationship' between two realities facing one another. To begin with, it has grasped nothing consciously. It is from the somewhat fortuitous linking of the two terms that a particular light has sprung, *the light of the image,* to which we are infinitely sensitive." Thus the value of the image "depends on the beauty of the spark obtained; it is in consequence a function of the difference in potential between the two conductors" (p. 52). In the rarefied atmosphere of surrealist automatism, images "alone steer the mind," which "is convinced little by little of the supreme reality of these images" (p. 53).

Gratuitousness necessarily heightens the degree of immediate absurdity in images born of automatism. In surrealist dialogue, it is a direct result of neglect of causal links between statement and response. This feature of surrealist communication, as opposed to reasonable communication, is well illustrated in the pages entitled "Le dialogue en 1928," and those published later as "Le dialogue en 1934."[24] In the former, Raymond Queneau's question, "What is Benjamin Péret?" elicits from Marcel Noll the reply, "A menagerie in revolt, a jungle, liberty." In the latter, Breton's inquiry, "What is reason?" receives from Eluard the answer, "It is a cloud eaten up by the moon." In every case, replies are delivered in total ignorance of the questions posed. Yet although the origin of both dialogues is so different from the sources of dialogue in *Vous m'oublierez,* a noteworthy parallel can be detected. It gives pertinence to a comment on "Le dialogue en 1934" by the surrealist Philippe Audoin: "One picks up curiously successful examples here which suggest the possibility of forms of communication at first sight aberrant, which nevertheless at the same time compromise

24. "Le dialogue en 1928" appeared in the magazine *La Révolution surréaliste.* "Le dialogue en 1934" was published in a special number of *Documents 34,* 'L'Intervention surréaliste' (Nouvelle Série, No. 1, June 1934), pp. 24–25.

the reasurring idea one has of 'real' dialogue and of 'what speaking means.' "[25]

"Le dialogue en 1928" and "Le dialogue en 1934" present findings resulting from a typical surrealist form of word game that, André Breton has remarked, "has always seemed to us poetically the most fabulous source of *undiscoverable* images."[26] The adjective underlined by Breton points to the most vital link between dialogue resulting from the arbitrary confrontation of question and answer and the dialogue of *Vous m'oublierez*, upon which automatism has left an indelible mark. In both instances we are provided with evidence of fidelity to the program outlined by Breton when he spoke of "giving language back its full purpose," that of "making cognition take a big step forward."[27] It is by recognizing how much importance both Breton and Soupault already attached to rationally undiscoverable images that with least delay we can relate *Vous m'oublierez* to a belief that finds expression through *Les Pas perdus*, in the course of an essay on *Les Chants de Maldoror*, by the way: "We know now that poetry must lead somewhere" (p. 80).

At the end of *Vous m'oublierez*, Parapluie reports that, although he can recall in detail visiting one of the castles on the Loire, he now finds it impossible to evoke memories that last as long as his two-hour visit. Recollected experience is less than adequate, then. Much more satisfying, we infer, are anticipated sights, unprecedented in past experience but foreshadowed by undiscoverable images of the sort in which Breton and Soupault seek to interest us. Just before the curtain comes down, these are given the right of way, as Parapluie advances to the proscenium, waving a red flag like the ones used by railroad crossing-keepers to halt traffic of one kind, going in one direction, so that another kind of traffic, heading somewhere else, may take precedence.

25. Philippe Audoin, "Jeux surréalistes," in René Alleau, ed., *Dictionnaire des Jeux* (Tchou, 1964), p. 482.
26. Cited in Robert D. Vallette, ed. Paul Eluard, *Le Poète et son Ombre* (Seghers, 1963), p. 185.
27. André Breton, "Les Mots sans Rides," *Les Pas perdus*, p. 167.

Roger Vitrac

Don't go to the theatre. Go to bed.[1]

"MAGIC has no secrets from Roger Vitrac, who is preparing a Theatre of Conflagration in which people die as in a wood," wrote Louis Aragon in the autumn of 1924.[2] By 1924 Vitrac had already written several playlets. His play *Les Mystères de l'Amour*, subtitled "a surrealist drama," had been completed in 1923. Published in November 1924, within a month of the first surrealist manifesto, it was to be staged in June 1927. Vitrac is one of the most prolific among the writers of Dada and surrealism attracted to the stage, an author whose contribution cannot be fully evaluated until his theatre has been weighed.[3]

Sanouillet speaks of "a play of Dadaic character" by Roger Vitrac, performed in 1920 while its author was completing his military service.[4] Called *La Fenêtre vorace* (*The Voracious Window*), it was lost subsequently. Nevertheless Béhar argues that, had the text survived, "it would without any doubt have permitted us to list Vitrac among the great apostles of the Dada spirit."[5] In the absence of evidence that might make this claim sound less exaggerated, we must confine our attention to material written a little later. By that time, Vitrac and Jacques Baron had decided to participate in the Dada visit to the church of Saint-Julien-le-Pauvre (April 14, 1921), where Vitrac introduced his young friend to Louis Aragon, whom he already knew slightly[6]

During the period when Aragon was writing *L'Armoire à Glace un*

1. Roger Vitrac, "Dormir," *Les Hommes du Jour*, April 28, 1923.
2. Louis Aragon, "Une Vague de Rêves," *Commerce*, No. 2, autumn 1924.
3. Vitrac's poetry is discussed in Henri Béhar, *Roger Vitrac: Un Réprouvé du Surréalisme* (Nizet, 1966), pp. 124–30; J. H. Matthews, *Surrealist Poetry in France* (Syracuse, N.Y.: Syracuse University Press, 1969), pp. 68–79.
4. Michel Sanouillet, *Dada à Paris* (Jean-Jaques Pauvert, 1965), p. 185.
5. Béhar, *Roger Vitrac*, p. 42.
6. Jacques Baron's account of the meeting (*L'An 1 du Surréalisme* suivi de *L'An*

beau Soir, Vitrac was at work on the brief fragment *Mademoiselle Piège,* on *Entrée libre,* and on *Poison,* all three dating from 1922.[7] Sanouillet treats the encounter with Aragon as proof that, for Vitrac, "contact with Dada was established" (p. 186). In his *Roger Vitrac* Béhar, too, gives us to understand that, more than anything else, meeting Aragon meant to Vitrac joining Dada (p. 44). There can be no question of denying Vitrac's early enthusiasm for Dada—*La Fenêtre vorace* aside, we recall that Jacques Baron's brother, François, has reported how he, René Crevel, and Vitrac would bring Dada manifestoes back to the barracks where they were stationed.[8] All the same, some caution is needed before we can advance in this area; as an interesting document shows.

In a Vitrac notebook containing reflections covering the period 1944–45, a sheet of paper outlines plans for bringing together certain of his early writings for the stage, introduced by a "preface under the general title: The Theatre of Conflagration." It is not possible to date these notes, which mention one play (*Victor*) not even begun when Aragon was already referring to the Theatre of Conflagration. But they make interesting reading even so.

Setting out to explain its title, Vitrac's projected preface would have offered not only a commentary on *Les Mystères de l'Amour* and *Victor,* but also comments on *Le Peintre* (*The Painter*)—his first text for the stage, published in January 1922—on *Entrée libre* (*Free Admission*), on *L'Ephémère* (a "phantasmagoria" dating from 1929), and on *Poison.* While *L'Ephémère* is followed by the parenthetical notation "scientific theatre," *Poison* is classified as "surrealism." Thus, although so far as we know Vitrac only sketched his preface, without ever developing it, his notes bring into focus a number of questions we must take up when dealing with his theatre.

---

dernier [Denoël, 1969], p. 45) corrects the version given by Sanouillet (*Dada à Paris,* pp. 185–86) who reports inaccurately that Baron introduced Vitrac to Aragon.

7. Two of the sketches appeared in *Littérature: Mademoiselle Piège,* Nouvelle Série, No. 5 (October 1922) and *Poison,* Nouvelle Série, No. 8 (January 1923). *Entrée libre* was published for the first time in the third volume of Vitrac's *Théâtre* (Gallimard, 1964), which also reprinted *Mademoiselle Piège, Poison,* and *Le Peintre.* Without acknowledgment to Gallimard, *Entrée libre,* presented as "a newly discovered surrealist play," appears in translation as an appendix to Nahma Sandrow, *Surrealism: Theater, Arts, Ideas* (New York: Harper & Row, 1972).

8. François Baron, *Les Frontières du Bonheur* (Gallimard, 1954) provides essential background information on Vitrac's activities at that time.

Vitrac's outline leads us to believe he had every intention of including *Poison* in his "Theatre of Conflagration." Supposedly, though, he
drew a distinction between this text, signed and dated on the manuscript December 4, 1922, and the plays that preceded it.[9] Presumably,
then, we are to infer that he recognized the presence of surrealism in
his theatrical writings only from *Poison* onward.

Like the unpublished verse collection of 1925, *La Lanterne noire*,
subtitled "Poèmes surréalistes," *Poison* is dedicated to André Breton.
This dedication and the care Vitrac took to separate *Poison* from his
earlier theatrical experiments suggest we ought to be able to detect a
radical change of manner or content—analogous to the change marking
La Lanterne noire after his volume of Symbolist verse, *Le Faune noir*—
when examining *Poison* side by side with, for instance, *Entrée libre* or
Le Peintre. Yet anyone expecting to be able by means of an examination of *Poison* to test Vitrac's fidelity to the principles underlying surrealist dialogue, as described in the first manifesto of 1924, is due for a
disappointment. As published on January 8, 1923, *Poison* was presented
to readers of *Littérature* as "a drama without words." The text bears
witness to something Jacques Baron has brought to our notice (p. 38):
Vitrac's fascination with silent movies. But the play cannot be considered the mere adaptation of early film technique to dramatic presentation. Rather, it reveals in its author appreciation of the film as an
essentially visual experience, imaginatively stimulating because unfet-
tered by reasonable commentary. Tableaux 7, 8, 9, 10, and 11 are devised to set off, in turn, the Arabic numerals 7, 8, 9, 10, and 11, each
inscribed on a card. The closest *Poison* comes to using speech is in its
twelfth and final tableau, described in one short sentence that makes
Vitrac's attitude plain: "The scene depicts a mouth which pretends to
speak." Throughout, our impression is that words are inadequate,
superfluous, even irrelevant. Thus *Poison* appeals to the eye primarily.
While it introduces sounds frequently, it makes no effort to explain
verbally the things it lets us see and hear.

All in all, Vitrac can never have intended *Poison* to gain recogni-

9. In his *Roger Vitrac* Béhar inaccurately dates *Poison* from February 4, 1922
(p. 164), and *Entrée libre* from November 18, 1924 (p. 166). The manuscript of
Entrée libre is signed and dated November 28, 1922.

tion as communicating surrealism in any but visual terms. The second tableau illustrates his method as well as any. It begins this way:

> The scene represents a bedroom in which the floor is covered with fragments of plaster. From the water pitcher on the washstand bursts a black spray of liquid. The sheets on the bed betray an enormous form. We hear the ringing of an alarm clock. The door opens and a horse's head appears. It sways about for a moment and the bed is mysteriously uncovered. A lot of smoke comes from it, momentarily darkening the room. When this has cleared away, we can see hair falling from the ceiling onto a diamond of exceedingly large size that has appeared in the bed.

Analogies are easy to perceive between the Vitrac passage we have just read and certain film scripts and scenarios signed by other surrealists.[10] Yet whether *Poison* warrants examination as theatre is debatable, surrealist though it is. Indeed—practical considerations aside—whether it lends itself to stage presentation is not the issue so much as whether staging it would provide the spectator with any more imagination stimulation than could be derived from merely reading Vitrac's text. In contrast, *Entrée libre* would surely gain from being enacted before an audience.

A one-act play, *Entrée libre* is divided into six tableaux, three preceding and three following a seventh that is, an author's note tells us, "the whole drama." Each of the six tableaux is the projection of a dream by one of the three characters. The first is Henri's dream, the second is Guillaume Roze's, the third is Hélène Roze's. After the fourth tableau, the characters dream again, in reverse order.

In his first dream, Henri ("I am invited to dinner to strangle children. No thanks, I don't break that kind of bread") encounters a rare bird (Hélène) in a forest. In the second tableau Guillaume dreams he is a sheep by the side of a lake ("I haven't forgotten my revolver. I've even tried shooting at a tree"), meets Henri, and reveals that he suspects his wife of misconduct. Next Hélène sees herself as a prostitute in a narrow Paris street, meeting both Guillaume and Henri. Despite the latter's plea ("Don't kill her, she has no hands"), Hélène fires on a young woman dressed for travelling and carrying a suitcase.

In the fourth tableau, Hélène is laying the table while Guillaume

---

10. See, for instance, the scenarios of Benjamin Péret in his *Le Gigot sa Vie et son Œuvre* (Librairie le Terrain Vague, 1957). Cf. J. H. Matthews, *Surrealism and Film* (Ann Arbor: University of Michigan Press, 1971), pp. 53–56.

reads his paper. Anxiety and foreboding seem to underlie Hélène's remarks as they wait for Henri. Guillaume remains calm until Henri has arrived and the niceties of sociability are behind them. "They sit down to eat. Suddenly Mr Guillaume Roze, who has his back to the audience, upsets the table. The lamp smashes. The stage is plunged into darkness. Pursuit. Cries." Hélène is heard crying "Don't kill her.[11] Guillaume, Guillaume, Guillaume. Help. Murderer. Murderer. Murderer." The curtain comes down.

Violence is still the theme of the fifth tableau, where Hélène sees herself as a news vendor, questioned by a policeman (Guillaume). When accused of an unidentified crime, she replies: "Officer, they dragged me by the hair and my head bumped on each step of the stairs. They left me in a meadow. It was warm. The grass was all red." The impression given in the sixth tableau is the same. It culminates with Guillaume (a bather) showing Henri (a sailor) something inside a bathing hut: the body of a woman, cut to pieces. The last dream, Henri's, takes place in a restaurant where a servant (Hélène) drops a pile of plates.

Entrée libre has one or two features in common with *Poison*, notably a thread of violence and particularly an element of distress: the fourth tableau of *Poison* lets us hear fire-truck sirens, while the fifth introduces us to a painter who, making a hole in the back wall of the set, pulls out a cable: "It seems that at the end of this cable is something light, but the wall collapses and a steamer advances on to the stage. An electric lamp placed in the bow gives distress signals." But its most distinctive aspect is the use of dream transcription. To Béhar, summing up his impressions in *Roger Vitrac*, *Entrée libre* appears as Vitrac's "first totally surrealist theatrical endeavor" (p. 166). True enough, the subject matter of this play does relate it to preoccupations from which, not long after its composition, organized surrealist activity was to ensue. Even so, the playwright himself denied *Entrée libre* the status of surrealism and, as his preface outline makes clear, intended to leave it out of his "Theatre of Conflagration" volume. The nature of this play suggests that there were good reasons for doing this.

11. Béhar speaks casually in his *Roger Vitrac* of "the death of Henri" (p. 167). Apparently he has not noticed the feminine gender in "Ne la tue pas," a phrase that echoes, by the way, Henri's cry in the third tableau: "Ne la tue pas, elle n'a pas de mains" ("Don't kill her, she has no hands"). The sixth talbeau lends support to the assumption that Hélène, not Henri, is the victim of the crime on the darkened stage of Tableau 4.

Despite the novelty of its form—which is significantly symmetrical, incidentally, evidencing controlled design—*Entrée libre* is a psychological study, utilizing dreams to cast light upon human motivation. By the standards of established drama, it is therefore eminently respectable in intent. Only here and there does it offer an inkling of the surrealist viewpoint, as when, right in the middle of the realistic dialogue of the central tableau, Guillaume announces, "A chronometer and a hat have been found on the Pont des Arts." It is noteworthy, all the same, that whereas a few phrases such as this do open the door on the inexplicable and the irrational in *Entrée libre*, they are extraneous to the main action, never of more than secondary importance.

This is where we begin to notice a major difference between *Entrée libre* and *Le Peintre*. The date appearing on the manuscript of the latter is the same as that given for *Poison*. Of course, we must assume that December 4, 1922, was when the text of the copy preserved in the Doucet library was completed, the text having been published a year earlier. Nevertheless, someone looking at Vitrac's theatrical writings for evidence reflecting an innovatory spirit might be forgiven for believing that internal evidence, present in *Le Peintre* more than in *Entrée libre*, authorizes his regarding the former as more likely than the latter to have been written about the time of *Poison*.

From the very beginning, the question of identity is of pressing concern in *Le Peintre*. A man seen painting a door in an entrance hall asks a child his name and then claims to bear that name himself. As one might expect, the man is challenged by the child. He replies, "It isn't true? (*Silence.*) You are right," then sets about painting the child's face red. Madame Parchemin appears, asks the same question, receives the same answer ("Maurice Parchemin"), dismisses it predictably as false, and is treated to the same response as her son—"It isn't true? (*Silence.*) You are right." The same punishment is meted out: this time the painter daubs both the child's face and the mother's. When a young man of twenty rings the door-bell and asks for Monsieur Parchemin, however, the painter assures him that Maurice Parchemin Sr is dead— "I killed him."

Throughout this farce, identity is a source of confusion. It introduces a bewildering element of ambiguity into every statement made by the painter. And the same is true of the things the young man says, once we have discovered that, although he claims to be Auguste Flanelle, his calling cards are, apparently, inscribed "Monsieur Glucose, dental surgeon, 31 Rue de Gaîté." Besides, it undermines confidence in the motives behind conduct for which we feel entitled to an explanation that eludes us.

A wild logic operates in *Le Peintre*, leaving the spectator perplexed. If Auguste Flanelle is really Monsieur Glucose, then the painter is perhaps right to address a black-bearded caller, who says he is Glucose, as Flanelle. Mr Glucose's attempt to have the painter arrested for an unspecified crime, which we suppose to be the murder of Maurice Parchemin, proves unsuccessful, though. He meets with ridicule from the two policemen who have accompanied him and receives . . . red paint on his face—despite, incidentally, the painter's assertion that he is using green paint ("What if I painted this door red, eh?").

The painter, who never leaves our sight, has openly confessed to murder. Yet when Madame Parchemin comes on, carrying the body of her son, who has died off stage in circumstances concealed from us, it is Maurice Parchemin Jr whom she accuses the man of having killed. The painter now paints his own face red and goes off, while Auguste Flanelle tries to take advantage of the situation: "Alone at last." For a while the bereaved mother is unresponsive. But she rises from her seat when Flanelle paints her likeness on a mirror. Little Maurice rolls to the ground, comes back to life and runs off, so giving us the opportunity to find out that his mother and Flanelle are indeed lovers. The painter returns, tearing off his beard: "Heavens, my husband." He treats his rival—whom he is now willing to call Flanelle—with courtesy. But as soon as the man has left, Parchemin attacks his wife. Their fight is interrupted by the arrival of their son, whose affectionate greetings on his mother's birthday bring about a tender reconciliation.

The play draws rapidly to an enigmatic close. Mr Glucose—now with a blond beard ("I have always been blond")—arrives with a gift ordered by Parchemin for his wife: a set of gold false teeth. The husband declares, "Mr Glucose, you have indulged in the most abominable of comedies," brushing off Glucose's protest: "I followed your instructions to the letter, Mr Parchemin." The only way Glucose can make amends, he is told, is to paint the door green—with the red paint Parchemin provides. Maurice Jr voices the question in every spectator's mind: "Why?" His mother reassures him, "You'll know that later, my boy."

A child may be resigned to waiting until he grows older to understand what has taken place in *Le Peintre*. But an audience requires something better than a deferred explanation for aspects of this play that cannot be credited to Monsieur Parchemin's taste for elaborate practical jokes (*farces*, in French). Things are not what they seem—we can accept this premise without reluctance. But reason offers some resistance to the corollary Vitrac would have us entertain: nor are things what they do not seem.

Only periodically does this play mirror reality after the fashion of theatrical convention. It provides elements borrowed from stock situation—the arrival of arresting officers, come to apprehend a criminal, a clandestine meeting between lovers, a glimpse of happy bourgeois home life—and presents these with enough irony (evidenced in the exploitation of verbal clichés, for example) to leave Vitrac's contempt for stage commonplace beyond question. Negligence with small details—why does Madame Parchemin, who was off stage when the painter confessed to having killed Maurice Sr, exclaim, "Oh! my God, you have killed my husband"?—confirms something Vitrac's use of stock materials like false beards and concealed identity suggests: that he enjoys misleading and confusing his public.

In *Le Peintre* Béhar responds above all to "a spontaneity [. . .] which truly leads to delirium" (p. 250). He ascribes the origin of this spontaneity to Dada, without considering every aspect of the matter. Thus when he speaks in his *Roger Vitrac* of the application of *Le Peintre* of "the secret principle of desire," used in defiance of "the laws formal logic" (p. 163), he is alluding to principles destined to be respected by surrealists at least as much as in Dada.

Béhar notes, of course, that Vitrac's play appeared originally in the third issue of *Aventure*, a magazine founded in November 1921, which Vitrac served as an editor. But when he insists in *Roger Vitrac* that "after giving *Le Peintre*, *Aventure* had nothing more to do, not being able to say anything more" (p. 48), he appears to have given insufficient attention to a salient paragraph figuring in an announcement of *Aventure* to be found in the monthly bulletin of the General Association of Paris Students, *L'Université de Paris*, on October 25, 1921: "This review, which, by the way, does not have a common cause with Dada, seeks to represent and express the most modern tendencies of the new French literature." Jacques Baron has confirmed this significant fact: The *Aventure* group was "rather reticent vis-à-vis Dada. [. . .] reticent because Dada at that time appeared to fall short of its destiny, as subsequent events have proved, and because we caught the scent of a sectarian spirit that favored pointlessly going one better."[12]

Vitrac's period of close contact with Aragon began, we remember, at the moment when the latter was beginning to find Dada less than satisfying. Like Breton and a few close acquaintances, Aragon was becoming conscious of that "absolutely new state of mind" to which he refers when introducing *Le Libertinage*. Vitrac was well prepared by his reservations about Dada to be responsive to what Aragon and his friends called *le mouvement flou*. Given the closeness of his relations with Aragon—they continued to be on cordial terms until Vitrac's dismissal from the surrealist camp in 1925—assumptions voiced by Béhar and Sanouillet regarding Vitrac's devotion to Dada appear tendentious. These critics' anticipation of signs of Dada in his earliest essays in theatre should not blind us to the important fact that *Le Peintre* foreshadows the major Vitrac plays of the twenties, *Les Mystères de l'Amour* and *Victor*. And these plays stand as indisputable proof that their author's reasons for siding with Breton, when the time came to choose between the future surrealist leader and Tristan Tzara, were not rooted in personal affection alone.[13]

As Béhar recounts events, Vitrac and Aragon worked at their theatrical texts on neighboring café tables, during the winter of 1922–23. In Vitrac's case, though, these circumstances prove something quite different from voluntary alignment with Dada orthodoxy. *Le Peintre* had been completed before his period of intimacy with Aragon commenced; early enough, in fact, to have exerted an influence, possibly, upon *L'Armoire à Glace*, which Aragon dedicated to him. In other words, *Le Peintre* may well have contributed to encouraging the cofounder of *Littérature* to prolong his search beyond the boundaries of Dada.

12. Baron, *L'An 1 du Surréalisme*, p. 34.
13. Discontented with Dada negativism as early as the beginning of 1922, Breton sought to organize a Paris Congress for the Determination of Directives and the Defense of the Modern Spirit, announced on January 3. On February 3, Tzara refused to join. Vitrac, however, was a member of the organizing committee. A letter from Breton to Picabia, dated February 18, 1922, mentions Aragon, Pierre de Massot, Jacques Rigaut, Baron, and Vitrac, when referring to "that common desire of ours to *close the file on* Dada" (omitted from the Breton-Picabia correspondence reproduced in Sanouillet's *Dada à Paris*, this letter is located in the file of the Congrès de Paris at the Bibliothèque Nationale; cited by Béhar in *Roger Vitrac*, p. 53). Vitrac's loyalty to Breton brought him under sharp attack from Ribemont-Dessaignes in the only issue of the magazine *Le Cœur à Barbe* to appear (April 1922). Later, Vitrac sided with Breton in his account of the *Soirée du Cœur à Barbe*, "Guet-Apens," published in *Les Hommes du Jour*, August 4, 1923. See pp. 37–38 above.

These background details help place *Le Peintre* in a somewhat different light from that in which a Dada work is to be viewed. They direct attention to one or two interesting facts. The first of these is that Vitrac made the acquaintance of André Breton as well as Louis Aragon in 1921, seeing the former occasionally during that year. Moreover, it was not as a participant in Dada scandal that Breton impressed Vitrac, we gather from a statement by François Baron. Alluding to the day when his younger brother and Roger Vitrac took part in the visit to Saint-Julien-le-Pauvre, Baron notes in his memoirs, "From that evening onward, we would often listen, stretched out on our beds, to Roger reading for us in his fine musical voice *Les Champs magnétiques* by Breton and Soupault or the poems of Aragon in *Feu de Joie*" (p. 71). It is noteworthy that the poems by Aragon read on those occasions— from the only Aragon verse collection available at that date—appeared on December 10, 1919, and so antedated their author's active participation in Dada. Even more noteworthy is the proof Baron supplies that Vitrac knew *Les Champs magnétiques* before he published *Le Peintre*.

Indication of tangible motivation, fully satisfying, is avoided in *Le Peintre*. We cannot explain away all its ambiguities: right to the end, Maurice Parchemin's green paint looks red to us. Meanwhile reminiscences of familiar dramatic situations—notably the recognition scene, satirized more than once—become ridiculous through displacement and inexplicable juxtaposition. All the same, none of these elements justifies detaching Vitrac's first play from what might be termed, by the end of 1921, a tradition of Dada theatre. To find signs that Vitrac was ready to take his place among those willing and able to treat Dada theatre as a stepping-stone to something else, we have to concentrate upon the brief interlude between Madame Parchemin and her lover:

> MADAME PARCHEMIN
> How you love me.
>
> AUGUSTE FLANELLE
> Yes. *He kisses her.*
>
> MADAME PARCHEMIN
> The palm tree.
>
> AUGUSTE FLANELLE
> Yes. *He kisses her.*
>
> MADAME PARCHEMIN
> The strawberry ice.

AUGUSTE FLANELLE
Yes. *He kisses her.*

MADAME PARCHEMIN
Madame Tiroir. The shabby dress.

AUGUSTE FLANELLE
Yes. *He kisses her.*

MADAME PARCHEMIN
The cabman.

AUGUSTE FLANELLE
Yes. *He kisses her.*

MADAME PARCHEMIN
25, Rue des Saints-Pères

AUGUSTE FLANELLE
Yes. *He kisses her.*

MADAME PARCHEMIN
Quite naked.

AUGUSTE FLANELLE
Yes. *He kisses her.*

The arrival of the painter, who promptly rips off his disguise, interrupts his wife's erotic daydream. Not, however, before Vitrac has had time to show that he has grasped the fundamental principle of surrealist dialogue as parallel monologues, exemplified in "Barrières" and soon to be granted more sustained illustration in *Les Mystères de l'Amour.*

However many questions are left unanswered by his preface outline, Vitrac's exclusion of *Entrée libre* and retention of *Le Peintre* should give no cause for concern. They are entirely consistent with the bias in favor of plays displaying surrealist tendencies that his "Theatre of Conflagration" would have displayed. Hence his preference for *Le Peintre* over *Entrée libre* points to an evolution in Vitrac's conception of drama. This invests *Les Mystères de l'Amour* ("my first play") with particular value as the first theatrical text to be published with the fully justified designation "surrealist" and quite independently of Dada.

In 1930 appeared a brochure called *Le Théâtre Alfred Jarry et l'Hostilité publique.* It is almost certain that this document, generally attributed to Antonin Artaud, was written by Roger Vitrac.[14] For this reason, the statement it contains on *Les Mystères de l'Amour* is especially interesting to us, particularly since—despite Vitrac's recent quarrel with Breton's group—it reflects no inclination to uproot the play from the context to which it belongs: "An ironical work which renders concrete on stage the disquiet, double solitude, dissembled criminal thoughts, and eroticism of lovers. For the first time, *a real dream* was realized in the theatre."[15]

The operative words here are "real dream," "renders concrete," and "realized in the theatre." *Les Mystères de l'Amour* illustrates its author's viewpoint on life by making audible human responses usually not articulated, and by acting out subconscious relationships not always of necessity rationally explicable. In putting his characters' fantasies on stage, without troubling to distinguish dream from reality and nightmare from diurnal activity, Vitrac proceeds much further than in *Entrée libre*. He now locates drama in confrontations precipitated by desire or fear, longing or revulsion, where dialogue delivers words normally unvoiced, so that his characters can "live as we dream" and "dream as we live."[16] *Les Mystères de l'Amour* invites us into the realm where surrealism reigns and where we come to understand what Breton meant when he spoke in his *Nadja* of "descending truly into the lowest depths of the mind, where it is no longer a matter of night falling or rising again (is this then daylight?)."[17]

Like the ready-made phrases conventionally employed to transmit the conditioned reflex of familiar emotional response, the banalities of

14. See the appendix "Lettres inédites d'Antonin Artaud à Roger Vitrac," in Béhar, *Roger Vitrac*, pp. 281–301.

15. Jacques Baron ascribes this quotation to Vitrac, without mention of Artaud, in *L'An 1 du Surréalisme* (p. 152). Apparently Eric Sellin is unaware of the evidence adduced by Béhar. In *The Dramatic Concepts of Antonin Artaud* (Chicago and London: University of Chicago Press, 1968, p. 141), Sellin attributes *Le Théâtre Alfred Jarry et l'Hostilité publique* to Artaud. He does not mention Béhar's book in either his text or his bibliography.

Les Mystères de l'Amour was first staged on June 2, 1927. Originally published in 1924 by Gallimard, it was reprinted by the same house in the second volume of Vitrac's *Théâtre* (1948).

Vitrac's stress on disquiet in *Le Théâtre Alfred Jarry et l'Hostilité publique* reminds us of his comment, "from the critical point of view, it was rather the period that followed Dada which, in my opinion, was the richest in experiments of all sorts. We lived then in anguish and disquiet." See his article "Le Monologue intérieur et le Surréalisme," *Comœdia*, March 17, 1925.

16. From the author's note in the 1948 Gallimard edition.

17. André Breton, *Nadja* [1928], rev. ed. (Gallimard, 1963), p. 35.

polite conversation go by the board. They succumb in Vitrac's play to explosive language and gesture that revitalize human attitudes by releasing them from habit and stereotyped courtesy.

Following a brief prologue, showing Patrice tracing lines in the mud of a public square after a rainstorm, the first tableau begins. It takes place in a stage-box, opening while the house lights are still on. Throughout this part of the drama Patrice and Léa occupy an intermediary position between the public and the stage where the spectator anticipated seeing the drama enacted, when he took his seat. Action has been displaced, brought forward, and is now under way closer than he expected. If without difficulty he can identify a stock situation, when he sees Patrice kneeling at Léa's feet and saying, "Accept these flowers," no theatrical precedent exists to reassure him before the gesture accompanying these words: Patrice slapping Léa's face. The young woman calls for her mother, not to complain, but to whisper the good news—"Mama! if you only knew, Patrice loves me." Patrice, meanwhile, has announced that he is going for a walk by the seaside and has sat down facing the audience. Within a few moments he is directing offensive remarks at members of the public.

Patrice's conduct at this point sets a precedent to be followed quite often as the drama unfolds. In this play, where action begins in a stage-box, moving up only later to the stage, the barrier separating the public from the spectacle frequently tumbles. The spectator finds himself denied the comfortable feeling of *distance* that is, he used to believe, an invariable condition of watching events enacted beyond the safety zone of the footlights. Patrice confides in the audience, "Léa loves me," delivering this aside at the top of his voice. At his urging, Léa makes a similar confession, shouting, "I love Patrice. Oh! I love his guts. Oh! I love this buffoon. Oh! I love this buffoon. From all aspects, from every seamy side, in all his shapes. Look at them, Patrice. Listen to them. Ha! ha! ha!" A voice from out front expresses a sense of outrage in which every member of the audience shares to some extent: "But why! Merciful heaven! Why? Is there something wrong with you?" As other spectators begin to intervene, their cries are punctuated by revolver shots, before the lights at last go down and silence is restored, temporarily.

Nothing, so far, marks a significant departure in *Les Mystères de l'Amour* from effects tried out by Breton and Soupault in *S'il vous plaît*. Very soon, however, the concept of theatrical dialogue is broadened. When someone in the audience declares aggressively, "Mr Patrice, you are a criminal," Patrice responds. Before long, Vitrac is questioning the fundamental convention of dramatic presentation when he allows his hero to say, "They are waving at us," and permits Patrice and Léa to wave back in friendly fashion. Involving his public directly, the playwright takes a significant step. He deliberately brings the "dream" on stage face to face with the "reality" in the auditorium, or, as Breton puts it in *Nadja*, "that which is very summarily opposed" to dream "under the name of reality" (p. 48). Practicing provocation as he elects to do, Vitrac increases the public's feeling of disorientation before the dislocated conversations of Patrice and Léa, in which at times neither seems to hear what the other is saying. In short, he draws his audience into the action so as to make them more keenly aware of being left out of things.

Although the lights have come on again, revealing that action is still confined to the stage-box, Léa behaves as if in her own dining room when warning Patrice and a rival, Dovic, to watch out for the furniture as they roll on the floor in a brutal fight. A few minutes later, she speaks to Patrice of being in their bedroom. Only now do the house lights go out and the footlights come up. There follows a brief illogical sequence involving an old and a young man whom we never see again, which could well have been modelled on the last act of *S'il vous plaît*. Understandably, a few spectators express disapproval. The theatre manager comes on stage to announce that the play is over. Unfortunately, we are informed, the author, a Mr Théophile Mouchet, has just killed himself. When the manager has gone off, someone out front calls for the author:

> The curtain rises. The author appears. He is in shirt sleeves. His face and clothes are covered with blood. He is roaring with laughter. He is laughing with all his might and holding his sides. The two curtains fall suddenly.

To leave the theatre at this point, as one seems to have been invited to do, means missing the second tableau. This takes place on a stage divided into three sets. On the Quai des Grands-Augustins in Paris, Patrice is seen as a lieutenant of Dragoons. Léa is carrying a doll. She says it is his child, but Patrice drops the baby in the Seine anyway. In his bedroom Lloyd George (played by Dovic, he looks like a certain British Prime Minister) lifts the sheets on a bed, showing Léa, who recognizes it with horror, the head of a little girl resting on the pillow. When he pulls the sheets right back to uncover the child, "It is naturally only a bust of flesh sawn off at shoulder level." In the presence of Léa and Patrice, Lloyd George proceeds to demonstrate his skill by sawing off the head of a young boy he has carried in under his arm: "That's quite a job, or I'm no judge."

This whole tableau is situated in a twilight zone where horror and laughter commingle—Vitrac, we notice, specifies that the flesh bust's role is a mute one—and where the dead and the living converse. Léa's mother and her late father join her and Lloyd George for dinner, while, upon the advice of Lloyd George, their daughter places Patrice's knees under the flesh bust to conceal that a crime has taken place. Patrice's head is now at liberty to withdraw to the top of a mirror-wardrobe from which it observes the domestic scene. To her dead father's annoyance, Léa finds the antics of Patrice's head so distracting that she finally has to cover it with a sheet of newspaper. "You'll really have to take an interest in my stories," Mr Morin comments petulantly, after being interrupted while telling one that begins quite promisingly: "Well, that night the sea was bad. We were catching sardines by the netful. But the darkness, the thunder, the lightning, and especially the niggers in the stokehold, not to mention the leopard . . ." Lloyd George goes off with him in the direction of the Quai des Grands-Augustins, agreeing that Léa is mad. Left alone, Léa and Madame Morin walk over to the bed from which slowly rise "two arms like two dead branches, but on which two enormous very white hands have blossomed." In spite of her mother's warning ("Oh! my child! Don't go near. She has leprosy"), Léa kneels by the bed, recognizes the victim's resemblance to herself, and concludes, "You really must agree that one doesn't die of love."

One finds it easiest perhaps to accept the second tableau as a nightmare dreamed by Léa. She has the last word, and we see her lying in bed as the next tableau opens the second act.[18] But Vitrac, we notice, does not tell us this is the case, in the way that he took care to do when including dreams in *Entrée libre*. He has given up establishing boundaries between the true and the false, the fanciful and the factual because, apparently, such boundaries no longer have any validity in his

18. In *Roger Vitrac* Béhar contends that it is important to understand that the second and fourth tableaux are dreamed by Patrice (p. 176). He does not explain, though, how he traces these sequences to Patrice's dreams.

estimation. This would explain why, after letting us see cotton wool take fire in Lloyd George's bedroom when Patrice's head passed close by in a dream sequence, now, in the real world of a conventionally decorated hotel room, Vitrac shows us Léa's hands burning Patrice's lips as he kisses them, and smoking as she goes over to the washbasin to plunge them into water. Neither of the lovers, we observe, finds this phenomenon any more difficult to accept than Léa's mother and dead father found events in the second tableau.

A butcher arrives to collect a parcel tied with string, left for him on the kitchen table. He grumbles that it is not worth his while to call again for so little: "Even if you were to give me the skin with the nails and hair, I'd not give you a penny more," he declares. Léa's evasiveness under Patrice's questions about this man and the reasons for his visit adds to the mystery pervading Vitrac's drama, just as the butcher's complaint contributes to the heavy atmosphere of monstrous violence in *Les Mystères de l'Amour*. The third tableau may provide less striking visual manifestations of mystery than when Lloyd George was on stage, but the behavior of Patrice and Léa is no less disturbing, in its way. Léa examining sights visible in Patrice's right eye, Patrice's account of a cryptic conversation with a neighbor in the middle of the night, the slaps he gives Léa, and, above all, the freedom granted words (the basic elements of conversation) in the remarks he makes to her—all this points to an emancipation of dramatic form to which Vitrac is evidently dedicated.[19] Meanwhile, summoned by Patrice, Dovic, and

19. In his book *Strindberg's Impact in France: 1920–1960* (Cambridge: Trinity Lane Press, 1971), Anthony Swerling argues that "the super-reality of Strindberg's comments on life can be opposed to the *non-sequiturs*, witticisms and incoherences of Vitrac's *actes gratuits*," and condemns *Les Mystères de l'Amour* for its "chaotic and often meaningless verbosity" (p. 60). Swerling apparently has not considered the nature of certain verbal effects (used by Vitrac as much in *Les Mystères de l'Amour* as in his poems) against the background of *Les Champs magnétiques* and *Vous m'oublierez*. Bringing Patrice a basket of dogs, sent by her mother, Léa explains in the first tableau, "Ma mère vous *enchien* ce panier de *voie*," so creating a neologism *enchien* and releasing *voie* ("way," "route") from *envoie* ("sends"). In the third tableau Patrice, wondering whether he will be all his life a clock (*une pendule*), adds, "Ou plutôt le pendule d'une pendule, ou mieux le pendu d'une pendule" ("Or rather the pendulum of a clock, or better still the man who has hanged himself from a clock"). Word play of this kind even connects statement and response. When Léa complains that Patrice is hardhearted and nasty—"Tu es dur, Patrice, tu es méchant"—Patrice treats the second adjective as a second-person singular verb form for which he has his own first-person form (*méchant* > *m'échine*) and replies accordingly: "Oh! I knock myself out [Eh! Je m'échine] as best I can, that's no one's business but my own. My spine [mon échine] is my own."

Madame Morin while Léa is off stage (giving birth to a son), the author has no helpful answer to give to Patrice's questions about how this play is to end: "Listen, my boy, your case interests me hardly at all. It hardly interests the public, either." The most the author will admit is that "in this case, I'd behave like you. But, in this case, permit me to withdraw." His brief visit has explained nothing, least of all Patrice's violent attack with a chair, which leaves Dovic and Madame Morin stretched out on the floor and the stage spattered with blood.[20] Patrice's only excuse is the one he gives Léa: "Yes, that's the way it is. I'm left alone and you see what happens."

Even when he is not alone, however, Patrice is somewhat unpredictable. Attempting to set his son on a pedestal over the fireplace, he allows the child to fall from his perch and kill himself. Evidencing a bewildering jumble of emotional responses, Léa exclaims, "Ha! Ha! Ha! . . . Murder! Murder! He over there, my lover, my Papa, my Papa, my Patrice, he's killed my Guigui, my Guigui, my Guillotin. (*Changing her tone.*) Incidentally, you could have given him another name. Infanticide." This final exclamation does not prevent her, of course, from telling a policeman who comes to investigate that the child caught measles when it fell.

The fourth tableau shows us Patrice as Mussolini and Madame Morin as a stranger in mourning. Madame Morin disappears as soon as she has entrusted her two dogs and child to someone she does not know— Léa, who finds the little boy looks like "the one I have at home, like my Patrice." Unable to get rid of the child, she gives us a chance to observe that, as she remarks, "A love is always a big nuisance." But this whole sequence, which lacks the inventiveness of the Lloyd George interlude, brings us nothing new. It was omitted from Artaud's 1927 production of *Les Mystéres de l'Amour*. Also omitted, more surprisingly, was the fifth tableau, which constitutes the whole of the third and final act.

As the fifth tableau begins, Léa is being brought down by hotel elevator, between two policemen, her hands bloody, her white dress in shreds. We learn that she has broken the mirror-wardrobe, demolished the dressing table, set fire to the drapes in her room, and strangled the goldfish. She has done all this, it appears, because Patrice did not keep

20. Vitrac lists both Théophile Mouchet, *auteur du drame*, and *L'Auteur* among the characters appearing in his play. The author we meet now and a little later is not the person represented earlier as having written the play.

a few unpractical promises, like taking her to the North Pole and giving her stars of his own fabrication. In the vestibule Léa demonstrates strange faculties, giving testimony to the magic power of words. She announces that a door will open of its own accord; it does so. She tells the policemen that they are going to say the word "light"; they do so in unison. As is the case with a similar prediction in Breton's *Nadja*, the door's obedience may seem a coincidence.[21] Meanwhile the policemen's willingness to humor a prisoner they think mad leads them to repeat readily enough the words "light" and "night," which she forecasts. But neither coincidence nor indulgence explains how Léa succeeds in summoning Patrice merely by pronouncing his name.

Patrice's arrival frightens the policemen off, literally freeing Léa and introducing an interlude involving several children. Now the conversation takes the direction followed later in "Le dialogue en 1928" and "Le dialogue en 1934":

> FIRST CHILD
> Mr Patrice, what do you bring in your shoes?
> PATRICE
> Elephants under the palm trees.
> SECOND CHILD
> And what about that lion looking at us?
> PATRICE
> That, my child, is liberty.
> THIRD CHILD
> And what about the automobile, is it for us?
> PATRICE
> It is unbreakable and deep.
> FIRST CHILD
> Are you giving us some new perfume?
> PATRICE
> Take these birds.

The first child is the son of the bakery horse, while the second is the offspring of his mother's sewing machine. The third, father of a colonel in the Zouaves, shoots the other two, then remarks to Patrice, "What do you expect, Papa, I was the father of a colonel of Zouaves by accident, but I will always be the son of love."

After listening to all this, the spectator may feel entitled to ask, as

21. See Breton, *Nadja*, p. 81.

Patrice now does, "What is going to become of me in this whole business?" Whatever answer suggests itself, it is clear that nothing is to be gained by looking to Patrice for elucidation of *Les Mystères de l'Amour*. He tells a strange tale about the harvesting of factory smokestacks. Then he tries to shoot the author with a revolver handed him by the latter, who comments, "Useless, my dear Patrice! Your bullets don't penetrate. And that's a pity!" When Patrice tries to return the revolver because it is of no use to him, the author insists on his retaining it: "If you don't want to do this for me, do it in the interest of the drama you are playing. I assure you that a last revolver shot is indispensable to the denouement."

Soon after presenting Léa with a revolver of her own, the author leaves, first whispering to Patrice, "A bit of good advice, my friend, use the piece. Your future depends on it." Has he told the truth? We are free to make up our own minds about this, since the play comes to a close before Patrice has the chance to use his weapon. During his final discussion with her, Léa fires her revolver and he cries, just before the curtain falls, "What have you done, Léa? What have you done? You have just killed a spectator."

A bullet pronounced harmless during an anti-Pirandellian conversation between Patrice and the author, on stage, becomes lethal when it passes the footlights on its way into the audience. Vitrac's parting shot is not pointlessly confusing, a mere gesture of defiance. Rather, it brings into focus the moral implications of his drama of frustrated love, while showing that the spectator's passive role in the theatre is no guarantee of safety where dream and reality cannot be kept apart. By the time *Les Mystères de l'Amour* is over, the public has been made to realize that, in the dream played out before them, verisimilitude has been sacrificed to the release of an emotional experience that makes its effect felt in the so-called real world. By the effort he brings to dispelling the illusion that his dream is to be treated as mere amusement, Roger Vitrac prepares the way in *Les Mystères de l'Amour* for *Victor, ou Les Enfants au Pouvoir*.

Vitrac collaborated with Paul Eluard and J.-A. Boiffard on the preface to the first issue of *La Révolution surréaliste*, which was launched in December 1924. He published nothing more in the original surrealist magazine before a text entitled "Consuella ou Méditations sur le Gouff-fre de Padirac," which he never completed. This text came out in the March 15, 1928, number. In the same issue appeared a short essay of Antonin Artaud's and a note by André Breton, making no secret of his disapproval of both Vitrac and Artaud. Shortly after, the surrealists turned out in force to protest when the Théâtre Alfred Jarry pro-duced *A Dream Play* by Strindberg. Then in 1929 Breton's *Second Manifeste du Surréalisme* made it official: Vitrac and Artaud had been expelled from the surrealist circle, dismissed contemptuously as "men of the theatre."

The circumstances surrounding the Théâtre Alfred Jarry produc-tion of a play by Strindberg and the surrealists' reasons for demonstrat-ing against it need not concern us at this point.[22] What is important is that by the time *Victor* was first performed, in late December 1928, Vitrac could no longer count himself a participant in the surrealist movement. All the same, he had not departed voluntarily. Nor had he done so because of some radical change in viewpoint, calling for free-dom of action denied him within surrealism. According to Béhar's *Roger Vitrac*, in fact, he would have welcomed reconciliation with Breton's group as late as 1928, at the time when he was writing *Victor*, which he completed a full year before its publication on April 25, 1929.[23] Furthermore, although he intended his play for staging by the Théâtre Alfred Jarry—it was mentioned in the production schedule for the 1928 season and was the last play put on by the Théâtre—Vitrac does not seem to have made any effort to eliminate surrealist elements that might be present in his text. On the contrary, *Le Théâtre Alfred Jarry et l'Hostilité publique* gives these elements the emphasis they deserve: "*Victor, or Children Take Charge*, a bourgeois drama in three acts by Roger Vitrac. This drama, sometimes lyrical, sometimes ironical, sometimes direct, was aimed at the bourgeois family, having as discriminants: adultery, incest, scatology, anger, surrealist poetry, patriotism, madness, shame, and death."

The very first line of the play offers an example of the kind of lan-guage manipulation that Vitrac—faithful in this to surrealism—prac-

22. Details are to be found in Breton's *Second Manifeste*, in Béhar's *Roger Vitrac* (pp. 142–43), and in Swerling's *Strindberg's Impact* (pp. 184–88). See also pp. 150–52 below.
23. Originally published by Robert Denoël, à l'enseigne des Trois Magots (1929), *Victor* was reissued by Gallimard in the first volume of Vitrac's *Théâtre* (1946).

tices in his theatre, as in his poetry. Minimal modification of the Biblical phrase *Et le fruit de vos entrailles est béni* permits Victor to say, "Et le fruit de votre entaille est béni":

VICTOR
. . . Blessed be the fruit of your gash.
LILI
To begin with, it's the fruit of your womb you ought to say.
VICTOR
Perhaps, but that's less vivid.

It is soon clear that Victor is not merely indulging a taste for the picturesque. In this "terribly intelligent" boy who has been a model child, a critical approach to language is just one expression of determination to effect some changes. In consequence, the apparently incoherent succession of words that, to his family's alarm, fall from his lips at one point in the first act—words he identifies as "the disordered elements of my next French composition"—exemplify his revolt against an environment where, until now, he has been an unprotesting conformist.[24]

Commenting on *Victor* in *Le Figaro* on November 11, 1946, at the time of its revival, Vitrac spoke of his play as "the myth of precocious childhood," explaining, "Victor simply dies on his ninth birthday . . . at the precise moment when he has a revelation of life, of life as it is. With its memories, its promises, its plots, its ephemerides . . . He couldn't live, you see, he was too intelligent."

Victor, originally subtitled "drame bourgeois,"[25] mounts a full-scale attack upon middle-class values such as no surrealist would repudiate.

24. "The most beautiful women in the world are imprisoned in their bloody lace, and the rivers rise up like charmed snakes. The man, surrounded by a general staff of wild animals, charges at the head of a town the houses of which march behind him, in serried ranks like artillery caissons. The flowers charge with panache. The troops uncurl their hair. The forests draw aside. Ten million hands copulate with the birds. Each trajectory is a bow. Each piece of furniture a military band" (I, 6).
25. When Victor dies the family doctor remarks callously, "And that's the fate of obstinate children." After the curtain has come down, two shots are heard. The curtain rises again to reveal Victor's father and mother lying at the foot of the child's bed, a smoking revolver between them. Lili the maid enters to deliver the last line of the play: "Mais c'est un drame!" In its specialized sense, *drame* designates a class of dramatic works intermediate between tragedy and comedy. Its theory was developed in the eighteenth century by Diderot, who conceived the *drame* as a serious presentation of the domestic problems of middle-class life. But in colloquial French "C'est un drame!" has the sense of "What excitement!" Thus irony and ambiguity reign as the play comes to a close.

In fact, the existence of this play confirms that among Vitrac's claims to recognition as a leading writer of surrealist theatre is this: his dramas are the very first in which a moral attitude consonant with surrealist views finds unequivocal and sustained expression.

The indictment underlying *Les Mystères de l'Amour* becomes explicit in *Victor*. In the latter, treatment of language and dramatic situation combine to communicate revulsion for bourgeois hypocrisy and horror at its stultifying effects. Even before the play was finished, Artaud commented enthusiastically, "In *Children Take Charge* the pot is boiling. The title itself indicates basic disrespect for established values. Through gestures at the same time burning and petrified, the play translates the disintegration of modern thought and its replacement by . . . by what? That, anyway, is the problem to which the play, *grosso modo*, replies: With what to think? And what remains? There is no common measure, no rank any more. What remains?" Artaud's production of *Victor* called for empty picture frames to be hung at the front of the stage. Allowing the audience to be conscious of looking through the fourth wall, he cast them in the role of voyeurs as well as of eavesdroppers.

In the first act, the madness of an adult, Antoine Magneau, and the anticonformist behavior of a child, Victor, introduce disruptive influences destined to trouble the even flow of middle-class existence in a manner all surrealists would commend as salutary. Even so, in order to unmask the features of the bourgeois outlook he finds detestable, Vitrac represents his hero's home life realistically. The play takes the form of a period drama set in the year 1909. The events it presents are exactly situated in time, occurring on September 12 between eight in the evening and midnight. On two occasions the playwright ironically authenticates his drama by citing the *Dictionnaire Larousse*. First he reproduces a biographical note on Bazaine, the French marshall who discredited himself during the Franco-Prussian war by surrendering the town of Metz to the enemy. Then he reproduces the dictionary's extravagant praise of the Third Republic. In addition Vitrac has explained, "I took the newspaper *Le Matin* for September 12, 1909. I cut out all the articles, then I proceeded to a 'collage' method as in Cubism."[26]

If the kind of collage used to *place* his play, historically, resembles the technique employed in Cubism, during one remarkable sequence

26. Statement made to Armand Gatti for *Le Parisien libéré*, cited in Béhar, *Roger Vitrac*, p. 187.

collage produces an unquestionably surrealist effect. The end of the second act shows us Vitrac's parents retiring for the night. Charles Paumelle reads aloud selections from the morning paper, finally coming to the serial: *Les Hommes de l'Air*, a "novel of sport and love" by Hughes Le Roux, Part Three, Episode Four, "Une très grande Dame." As Paumelle reads of the arrival of an excitingly beautiful woman in the bedroom of the athletic hero, we see the very scene described by Le Roux acted out between Victor's father and a mysterious woman visitor. Emilie Paumelle's weeping testifies to the extremely important fact that we are not merely witnessing a fantasy in which her husband indulges. We are in fact present at the materialization of his erotic dream.

No doubt it would be distorting the play to interpret every aspect of *Victor* in the light of surrealism alone, so denying its value as a projection of Vitrac's personal experience, for instance. All the same, the essential ingredients it brings together are entirely consistent with surrealist principles. Present at the 1946 revival of this drama focusing attention on a nine-year-old social misfit, almost six feet tall as the action begins and growing taller as we watch, André Breton could only have approved of Vitrac's illustration of the following dictum from the *Manifeste du Surréalisme:* "it is perhaps childhood that comes closest to the true life" (p. 56). Besides, the handling of the elements assembled in this play is deserving of the highest praise from the surrealists. Vitrac, who declared in *Comœdia* on January 27, 1925, apropos of Strindberg, that theatrical activity belongs to the realm of dream, does not waver, between *Les Mystères de l'Amour* and *Victor*, in his conviction that dreams are tangible and merit presentation upon the same footing as objective reality. Charles Paumelle's dream bears witness to his creator's readiness to demonstrate this conviction. Moreover it proves Vitrac's ability to do so within the framework of a dramatic technique that is conventional on the surface only.

Criticizing *Victor* for "a lack of necessity," as one commentator has done,[27] betrays a misunderstanding of the nature of Vitrac's undertaking in his theatrical works influenced by surrealism. To Vitrac, necessity is not primarily dramatic, even though his command of dramatic technique is so exceptional that Béhar feels it fair to say that Vitrac stands apart from Breton, Aragon, and Ribemont-Dessaignes

27. Fred Roge, "Scandale de tout Repos," *L'Etoile du Soir*, November 28, 1946.

because he always thinks of the staging of his "poetic plays."[28] The necessity governing action in Vitrac's early plays is one that takes its origin in the playwright's firm belief that dream and desire are as worthy of our attention as what we habitually call reality. Not dramatic necessity, therefore, but recognition of the conflict produced by the imposition of repressive limits upon our desires and dreams explains the tragic progress of *Les Mystères de l'Amour* and of *Victor*. As the "Author's Note" comments in introduction to the former:

We know very well that everything must be said. Clearly? Why?
Everything lies in understanding one another.
Here we have a dialogue of echoes.

With *Victor* behind him, Vitrac could no longer see any hope of reconciliation with surrealism. Treated harshly in the *Second Manifesto* by Breton who never retracted and did not even soften his accusations, as he was to do when speaking subsequently of several others whose excommunication was made public in 1929, Vitrac was one of the very first to demonstrate how love for Breton could turn to hate. He made a violent contribution to a scurrilous collective attack on the surrealist leader that appeared in January 1930 under the title *Un Cadavre (A Cadaver)*. It was entirely consistent with the emphasis reflected in his surrealist plays that Vitrac's text should stress moral issues. Called "Moralement Puer" ("To Stink Morally"), it marked Vitrac's definitive separation from surrealism.

Vitrac went on to write other plays, and he stands out as the only person associated with surrealism who ever sought to make a career for himself as a dramatist, meanwhile seeking consolation in absinthe. Béhar views his work as a whole as permanently marked by the sufferings reserved for an "outcast from surrealism," and attempts to plead that responsibility for Vitrac's subsequent failure rests on other shoulders than his own.[29] In contradiction with Béhar, might one not entertain the hypothesis that Vitrac's talent as a playwright faded because, after his initiation into surrealism, he went on to aim at success with a public for whom he had shown no regard, while writing the two plays for which he will be remembered longest and upon which the stamp of surrealism is clearly visible?

28. Henri Béhar, *Etude sur le Théâtre dada et surréaliste* (Gallimard, 1967), p. 253.
29. This is the thesis defended in Henri Béhar's *Roger Vitrac*.

Antonin Artaud and the
Théâtre Alfred Jarry

The Théâtre Alfred Jarry was
created to use the theatre
and not to serve it.[1]

OF ALL THOSE whose names have been linked with surrealism, for whatever length of time, Antonin Artaud is without doubt the one generally associated most readily with the stage. The immense influence his theories have come to exert over the theatre in the second half of the twentieth century is self-evident. Less clear is the extent to which the ideas embodied in his conception of the Theatre of Cruelty may be traced to surrealism. Specifically, the relationship between the principles underlying the Théâtre Alfred Jarry, of which Artaud was cofounder, and those advocated in surrealism has been subject to contradictory evaluation. At one extreme, Henri Béhar assures us that, after 1930, Artaud's theatrical ambitions developed directly from the propositions underlying the Théâtre Alfred Jarry—and that means, ultimately, from surrealism.[2] At the other, Eric Sellin, discussing Artaud's dramatic concepts, declares that "for all intents and purposes his surrealist period ended in 1927."[3] Meanwhile the surrealist origins of

1. Antonin Artaud, *Manifeste du Théâtre Alfred Jarry*, 1928 Season.
2. Henri Béhar, *Etude sur le Théâtre dada et surréaliste* (Gallimard, 1967), p. 244. Unless otherwise indicated, all references to Béhar are to this work.
3. *The Dramatic Concepts of Antonin Artaud*, p. 75. Unless otherwise identified, all page references are to this work of Sellin's.
Sellin hastens over the ideas behind the Théâtre Alfred Jarry, concentrating upon those that underlie Artaud's Theatre of Cruelty. He tends to dismiss Artaud's connections with surrealism as unworthy of attention, discounting its influence. This has not prevented him from contributing an article entitled "Antonin

Artaud's first play, *Le Jet de Sang* (*The Spurt of Blood*), have never been established with any degree of clarity.

As early as 1923 Artaud became interested in what André Breton was doing. In 1924 he became a member of the newly formed surrealist group, although his name does not figure, as does Vitrac's, among those mentioned in the first manifesto as having "given proof of ABSOLUTE SURREALISM." Among the early surrealists he distinguished himself as the author of some of the most violently aggressive open letters signed by participants in the movement, earning this praise from Breton in *Entretiens:* "no one had more spontaneously put his means, which were great, at the service of the surrealist cause" (pp. 107–8). It was Artaud, commended by Breton for his uncompromising fury "which spared so to speak no human institution," who in 1925 drew up a statement on the activities of the Bureau of Surrealist Research, opened on the Rue de Grenelle in Paris in 1924. When, having closed its doors to the public in 1925, the bureau continued to operate in private, he became its director. To Artaud fell also responsibility for preparing the April 1925 number of *La Révolution surréaliste*, the last issue to appear before Breton took over the magazine and edited it himself from the fourth number onward.[4]

All that Artaud wrote, during his period of enthusiastic support of the ideas set forth in Breton's *Manifeste du Surréalisme*, shows him to have been unreservedly committed to the cause he had espoused. To insist, as Sellin does, that Artaud "made no changes in himself, no adjustment, to become 'surrealistic'" (p. 74) and so to imply that Artaud's outlook was in no way modified through contact with surrealism proves nothing, one way or the other. This makes Artaud's case by no means as exceptional as Sellin and Virmaux (p. 129) apparently believe.

Artaud and the Objectified Language of the Stage" to a special issue of *L'Esprit créateur*, 6, 1 (spring 1966), pp. 31–35, on the theme of surrealist literature. In that text, which has found its way into his book, the word "surrealism" does not appear even once. As for Alain Virmaux, his discussion of Artaud and surrealism takes up two paragraphs in a text of 240 pages: *Antonin Artaud et le Théâtre* (Seghers, 1970), p. 129.

4. The April 15, 1925, number contains the Address to the Pope, the Address to the Dalai-Lama, the Letter to the Schools of Buddha, the Letter to Directors of Insane Asylums, the Letter to the Rectors of European Universities—all written by Artaud. These texts, together with the statement on the activities of the Bureau of Surrealist Research, all appear in Artaud's *Œuvres complètes*, Vol. I (Gallimard, 1956). They appear also in Maurice Nadeau, *Histoire du Surréalisme*, II, *Documents surréalistes* (Aux Editions du Seuil, 1948).

What really counts is that, for a while, surrealism offered Artaud encouragement to demand complete satisfaction of needs that he, Breton, and their friends all had in common.

If we examine, for example, Artaud's statement on the activities of the Bureau of Surrealist Research, we find nothing suggesting either that he had significant reservations about the action to be taken in furthering surrealism's aims, or that he brought any remarkably distinctive proposals to the pursuit of surrealist ambitions. We do not even come across proof that he was possessed of exceptional gifts for achieving these aims, however talented he proved to be at giving them vehement expression. Antonin Artaud's definition of the problems facing surrealists and his recommendations for handling these were entirely orthodox, substantively distinguishable in no way from what others in the movement were saying during the mid-twenties. Speaking of the surrealist revolution, for instance, he asserted:

> This revolution aims at a general devaluation of values, at the depreciation of the mind, at the demineralization of evidence, at the absolute and renewed confusion of tongues, at changing the level of thought.
> It aims at breaking and disqualifying logic, which it pursues unto the eradication of its original entrenchments.

While still a willing participant in surrealism, Artaud published his first play, *Le Jet de Sang*, in his *L'Ombilic des Limbes* of 1925. Confined to this one text, tangible evidence of his ideas on theatre during the period when he was directly involved in surrealist activities is limited. But it is no less so, proportionately speaking, than the evidence Artaud was able to bring forward in support of his conception of the Theatre of Cruelty, when he decided to found his Théâtre de la Cruauté in order to stage his only full-length play, *Les Cenci*—an adaptation from Stendhal and Shelley—in May 1935. If, then, there is a major difference between his contribution to the theatre during his time as a surrealist and later on, it is this: while militating for surrealism, Artaud, who within a decade was to distinguish himself as one of the most original theoreticians of the theatre, advanced not a single observation upon the principles according to which *Le Jet de Sang* had been written, either in explanation or in defense of what he had tried to do.

Of course, we must bear in mind that Artaud felt drawn to the theatre before he made Breton's acquaintance. Coming to Paris from his home town of Marseilles in 1920, he attracted the attention of A.-F. Lugné-Poë, director of the Théâtre de l'Œuvre, who gave him a small role in Henri de Régnier's *Les Scrupules de Sganarelle*. In 1921, Artaud made contact with Charles Dullin, for whom he played a variety of roles at the Théâtre de l'Atelier. He also acted with the Georges and Ludmilla Pitoëff troupe at the end of its 1922–23 season and during the 1923–24 season. At about the same time he began to find roles in films.[5] All the same, in the absence of proof that, by the time he joined surrealism, Artaud had already begun to view the theatre in a way that would set him apart from those with whom he was about to consort voluntarily, there is no reason to treat *Le Jet de Sang* as anything other than an attempt to bring surrealism to the stage. Indeed, where–as a consequence of Artaud's direct experience of stage productions–one might expect to see signs that the author of *Le Jet de Sang* was not only far more aware of the needs of the theatre than his fellow surrealists but also much more responsive to them, we encounter instead indisputable evidence of unwillingness to compromise surrealist iconoclasm through any concession at all to the practicalities of staging. We are reminded in this play, therefore, of an affirmation made by Artaud in his statement on the activities of the Bureau of Surrealist Research, an affirmation that noticeably stressed the negative rather than the positive aspects of the surrealist program: "Surrealism, rather than beliefs, registers a certain order of repulsions."

Le Jet de Sang has not fared well with the critics.[6] So we find our-

5. Artaud acted in films from 1922 to 1935. For his contribution to surrealism as a writer of film scripts and scenarios, see J. H. Matthews, *Surrealism and Film* (Ann Arbor: University of Michigan Press, 1971), pp. 59–66; Virmaux, *Antonin Artaud et le Théâtre*, pp. 155–57.

6. Possibly out of an antagonism for Breton clearly reflected in his book (see pp. 71–74), Sellin is eager to detach Artaud from surrealism. As a result, he makes the following attempt to dismiss both *Le Jet de Sang* and *La Pierre philosophale*, which Artaud wrote between 1930 and 1931: "In the early works we have the seemingly irrational profusion of sundry objects such as those that fall from the sky in *The Spurt of Blood*, and the unrealistic use of mannequins as in *The Philosopher's Stone* when Isabelle pulls the effigy of Doctor Pale from under her skirts when she has been caught making love to Harlequin. Perhaps these incidents have some symbolic value, but it is difficult to disentangle the elements true to Artaud's concepts from those which seem to derive from his association with the surrealists" (p. 125). A footnote (p. 150) shows that Sellin is content to dis-

selves seeking an explanation for the general reluctance displayed by commentators to discuss this play. One may be found, it seems, if we consider Sellin's criticism of the stage directions Artaud places just after the action has begun with an avowal of love between a young man and a young woman:

> A silence. We hear something like the sound of an immense wheel turning and setting off a wind. A hurricane breaks them apart.
>
> At this moment, we see two astral bodies come into collision and a series of legs of living flesh falling with feet, hands, hair, masks, colonnades, doorways, temples, alembics, falling, but more and more slowly, as if they were falling in a vacuum, then three scorpions one after the other, and lastly a frog, and a beetle that comes to rest with heart-rending slowness, sickening slowness.

The young man cries, "The sky has become mad." But this, apparently,

---

miss *Le Jet de Sang* as having a "surrealist comic opera atmosphere" and as "either an imitation or a pastiche" of Guillaume Apollinaire's *Les Mamelles de Tirésias*, written between 1903 and 1916.

So far as one can tell, Michael Benedikt disagrees (Michael Benedikt and George Wellwarth, *Modern French Theatre: The Avant-Garde, Dada, and Surrealism* [New York: Dutton, 1964]). Making the unsettling error of asserting that in 1927 *Le Jet de Sang* was "produced at the Théâtre Alfred Jarry"—wherever that might be—Benedikt comments that it is "one of the few original works we can turn to in order to see what Artaud may have ideally thought of as drama, in any conventional sense" (p. xxix). Apparently Béhar inclines to the same opinion, for he writes, just as vaguely, that *Le Jet de Sang* is "one of the rare works which permits [*sic*] us to see what Artaud understood, in the absolute, under the name of drama" (p. 231). And there is good reason for this agreement. Without acknowledging his debt, Béhar is obviously paraphrasing Benedikt, who continues with the comment that Artaud "seems to envision this play in terms of a vocabulary of pure theatrical impossibility." Béhar's version runs: "One has the impression that this play is theatrically impossible." Where Benedikt remarks, "Here we have the disintegration of all values imposed by civilization spectacularly symbolized in the tumbling down of live pieces of human bodies, and whole temples," Béhar echoes, "The best-established notions of our civilization are disintegrated in it." He stops short of finding, as Benedikt does, " 'theatre of cruelty' in the frenziedly discontinuous activity which characterizes the entire play." But no more than his American predecessor does he speak of surrealism when summarizing the main features of *Le Jet de Sang*. As for Gérard Durozoi, his only comment on *Le Jet de Sang* is that it is a "playlet parodying Salacrou" (*Artaud: L'Aliénation et la Folie*, Larousse, 1972, p. 72).

The most that can be said in favor of Béhar, Benedikt, Durozoi, and Sellin is that they do at least mention Artaud's first play. Martin Esslin, on the other hand, does not bother to do so (*The Theatre of the Absurd* [1961], rev. ed. [New York: Doubleday, Anchor, 1969]). His pages on Artaud typify a critical trend that can develop most freely, it would appear, only at the expense of even a passing reference to *Le Jet de Sang*.

is not enough to placate Sellin who, despite the fact that *Le Jet de Sang* was staged in London by Peter Brook in 1964, complains, "This is as unstageable as it is unscientific. Furthermore, it is strangely static in essence and—like so many scenery descriptions by surrealist playwrights—reminds us more of a Max Ernst collage than a blueprint for dramatic action."[7]

It would be helpful to know which playwrights Sellin has in mind, since at least one of those he mentions in his article—Jean Cocteau—certainly had nothing to do with surrealism. All the same, the drift of his argument does not escape detection. Nor do its consequences elude us. To anyone looking to *Le Jet de Sang* to provide "a blueprint for dramatic action"—looking, in other words, for ideas that can be expected to contribute materially to giving the theatrical event new direction—Artaud's first play must necessarily offer little excitement. Far from helping supply the theatre with the kind of impetus most drama critics are equipped to measure, *Le Jet de Sang* exemplifies surrealist anti-theatre. To the very extent that such critics find it worth no more than a brief mention, it is valuable to those concerned with the role of theatre in surrealism.

Surrealism places in our hands the only instrument sensitive enough to register accurately the effects obtained in *Le Jet de Sang*. Speaking of surrealism in the course of his comments on the Bureau of Surrealist Research, Artaud pointed out most pertinently, "But, in the final analysis, it is in the mind, it is from within that it is judged, and, faced with its thought, the world does not carry much weight." The stage directions Sellin has condemned rest neither upon science, which he invokes to dispose of them, nor upon admission of the primacy of practical considerations in theatrical production. Instead, they take their meaning from an attitude reflected in what Artaud has to say about surrealism:

> In the name of an inner liberty, of the exigencies of its peace, its perfection, its purity, it spits on you, world given over to dessicated reason, to the bemired mimetism of the centuries, and who have built your houses of words and established your lists of precepts where the surrealist spirit, the only one to which we owe being uprooted, can no longer explode.

It is surely in relation to this affirmation of faith in the power of

7. Eric Sellin, "Surrealist Aesthetics and the Theatrical Event," *Books Abroad*, 43, 2 (spring 1969), p. 171.

surrealism to release man from inherited and inculcated thought processes that we must consider the instructions given in *Le Jet de Sang* at a time when a violent storm is raging on the darkened stage: "At a given moment an enormous hand seizes the bawd's hair which catches fire and grows visibly." The bawd, we notice, recognizes the "gigantic voice" that orders, "Bitch, look at your body!" as her clothing becomes transparent, showing her in hideous nudity. She exclaims, "Leave me, God." All the same, instead of accepting divine retribution as just, "She bites God on the wrist," causing an immense spurt of blood to strike the stage. Such unexpected behavior indicates that Artaud's play was not written to reaffirm familiar moral precepts. So does the fact that, when the footlights come up again, everyone else—including a priest—lies dead, while the bawd, still very much alive, is talking to the young man "as though at the extreme point of a love spasm."

It is not in staging alone, therefore, that Artaud calls for rejection of convention in *Le Jet de Sang*. He demands no less radical a change in our predispositions with respect to dramatic action. As the play opens, the banal exchange of stock phrases between lovers is given new vitality, taking an inhabitual direction. As each of the two characters varies pitch, when delivering lines stripped of all vestiges of novelty, words we know only too well assume a strange aspect, thanks mainly to arbitrary emphasis. This is not attributable to psychology so much as to the degree of intensity granted the sounds we hear.

Sellin speaks accurately of "new tonalities" being "sprung from the traditional rhythms of speech by the artificial registers employed" (p. 118). Where we cannot follow him is in treating this effect as "perhaps more silly than dramatic." In fact, his first adjective betrays Sellin's prejudice toward a mode of drama that concerned Artaud little, if at all, during the writing of *Le Jet de Sang*. Meanwhile something that to a critic of Sellin's persuasion seems silly is revelatory of a characteristic feature of surrealist dialogue, as described in the first manifesto. Examination of the examples furnished in Breton's text reveals that the *exchange* authorizing us to speak of "dialogue" is not necessarily of the kind that takes meaning from the logical advancement of a plot. Indeed, by standards usually considered applicable in drama, dialogue of the sort in question is stationary, not progressive. Halting rational intercourse, it replaces this with a confrontation that merits classification as poetic, surrealists agree, by virtue of its nonconsecutive nature.

After the hurricane has separated the lovers at the beginning of *Le*

Jet de Sang, a medieval knight and a swollen-breasted wet nurse, who may or may not be the young woman's parents, trade insults. Now the young man returns, declaring, "I have seen, I have known, I have understood," but without making any attempt to share his insights with the audience. In his continuing quest for the young woman he has lost, he receives no assistance or encouragement from figures of authority like a beadle and a priest, who remarks significantly, "We don't see it that way" (literally: "We don't hear it with that ear").

Although capable of retaliating against God with impunity, the bawd cannot distract the young man with her amorous conduct. He hides his head in his hands, while the wet nurse returns, flat-chested now and with the corpse of the young woman under her arm, like a package. A momentary diversion occurs. The knight demands the Gruyère cheese we saw him eating earlier. "There you are," says the wet nurse, lifting her skirt. Unaccountably reduced to marionettelike stiffness in his movements, the young man pleads in a ventriloquist's voice, "Don't hurt Mummy." The knight displays horror as a large number of scorpions "come out from under the wet nurse's dress and begin to swarm into her sex which swells and splits, becomes vitreous, and flashes like a sun." The young man and the bawd run off together "like trepaned people," while the young woman, miraculously returned to life, has the closing line of the play: "The virgin! ah that's what he was looking for."

Just as significant as the shock administered to conventional religious feeling through the element of blasphemy introduced quite casually in *Le Jet de Sang* is the shock it offers well-established assumptions about the structure and function of drama. On the technical plane no less than on the moral plane, this play faithfully reflects the surrealist attitude. Thus the discontinuous character of *Le Jet de Sang* is entirely in accord with the belief common to surrealists that sustained plot development is not mandatory in the theatre. On the contrary, it seems to them that plot consistency may be sacrificed without hesitation or regret to more pressing concerns. If, for instance, we look at that part of the play where Artaud appears content to mingle horror with the scabrous, when the scorpions swarm under the wet nurse's skirt, there is reason to believe that this spectacle is by no means as gratuitous as it appears at first.[8] True, no explanatory statement is to be found in the

8. Readers who know *Le Jet de Sang* only in George E. Wellwarth's translation

stage directions, and none is made in the dialogue. In fact we should have no guidance from the author when interpreting this part of *Le Jet de Sang*, had not Artaud later drawn up a scenario for a play called *La Conquête du Mexique* (*The Conquest of Mexico*), which was to have been the first of his Theatre of Cruelty productions. In the outline for the third act of *La Conquête du Mexique* occurs the sentence, "Montezuma cuts through true space, splits it open like a woman's sex to make the invisible spurt from it."[9] In the last verb we hear a distinct echo of the title *The Spurt of Blood*. Even without this, however, the recurrence of the arresting image of splitting a woman's sex would suffice to bring to our notice an allusion that illuminates the whole of *Le Jet de Sang*.

It could well be that only the passage of time made it possible for Artaud to recognize, in the bold image from *Le Jet de Sang* to which he returned after 1930, the projection of a need to bring the invisible forth from the visible. In the circumstances, it might not be wise to credit him with full awareness of what he was doing, while working on his first play.[10] But if we may suppose he was less than clear in his mind about the implications of what he was saying, this still does not detract from the validity of *Le Jet de Sang* as an expression of surrealism. On the contrary, under these conditions that play might be regarded profitably as testimony to Artaud's refusal to set reasonable bounds upon a drama he was writing at a time when, as he noted in his open letter to the Schools of Buddha, "We are suffering from a rot, from the rot of Reason."[11]

(Benedikt and Wellwarth, *Modern French Theatre*, pp. 221–26) should note that this translation is defective. Wellwarth renders Artaud's sentence "Alors une multitude de scorpions sortent de dessous les robes de la nourrice et se mettent à pulluler dans son sexe qui enfle et se fend [. . .]," as "An army of scorpions comes out from under the nurse's dress and swarms over his [i.e., the Knight's] sex which swells and bursts [. . .]."

9. Artaud's preliminary notes for *La Conquête du Mexique* were published with his manifesto *Le Théâtre de la Cruauté* (Société Anonyme du Théâtre de la Cruauté, 1932). The scenario from which the sentence cited here is borrowed was published for the first time in *La Nef*, Nos. 63–64 (March–April 1950), 'Almanach surréaliste du Demi-Siècle.'

10. However, it is worth noticing that in "A Table" (*La Révolution surréaliste*, No. 3, April 15, 1925), Artaud wrote, "Through the splits in reality, henceforth inviable, speaks a world obstinately sibylline."

11. Cf. "A Table," where Artaud declared, "Woe betide your logics, Gentlemen, woe betide your logics, you do not know how far our hate of logic can take us," and argued, "Our attention must not be drawn too much to the chains that bind us to the petrifying imbecillity of the mind." At the end of this text

Be that as it may, we have no difficulty tracing the orientation of Artaud's thinking during the period to which *Le Jet de Sang* belongs. We can do this most conveniently through the open letters he drafted for the surrealist group to issue as collective challenging statements. Thus the one addressed to the directors of insane asylums—particularly noteworthy, when we recall how many years its author was to spend as a patient in mental institutions—begins accusingly, "Laws and customs grant you the right to measure the mind. This dangerous sovereign jurisdiction you exercise with your intelligence. Forgive us if we laugh." Soon Artaud is asserting, "We do not admit that the free development of a delirium should be hindered. It is as legitimate, as logical as any other succession of human ideas or acts." And a moment later he affirms "the absolute legitimacy" of insane people's conception of reality and of "all the acts stemming from it."

Being attentive to Artaud's approach to life as a surrealist means something quite different from getting ready to write off his first play as proof of mental imbalance. The value of the open letter just cited lies elsewhere. It establishes the relative unimportance, from where he stands beside the surrealists, of rational criteria, both in the creative act itself and in interpretation of its fruits. Without risk of ascribing undue importance to *Le Jet de Sang*, therefore, we can safely claim that its significance lies in the following areas. This is a text in which premeditation is sufficiently questionable—here and there, at all events—for spontaneity of an irrational nature to be a feature of the creative process we cannot discount, when asking how the play came to be written. When we ask, next, why it was written, we have to recognize that *Le Jet de Sang* poses a question regarding the nature of reality that is fundamental to surrealism, and does this whether or not we estimate that conscious intent is largely absent here. "Existence is elsewhere," declares Breton at the very end of his *Manifeste du Surréalisme*. "We are not in the world," observes Artaud, after Rimbaud, as he condemns the Pope in an open letter for being "confined to the world." When, finally, we ask how Artaud's drama was put together, with what degree of concern for character and plot, we cannot help noticing the effects of an underlying spirit of rejection likely to promote consternation and epitomizing the surrealist approach to dramatic form.

language is called "a means of madness, of eliminating thought, of breaking down, the labyrinth of unreason."

Le Jet de Sang conforms to the anti-aesthetic of surrealism so faithfully that someone thoroughly familiar with the latter's demands upon the theatre is likely to find this play offers him no real surprises. Indeed, such a viewer might reasonably expect that Antonin Artaud could have gone on producing texts just as representative of the surrealist outlook as his first play, in which there are no signs that he was finding the surrealist mode irksome or inadequate to his needs. However, while internal evidence in his drama does foster the belief that Artaud could have remained faithful to surrealism, certain events taking place soon after *Le Jet de Sang* was published made continued fidelity impossible for its author.

In 1927, after much soul-searching, five members of the surrealist group, Aragon, Breton, Eluard, Benjamin Péret, and Pierre Unik, joined the Communist Party, determined to give political expression to the surrealist revolution. Explaining their reasons in a public statement printed under the title *Au Grand Jour (In Broad Daylight)*, they took the opportunity to attack two former members of their circle "in the name of a certain principle of honesty which, in our opinion, must come before everything else." These two were Philippe Soupault and Antonin Artaud.

The accusations against two formerly valued members remained generally vague. Only one of their shortcomings was specified: "their *isolated* pursuit of the stupid literary adventure." Years later, Breton was to comment less abruptly upon his reservations vis-à-vis Artaud. Referring to the celebrated open letters for which Artaud was responsible, Breton remarks in *Entretiens*:

> However [. . .] it did not take me long to become disturbed by the atmosphere they created. [. . .] I had the impression that, without quite knowing it, we had caught a fever and that the air was becoming rarefied about us. [. . .] This new direction, half-liberative, half-mystical, was not quite mine and I came to regard it rather as a dead-end than as a new direction (I was not the only one, by the way). (p. 109)

Only when he criticizes the "verbal" nature of these documents in *Entretiens* does Breton come close to justifying the attack made in *Au Grand Jour*. What he says does go a little further, though, toward helping us understand how ridiculous political involvement must have seemed to Artaud, who confided in one of his letters, "*I can say, truly,* that I am not in the world, and this is not a mere attitude of mind."[12]

Artaud's response to *Au Grand Jour* was not long delayed. It took the form of a privately printed counterattack, *A la Grande Nuit ou Le Bluff surréaliste* (*In the Darkest Night or The Surrealist Bluff*), dated June 1927.[13] As one might anticipate, where the authors of the former talk of him as having been expelled, Artaud speaks of having withdrawn voluntarily because surrealist action has become sterile, whatever the framework selected for it. Hence he is led to define surrealism from the standpoint of his own demands upon it. "The revolutionary forces of any movement," he comments, "are those capable of throwing the present basis of things off axis, of changing the angle of reality." While certain surrealists now feel constrained to consider the social implications of their attitude of revolt, Artaud avers, "I am speaking of a metamorphosis of the inner conditions of the soul." This is how he comes to refer to surrealism in terms that set *Le Jet de Sang* in perspective, as "that conflagration of the basis of all reality," insisting that for him, "It is a matter of that shift in the spiritual centre of the world, of changing the levels of appearances, of that transfiguration of the possible which surrealism was to contribute to provoking. All matter begins in spiritual derangement."

The longer he talks of surrealism, the more clearly Artaud indicates the nature of the motivation from which his first play originated. Surrealism, he declares, was never to his mind anything but "a new sort of magic." Imagination and dreams are "that intense liberation of the unconscious which has as its aim to bring flowing to the surface of the soul that which the soul is accustomed to keep hidden," with consequent "profound transformations in the scale of appearances, in the value of signification and the symbolism of the object created." Thus the beyond, the invisible "push back reality." Taking issue with those he feels no longer have anything in common with him, Artaud announces, "They can howl as much as they like in their corner and say

12. See Antonin Artaud, *Correspondence avec Jacques Rivière* (Editions de la N.R.F., 1927), letter dated May 25, 1924. Readers of *L'Ombilic des Limbes*, where *Le Jet de Sang* finds its place, will recall Artaud's early affirmation, "Where others propose works I claim nothing other than showing my spirit" (he uses the word *esprit*, which means 'mind' as well as 'spirit').

13. *Au Grand Jour* appeared under the imprint Editions surréalistes. The text is reproduced in Maurice Nadeau's collection "Documents surréalistes" (pp. 95–111), followed by the text of *A la Grande Nuit* (pp. 112–19). The latter appears also in Artaud's *Œuvres complètes*, Vol. I, pp. 281–91.

it is not this, I will reply that for me surrealism has always been an insidious extension of the invisible, the unconscious within reach. The treasures of the invisible unconscious, become palpable, lead the tongue directly in one spurt."

What is interesting above all is that Artaud's definition of surrealism is still quite orthodox. It presents no noteworthy divergence from the one that continued to be defended by the surrealists after his departure and regardless of the need felt by some of them to extend their protest against the reality principle to the plane of social reality. In other words, had Artaud not quarrelled with the surrealists over politics, it would not be difficult at all to imagine him capable of writing a play after *Le Jet de Sang*, no less expressive of the surrealist point of view while yet communicating his own preoccupation with "the equivocal, fathomless domain of the unconscious" with its "signals, perspectives, glimpses, a whole life growing when one stares at it and showing itself capable of still disturbing the mind."

Something else noticeable is that, when attacking his former friends, Artaud speaks of their having sacrificed spiritual revolt to social revolution. He is content to allude regretfully and with no sign of insincerity to "that magnificent power of evasion" to which, it seems to him, surrealists held the secret. Nowhere in *A la Grande Nuit*, though, does he face and attempt to meet the accusation that he has already betrayed an interest in creating literature, a commodity most suspect in surrealist eyes. Meanwhile, the authors of *Au Grand Jour* ignore, just as he does, a factor that contributed measurably to bringing about a deterioration in Artaud's relationship with the surrealist group. Neither *A la Grande Nuit* nor *Au Grand Jour* mentions the Théâtre Alfred Jarry, founded by Artaud, Vitrac, and Robert Aron in September 1926, fully eight months before *Au Grand Jour* appeared in May 1927.

The history of the Théâtre Alfred Jarry is worth reviewing here for two reasons. First, it permits us to examine the relation to surrealist principles of the theatrical concepts Artaud and his friends were defending. Second, it gives us an opportunity to learn, through surrealist reaction to what Artaud was doing, how surrealists felt during the years immediately following the first manifesto about the theatre as a medium for communicating with the public at large.

The Théâtre Alfred Jarry was to have staged its first production in early 1927. Already in October 1926 the following unsigned text had been given to the newspapers:

> A group of young writers brought together to revive the idea of an absolute theatre is going to found a new theatrical company, under the name Théâtre Alfred Jarry. Their efforts are directed toward creating a theatre which will develop in the direction of complete liberty and which will have no other aim than satisfying the most extreme demands of the imagination and of the spirit. For them, the theatrical event can no longer rest upon an illusion but corresponds to a reality of the same order as the other tangible realities.

To promote interest in the Théâtre Alfred Jarry it was decided that a public lecture should be given. This was delivered by Aron at the Ecole des Hautes Etudes on November 25, under the title "Genèse d'un Théâtre." In the absence of Aron's text, which was not preserved, we have to rely for a report of the content of his talk upon a review published by Guy Crouzet in *La Grande Revue*'s December 1926 issue. Aron spoke of "a free exchange between the stage and the auditorium," stressing removal of the barriers traditionally marked by the footlights. "From each play must result the creation of a world," imitation of everyday acts and gestures being replaced by "the limitless freedom of dream and the spirit."

A circular letter signed by Yvonne Allendy on December 12, 1926, records that, when Artaud and his friends came to visit her and her husband on September 26, 1926, asking for assistance in raising funds, they wanted to found a theatre dedicated to putting on "a programme including plays by Jarry, Strindberg, Roger Vitrac, etc."[14] As it happened, Artaud never produced a play by Jarry, whom the surrealists revered. After a first spectacle in which all three co-founders were represented, a second, given on January 14, 1928, consisted of Pudovkin's film *Mother*, banned in French movie houses, and unauthorized presentation of an act taken from a play not identified in advance but in which Breton recognized *Partage de Midi* by Paul Claudel, French Ambassador to the United States or, as Artaud called him from the

14. See Antonin Artaud, *Œuvres complètes*, Vol. II (Gallimard, 1961, p. 270, n. 29.

stage, when keeping his promise to name the author of the play, "an infamous traitor." Then came Strindberg's *A Dream Play* (June 2 and 9, 1928). Finally Artaud produced Vitrac's *Victor* on December 24 and 29, 1928, and January 5, 1929.

The Théâtre Alfred Jarry's was a mixed program, one that could hardly be expected to appeal to the surrealists in its entirety. Artaud, of course, had ceased to care about pleasing Breton and his associates. Had this not been the case, it would be less interesting to observe how closely the principles underlying the ideas upon which the Théâtre Alfred Jarry rested parallel those we have found to be characteristic of surrealist practice in the theatre. Much remains vague in what we know of Aron's lecture. The same is true of the statement given to the press. Yet in the original plans for a new theatre outlined by Artaud, what we notice above all is that the most concrete proposals relate quite closely to those exemplified in plays of surrealist inspiration.

The aim of the Théâtre Alfred Jarry, Artaud informs us, is that "everything obscure in the mind, buried deep, unrevealed should be manifested in a sort of material projection, real." Still true to surrealist principles, he asserts, "In the theatre that we want to produce, chance will be our god." He expresses contempt, meanwhile, for "all theatrical means properly so called," for "all that constitutes what people generally agree to call the *mise en scène*, like lighting, sets, costumes, etc.," insisting that the Alfred Jarry Theatre is intended for "all those who do not see in the theatre an end but a means, all those disturbed by concern for a reality of which the theatre is only a sign." In short, the Théâtre Alfred Jarry was created, he declares, "in reaction against the theatre."[15]

Not surprisingly, Jarry's example appealed to Artaud as much as to the surrealists. Like them, he saw in the author of *Ubu Roi* a man who "was able to contemplate the abolition of the theatre."[16] For this reason, *Ubu Roi* meant very much the same to Artaud as to those from whom, in helping found the Théâtre Alfred Jarry, he was asserting his independence. Thus it was respect for Jarry and for what he had made possible in the theatre that maintained continuity in Artaud's theatrical principles, when he left the surrealist group.

15. See Artaud, *Œuvres complètes*, Vol. II, pp. 16, 17, 22, 27, 33.
16. Jacques Robichez, "Jarry ou la Nouveauté absolue," *Théâtre populaire*, No. 20 (September 1, 1956), p. 94.

Persuasive evidence of continuity in Artaud's ideas at the time when, moving away from surrealism, he was planning a new theatre is the first spectacle presented by the Théâtre Alfred Jarry on the stage of the Théâtre de Grenelle, June 1 and 2, 1927. It consisted of three plays—Aron's *Gigogne*, Artaud's *Ventre brûlé ou La Mère folle* (*Burnt Belly or The Mad Mother*) and Vitrac's *Les Mystères de l'Amour*—of which the last was by far the most substantial. In the brochure *Le Théâtre Alfred Jarry et l'Hostilité publique* Aron's play is described as "written and presented with the systematic purpose of provocation." It was never published. Artaud's musical sketch, "a lyrical work that humorously denounced the conflict between cinema and theatre," was not preserved either, and was a modest effort.[17] Vitrac's is the only play of the three to have been published. It came out, we recall, in November 1924, within a month of Breton's *Manifeste du Surréalisme*, two and a half years before its production under Artaud's direction.

Artaud and Vitrac met in 1924, within the surrealist group and a year after *Les Mystères de l'Amour* was completed. They became close enough to spend their summer vacation together in 1925. Upon their return to Paris, each submitted an article to *La Nouvelle Revue Française*. Publication of Vitrac's, a note on *L'Ombilic des Limbes*, was delayed until December, but Artaud's laudatory review of his friend's play appeared in the September 1925 issue. Artaud's admiration for *Les Mystères de l'Amour* led him, in the hope of seeing it staged, to approach Lugné-Poë. However, arrangements to present it under the latter's direction in December 1925 fell through. In November 1926 Robert Aron's lecture on the Théâtre Alfred Jarry was followed by readings from Jarry, Raymond Roussel, and *Les Mystères de l'Amour*. Meanwhile the previous month Vitrac's play had been mentioned as figuring in the first Théâtre spectacle announced in the press for production at the Vieux Colombier on January 15, 1927. When lack of funds halted plans for January, Yvonne Allendy and her husband set about raising money that permitted Artaud to begin rehearsal of Vitrac's drama in May 1927, at the Théâtre de l'Atelier, where Dullin made space available.

The dates speak for themselves and really should leave no room for confusion. Nevertheless commentators have tended to ignore them

17. Robert Maguire's reconstruction of the play, based on recollections of the performers, in his dissertation "Le Hors-Théâtre" (1960), is reproduced in Virmaux, *Antonin Artaud et le Théâtre*, pp. 319–20.

when interpreting the relationship of Vitrac's "surrealist drama" to Artaud's ideas on the theatre.

Indisputably, Artaud was preoccupied with *Les Mystères de l'Amour* for quite a time before he produced it in 1927. However, to some observers his interest appears directly influenced by his own exclusion from surrealism in November 1926. Specifically, their comments reveal their judgment to have been affected by the postscript, dated January 8, 1927, to Artaud's *Manifeste pour un Théâtre avorté* (*Manifesto for an Aborted Theatre*), published in the *Cahiers du Sud* (February 1927) after its author had reached the conclusion that financing the Théâtre Alfred Jarry would be impossible. This postscript takes up the surrealists' contention that Artaud and Vitrac were engaged in literature and, by their efforts to establish a theatre, had proved themselves to be counter-revolutionaries. Implying that, being no longer associated with surrealism, he and Vitrac had ceased to be indebted to it, Artaud appears to be inviting reactions that are, at best, ambiguous.[18]

The truth is that, to explain the steadfastness of Artaud's faith in Roger Vitrac's play *Les Mystères de l'Amour*, we have to look beyond their friendship. We have to recognize the compelling influence of ideas about the nature and function of theatre that derived from sur-

18. Michael Benedikt, for example, remarks, "It remained for a play by Roger Vitrac, *The Mysteries of Love*, written about 1924 [*sic*], and directed by Antonin Artaud at the Théâtre Alfred Jarry in 1927, to represent both the culmination of the Surrealist drama and at the same time bring Artaud's own dramatic theories effectively to the stage" (p. xxix). Benedikt does not say in so many words that Vitrac's play was written to illustrate Artaud's theories, any more than he asserts that the latter depart in some way from surrealism. All the same, inferences may be drawn from his comments, and from his use of quotations borrowed from Artaud to explain *Les Mystères de l'Amour*, which conflict with the incontrovertible fact that Vitrac wrote his play before he even knew Artaud. It is interesting, then, to see Béhar go even further than Benedikt. Arguing that agreement between Artaud and Vitrac was not accidental, in his *Roger Vitrac: Un Réprouvé du Surréalisme* (Nizet, 1966), he shows complete disregard for chronology when declaring that "it rests on a certain number of preliminary reflections about the function of the theatre which they viewed in the same way, at the same date" (p. 170).

Béhar's mistake in treating Vitrac's 1923 play as contemporary with the theories underlying Artaud's involvement with the Théâtre Alfred Jarry is a revealing one. Such an error could not possibly have been made if *Les Mystères de l'Amour* and Artaud's theorizing in 1927 did not have a common origin in surrealist thought. In the final analysis, what matters is that Vitrac's play appeared to Artaud very well suited to staging by the Théâtre Alfred Jarry because the director's thinking had not yet evolved appreciably away from fundamental principles inculcated by surrealism, according to which *Les Mystères de l'Amour* had been written.

realist thinking, in Artaud's case as much as in Vitrac's, far more than from anywhere else. Personal differences aside, it seems at first conceivable that Artaud might have been capable, if not of placing the Théâtre Alfred Jarry at the service of surrealism, then at least of welcoming those surrealists who wished to take advantage of a stage where their plays would have been guaranteed sympathetic presentation by a director sensitive to their aspirations in drama. To see why speculation of this kind is inadmissible, we must look at the facts more closely.

In advance of his disagreement with the group over politics, Artaud took a step in 1926 that carried him outside the surrealist circle. Not only did he show willingness to risk censure for collaborating with Vitrac, expelled more than a year before, but he also demonstrated his readiness to devote himself to a project tempting to no other surrealist: he was preparing to involve himself in a theatrical venture that inevitably entailed commercial considerations. Moreover, he freely admitted in *Théâtre Alfred Jarry, 1ʳᵉ Année*, "the works we shall put on belong to literature." Confessing a tendency toward literature of which he stood accused by the surrealists, Artaud went on to employ the unfortunate phrase "pure theatre," far too evocative for surrealist taste of the abbé Brémond's "*poésie pure*." In the circumstances he could not hope to escape suspicion from former friends who had not ceased to fear the concessions they felt must attend any effort to meet the public on terms other than their own. Indeed one has the distinct impression that Artaud's conduct was calculated to provoke the surrealists to caution and to keep at a distance those with whom he was no longer associated.

While, to begin with, it may seem pure coincidence that Artaud and Vitrac waited until they had severed contact with surrealism before attempting to found a theatre, this is hardly likely. The reaction they would have stirred up by taking such a step earlier is easy to imagine, so fearful was Breton of compromising the demands of surrealism in ways he soon had cause to believe that Artaud and Vitrac were quite willing to accept: not only did they stage a Strindberg play with the backing of the Swedish Embassy, but they even called in the police to prevent the surrealists from disrupting the performance.[19] Anger at Artaud and Vitrac had the effect of blinding Breton and his followers to the simple fact that, in some significant ways, the Théâtre

19. Breton did not forgive Artaud publicly for this action until 1946. See the "Avertissement" written for the reprinting of the *Second Manifeste du Surréalisme* (1946).

Alfred Jarry stood for the same things as they. Thus not one of them would have raised any objection to adding his signature to the following statement, had it not been written by Artaud in his *Manifeste pour un Théâtre avorté* of 1927: "Everything belonging to the illegibility and magnetic fascination of dreams, all this, those dark layers of consciousness which are all that preoccupies us in the mind, we want to see it radiate and triumph on stage, content to lose ourselves and to expose ourselves to a colossal failure."

On the face of it, then, the surrealists had only themselves to blame for not appreciating the possible benefit to their movement of active cooperation with Artaud. From one important point of view, however, they had good reasons for withholding their support. From the surrealist standpoint Artaud and Vitrac appeared altogether too inclined to pursue in the theatre alone their effort to attain those ambitions that they had in common with surrealism. In this sense, they fully deserved categorization as "men of the theatre." Their dedication to a medium they hoped to serve while making it conform to their special requirements had a consequence that no surrealist could envisage for long without alarm. "Before thinking of his ideas," remarked Artaud, when announcing *Victor* in the program of the Théâtre Alfred Jarry's 1928 season, "Roger Vitrac, like any good dramatic author, thinks of the theatre but remains at the same time close to his thought." Essentially, it was the question of precedence that separated the surrealists' values from those Artaud was defending by reference to Vitrac's theatre.

Weighing this question, the surrealists did not take long to find both Artaud and Vitrac guilty of "*arrivisme ignoble*."[20] The offhand manner in which this judgment is delivered in the course of a 1929 article not aimed primarily at taking Artaud and Vitrac to task, tends to conceal its central importance with regard to the special problems the theatre raises for surrealists. To the extent that Artaud credited Vitrac with placing concern for his medium above dedication to the material that medium was to communicate, he removed Vitrac's plays from the context of surrealist endeavor, situating them instead in rela-

20. See Aragon and Breton, "A Suivre: Petite Contribution au Dossier de certains Intellectuels à Tendances révolutionnaires (Paris 1929)" p. xxii. Among those attacked in "A Suivre" was Georges Ribemont-Dessaignes (see pp. xxix-xxxii), who had collaborated with Artaud and A. Barsalou on the pamphlet *Point final*. This text reaffirmed opposition expressed in *A la Grande Nuit* to the surrealist conviction that revolution must find expression on the social plane. *Point final* was made public for the first time in *Le Magazine littéraire*, No. 61, in February 1972.

tion to the demands drama imposes upon writers. If it were true that, as Béhar wants us to believe, the original purpose of the Théâtre Alfred Jarry was simply to "contribute to ruining the theatre as it exists by specifically theatrical means" (p. 236), then the surrealists could only have applauded Artaud's undertaking. But Artaud necessarily fell into disfavor with them when attempting to make a contribution to the medium of theatre, rather than requiring the theatre to comply with standards given precedence in surrealism.

Criticizing Vitrac in an undated letter, Antonin Artaud wrote, "If you want to make a theatre to defend certain ideas, political or otherwise, I will not follow you in that direction. In the theatre only that which is theatrical interests me, to use the theatre to launch any revolutionary idea (except in the domain of the spirit) seems to me the basest and most repugnant opportunism."[21] Less important to us as a sign of the growing disagreement that finally came between Vitrac and Artaud, this letter is valuable as an expression of its author's point of view, which is, he concedes, "the point of view of a stage director if you like, but basically theatre is everything that has to do with staging, [. . .]."

Henri Béhar talks of a "tragic misunderstanding" between the promoters of the Théâtre Alfred Jarry and the surrealists. But for this, he contends, Artaud might have furthered the cause of surrealism in the theatre, much as Antoine had served that of naturalism, and Paul Fort and Lugné-Poë had served Symbolism (p. 227). But we can follow this line of reasoning only if we gloss over the serious differences that, above and beyond personal disagreements, set Artaud the man of the theatre apart from his former associates. These differences make clear why, from the early days of group action, the surrealists shunned contact with professionals who might have brought their form of theatre to public notice.

Marc Alyn does not paint a true picture when, remarking that Vitrac's passion for the theatre separated him from his surrealist friends, he remarks, "The condemnation of Roger Vitrac by André Breton in the *Second Manifesto* translates by the way a wider incomprehension, which is that of surrealism with regard to the theatre."[22] All that Alyn brings to light here is his own incomprehension of the surrealist attitude toward theatre, an inability to appreciate that surrealists place their beliefs, and the consequences of these, before the requirements

21. Quoted in Béhar, *Roger Vitrac*, pp. 289–90.
22. Marc Alyn, "Vitrac l'Oublié," *Le Figaro littéraire*, January 21–27, 1965.

that the drama conventionally imposes, first on the author and second on the director of his play. In so doing, all surrealists feel justified, as Breton did, in weighing the "moral value" of an action like the one Artaud took when seeking support for the Théâtre Alfred Jarry by presenting a program designed to please the Swedish Embassy. Similarly, in his *Roger Vitrac* Béhar treats the surrealists' attack on Artaud and Vitrac as indicative of "a condemnation of the theatre in general." Passing over the fact that other surrealists agreed with André Breton, Béhar proceeds to suggest that the reasons behind condemnation of both Artaud and Vitrac and, through them, of the theatrical genre, may have been an aversion peculiar to Breton: "Only the bad taste—or the absence of taste—of Breton on the subject (as with respect to music) explains the negative attitude of the surrealists toward the Théâtre Alfred Jarry" (pp. 102–3).

According to Béhar, proof of Breton's lack of appreciation for the theatre can be traced to *Nadja*, where the surrealist leader frankly confesses that Paul Palau's *Les Détraquées* is the only dramatic work he is willing to remember (p. 35).[23] To give his argument substance, Béhar suppresses Breton's all-important qualification, "I mean: written solely for the stage." In his hurry to impugn Breton's judgment, Béhar fails to point out that the author of *Nadja* does not admit to being interested in *Les Détraquées* on the level at which his taste seems to invite ridicule. Summarizing the play, surrealism's principal spokesman insists that the plot is hardly the main attraction for him. The special appeal of this potboiler lies in the discovery Breton makes that, without knowing it, Palau has produced a text that solicits "conjectures" of a kind without analogy in any other play written "solely for the stage." When we evaluate Breton's response to Palau's play, therefore, the following considerations are of paramount concern.

The question raised by Breton's affection for *Les Détraquées* is not one of taste, but of imaginative responsiveness, as fostered within surrealism. Thus Béhar's diversionary tactics are of no avail in concealing the important distinction Breton, as a surrealist, brings to our attention between plays written to meet the requirements of the stage and those valuable to him because, although they may be technically imperfect, they nevertheless stimulate imaginative activity productively. To put it another way, *Les Détraquées* compels Breton's admiration because it

23. The first number of *Le Surréalisme, même* (1956) testifies to the abiding appeal of *Les Détraquées* for the surrealists. It reprints the complete text of the play.

inadvertently meets the extra-theatrical criteria that are of prime importance to him, as they must be to all surrealists for whom the theatre can be valid only in the degree that it refuses to be circumscribed by the limits of stagecraft.

"The Théâtre Alfred Jarry was created to use the theatre and not to serve it," declared a manifesto announcing its 1928 season. If only Artaud had kept to this plan of campaign, he might still have gained the surrealists' confidence. However, the scope of the program he was able to see through to production was altogether too limited to command the surrealists' trust. From within the surrealist camp it seemed that he was doing more to confirm deep-rooted fears about the sad consequences of a public theatrical venture than to allay misgivings. Meanwhile, more and more inclined to speak as a director, Artaud was falling into a role that promised to make the Théâtre Alfred Jarry serve theatrical demands oftener than it subverted them. Counselling Vitrac, while *Le Théâtre Alfred Jarry et L'Hostilité publique* was in preparation, Artaud spoke pointedly of "the essential *theatrical* domain which does not interest you solely, I know, but from which I don't want to move, so far as the Théâtre Alfred Jarry is concerned." Voicing his reservations about Vitrac's latest play, *Le Coup de Trafalgar*, on November 5, 1930, he asserted pedantically, "Finally a play is not a mere exposition nor even merely a development of characters around nothing." Related criticisms in other letters written the following year[24] all reflect the same bias: demanding consistency of character and motivation, Artaud was challenging Vitrac to conform to standards that surrealists felt entitled—not to say obligated—to ignore.

The last of these letters takes us into a period when the Théâtre Alfred Jarry had already ceased to be active and when the friendship between Artaud and Vitrac was soon to be terminated so acrimoniously that the two refused to meet at the time of *Victor*'s revival in 1946. Long before that period, the surrealists had registered their profound disapproval of Artaud in whom they eventually were to forgive the poet, but not the man of the theatre.[25]

24. All these letters are reproduced in Béhar, *Roger Vitrac*, Appendix 2.
25. Georges Hugnet omitted Artaud from his anthology of surrealist poetry. Benjamin Péret, however, restored Artaud to his rightful place in *La Poesia surrealista francese*. Artaud is represented also in Aldo Pellegrini's anthology. Jean-Louis Bédouin, in his selection of surrealist poems, comments on the break with surrealism marked by Artaud's *A la Grande Nuit:* "This break will not prevent Artaud from remaining faithful to the spirit of surrealism which he will have contributed to disseminating" (p. 49).

Georges Hugnet

We spend our lives on the lookout
for adventure. No. Not adventure, no.
Surprise, yes, surprise.[1]

IN DADA AND SURREALIST LORE the name of Georges Hugnet comes up
for the first time in connection with Roger Vitrac's *Victor*. It is said
that Hugnet was the person who reportedly threw stink bombs during
the dress rehearsal, giving added but unwelcome realism to the scene
in which a minor character, Ida Mortemart, displays her unfortunate
affliction: uncontrollable flatulence. Best known as the compiler of the
first anthology of surrealist poetry, in which he is represented, Hugnet is also the author of a dramatic essay, *La Justice des Oiseaux* (*The
Justice of Birds*), printed in the magazine *L'Usage de la Parole*,[2] and
of two plays published together in 1930, *Le Droit de Varech* (*Wreck
Rights*) and *Le Muet ou Les Secrets de la Vie* (*The Mute or The
Secrets of Life*).

Dated April 1927, *La Justice des Oiseaux* is, in the context of surrealism, the least interesting of his writings for the stage. Set in a pet
store, it tells how the owner, Harmann, who specializes in teaching
parrots how to talk (*l'usage de la parole*), locks up his seventh wife,
Adèle, when her curiosity is aroused by suspicious sounds emanating
from behind a door. Inexplicably using phrases they have never learned
from Harmann, the parrots obligingly alert an off-duty policeman to
the crime. The policeman releases Adèle and, with her, other women
who must be Harmann's previous wives.

The weighty atmosphere of menace that holds our attention in

1. Georges Hugnet, *Le Muet*, in *Le Droit de Varech*, précédé par *Le Muet ou
Les Secrets de la Vie* (Editions de la Montagne, n.d. [1930]).
2. See *L'Usage de la Parole*, 1re Année, No. 1 (December 1939), pp. 11–12.

Aragon's *L'Armoire à Glace* is absent from *La Justice des Oiseaux*. Although Harmann's parrots have an impressive command of French and reasoning powers to go with it, their conduct does not lift this play out of the category of fanciful fairy tales. And so Hugnet's text fails to qualify for recognition as one of the "almost fairy tales" for which Breton appealed in his 1924 *Manifeste du Surréalisme* (p. 29). Only by his earnest insistence upon the liberative function of words does Hugnet give signs of appreciating what surrealism stands for and of being ready to take his "first steps into the unexplored lands of the marvelous."[3]

The action of *Le Muet* is situated in 1927, "in Paris and elsewhere." This play opens against a conventionally realistic background. In a bourgeois dining room a young man sees and listens to two beautiful women. These supposedly uninvited visitors remain invisible to his father, who cannot hear "the theatrical and fresh words" they utter. While the father is absent from the room, the young man takes a revolver from his pocket, locks it in a drawer, and throws the key out of the window "so as not to be tempted," he explains a few moments later, "to massacre my family, my whole family." The father fears his son has become deranged, apparently having cause to be concerned. Soon the young man is dictating a nonsensical but vaguely threatening telegram, before throwing a second revolver from the window. However, when a police inspector arrives in response to the father's request, he arrests the parent, not the son.

The arrest of the father goes unexplained, but it is quite consistent with the movement of the first tableau in *Le Muet*. Here from the moment when the audience is allowed to share with the young man the privilege of seeing and hearing the mysterious women who are his "only reason for living," the normal is overturned. Hugnet's preference for the improbable over the probable is further demonstrated in events occurring after the young man has thrown his weapon into the street.

Bleeding from the forehead, a man enters. He has been hit by the revolver, yet states with scrupulous politeness that he does not hold this against the nameless young man. "But the most serious thing is that you made me kill my daughter," the blow to his head having activated the trigger. The young man recognizes in the name of the daughter, Æmilia, the one written down for him by the Mute ("who seems to preside over events," Hugnet comments) on a piece of paper

3. Georges Hugnet, *Petite Anthologie poétique du Surréalisme* (Editions Jeanne Bucher, 1934), p. 11.

he must save forever. Hence the young man's fear is that the accident may prevent him from knowing a secret in which his destiny is tied up with Æmilia's. Brought in on a stretcher, the young woman revives. However she refuses to stay: "Would you have recognized me," she asks, "if you had not almost killed me by chance and indirectly [*par ricochet*] and if the Mute had not made known to you my name, that first step toward the light? Farewell, you will have to search for me again."

At the end of this first tableau, the everyday order is turned to ridicule as we see the father, who has committed no crime, meekly obeying an arresting officer who may or may not be an imposter.[4] The play proceeds in a manner illustrative of Hugnet's preoccupation with imposing values of his own. "Let us say this," he remarks significantly in his *Petite Anthologie poétique du Surréalisme*, "if surrealism finds in our time so many detractors, this is because, demanding too much, it threatens established order, this is because it lays down in principle everything that cuts the bridges behind it" (p. 20).

The second tableau finds the young man visiting a fortune-teller. He is intent upon hearing if doing so will defend him from his past. Everything he is told about his present he denies, much to the annoyance of the fortune-teller who continues with vague, unconvincing promises about future bliss in distant lands. A strange card she has never seen before turns up in her Tarot pack, unveiling the young man's future, she claims. But when, conquering his fear, he asks her to speak out, she says she cannot. As their conversation proceeds, the young man remarks that they are both lying. Soon he declares, "You have no right to disturb my life, to change its direction, to interfere with it because you know my destiny." He is now wholly taken up with his suspicion that someone is listening behind a curtain. After a moment's violence, brought on by the discovery that the curtain conceals a crow, he falls to the ground as though in a faint. The fortune-teller confesses she knew he would come one day, "but I put all my hope in deception with the cards. Or in trickery."

The man injured in Tableau One arrives, asking for Mademoiselle Æmilia who, he asserts, looks like his dead daughter. The young man, whom the caller has only a vague recollection of having seen before,

4. The inspector introduces himself as Stanislas Boutemer. The title of Hugnet's first published volume is *Les Poèmes de Stanislas Boutemer* (Editions Th. Briant, 1928).

assures him he is on the wrong floor and shuts the door in his face.

Just as she denied earlier having a daughter, so now the fortune-teller denies any knowledge of the identity of Æmilia, even though she confesses to the realization that "what must happen is about to take place." While the young man rests in an armchair, the curtain is drawn back to reveal Æmilia. Lovingly she caresses the young man's head, ignoring her mother's appeal to leave him: "You have chosen according to your destiny," the fortune-teller comments, "I know what is going to happen. You have lost your mother." The elder woman leaves by a door through which the injured man returns once again: "At last Æmilia, I find you again at last. You whom I killed by accident and who know how to outlive yourself." Informing him she is no longer Æmilia, the young woman sends him away, remaining with the young man as the curtain comes down.

In the second tableau coincidence, not clairvoyance, provides the young man with the key to his situation. The fortune-teller he consults makes every effort to impede his progress toward self-knowledge. But even as she seeks to conceal the presence of Æmilia from him, she appreciates that she cannot divert the course of events, dictated in this melodrama by beneficent chance.

"When surrealism interrogates chance," Hugnet was to point out not long after writing *Le Muet*, "it is to obtain oracular replies."[5] The hero of his play is a representative surrealist figure in this respect, that he is attuned to "a signal of invisible complicity" to which Breton shows himself attentive in *Nadja*. Like Aragon in *Le Paysan de Paris* (1926), this young man lives "by chance, in the pursuit of chance, which alone of all the divinities [has] succeeded in retaining its prestige."

Seeing Hugnet's young man in the light of his unquestioning obedience to the dictates of chance helps us avoid error, when it comes to evaluating the way in which the plot of *Le Muet* is constructed. The author repeatedly has recourse to coincidence. It is given so much emphasis in his melodrama that it disposes of any illu-

5. See J. H. Matthews, *An Introduction to Surrealism* (University Park: Pennsylvania State University Press, 1965), p. 99. Cf. Breton's comment on Monsieur Létoile who appears in *S'il vous plaît*: "In actual fact, it is quite true, he expects no one since he has made no appointment, but the very fact that he adopts this ultra-receptive posture shows that he counts in this way upon helping chance, how shall I put it, putting himself in a state of grace with chance, so that something may happen, so that someone may come along" (*Entretiens, 1913–1952* [Gallimard, 1952], p. 136).

sions we may have had, upon seeing the first scene open in a realistic middle-class environment, regarding Hugnet's willingness to confine action within the bounds of credibility. Indeed, the value of *Le Muet* lies in the instinct it expresses to exceed those bounds and to demonstrate their irrelevance to the drama of human existence. Here chance is not merely a theatrical device used for sustaining interest or reviving it when there is danger of its flagging. Chance is a token of a view of life to which the playwright, as a surrealist, is committed. For this reason, a structural element traditionally regarded in the theatre as a valid means, when judiciously used, of drawing and holding attention, is utilized in total indifference to verisimilitude. It is applied in defiance of common sense, and far less out of concern for theatrical needs than with the intention of projecting a conception of life based, against reason, in surrealist convictions.

As we ask what Hugnet is doing, we come to recognize in the role granted chance throughout *Le Muet* an indication that this play centers upon desire in order to show how desire finds an outlet, and with what consequences. Thus the young man's feeling of alienation, separating him from his family as the play begins, betokens a sense of loss that makes him sensitive to the presence of two visionary figures, whom his parents can never see because they have no need to do so. The underlying force motivating this young man's behavior is that sense of paradise lost in which surrealist pessimism about the current circumstances of man's mode of existence takes root. However, thanks to encouragement from beneficent chance, his feelings of estrangement do not immobilize Hugnet's hero in helpless frustration. Instead they are channelled into an activity bearing witness to surrealist optimism about man's capacity to attune the world to his needs. In the central character of Hugnet's play, we see fostered undeviating determination to reconcile desire and reality. For this reason, *Le Muet* illustrates how, in surrealism, chance becomes a double key—to man and to his world.

The further the play proceeds, the more anti-reasonably it solicits our participation, aspiring to coherence on the level of dream, not conventional reality. This melodrama finds its center of gravity in desire, projecting its demands upon the objective universe where chance works assiduously to prepare the way for their satisfaction. In this case poetry, as this word applies in surrealism, resides in the triumph of dreams over all obstacles, effected in such a way as to impose upon apparently unrelated encounters and incidents the coherence of desire fulfilled. As Breton intimates in his *Les Vases communicants*, it lies in surmounting "the depressing idea of the irreparable divorce between action and dreaming,"[6] thanks to the role surrealism reserves for something Breton calls in the same context *"capillary tissue."* This has an essential role: to "ensure the constant exchange which must be produced in thought between the exterior world and the interior world, an exchange which necessitates the continual interpenetration of waking and the activity of sleep" (p. 189). As he pursues in Æmilia the object of his desire, Hugnet's young man permits us to appreciate the function of the dream for surrealists in "liberating the individual," as Breton comments in his *L'Amour fou*, "from paralyzing affective scruples, confronting him and leading him to understand that obstacles he might consider insurmountable have been cleared."[7]

Discussing something that, borrowing Hegel's terminology, he calls phenomena of "objective hazard," Breton once expressed the conviction that such phenomena come into play only "when it is the heart, not the mind, which is alerted."[8] So far as we see Hugnet's young man uncritically responsive to chance, we find the author of *Le Muet* in agreement with Breton. He uses chance as a unifying factor, to the detriment of reason and to the advantage of irrational feelings, as he entices us step by step into the "unexplored lands of the marvelous" to which he believes surrealism destined to lead.

At the beginning of Tableau Three we are told that Æmilia and the young man have joined a travelling circus. On a country road the young man encounters a sailor. This man confesses to having just fractured his wife's skull upon impulse, and is surprised to find Hugnet's hero not only aware of the crime but also capable of putting into words feelings that he, the murderer, was not conscious of having at the time of the crime. Saying his wife's name is Æmilia, the sailor is much surprised to detect her likeness in a drawing in the dust made by the young man before his arrival. The sailor notes too the heel mark left by the artist on Æmilia's portrait when the young man made the discovery that it had no heartbeat.

While describing the murder he has not witnessed, the young man

6. André Breton, *Les Vases communicants* (Editions des Cahiers libres, 1932), p. 198.
7. André Breton, *L'Amour fou* (Gallimard, 1937), p. 46.
8. André Breton, "Henri Rousseau sculpteur?" *La Brêche: Action surréaliste*, No. 1 (October 1961), pp. 13–14.

has referred to Æmilia's head as falling on her shoulders "like a teal that has just been killed." Now as the sailor examines the heel mark in the dust, we hear a shot off stage, and a dying teal falls onto the heart in the drawing. Before leaving to rejoin his ship, the sailor presents the young man with a photograph of his wife, in whom the hero recognizes his own Æmilia, who now enters, dressed as a dancer. Æmilia meanwhile recognizes herself in the drawing on the ground, for this is how she has seen herself in her dreams, blood behind her ear and a dead bird in place of her heart.

When a hunter has claimed the teal, the young man ascertains that Æmilia was indeed hidden behind the curtain in the second tableau. She knew he would come to her mother's, apparently, and loved him, she admits, even before he arrived and while, although still a virgin, she walked the streets. Æmilia brushes aside his words of regret at not having been given the chance to meet her in her role as prostitute: "No, you wouldn't have known me that way. If I'd met you at night on the street, I'd have hidden in a doorway to slip away from you once again, to run away from you . . ." The young man muses, "I don't know. I no longer know where I knew you, where the others knew you, I don't know if I know you. And yet I can draw your portrait from memory, without the help of any photograph." The power to formulate a reasonably acceptable explanation eludes him. But the important ability to conjure up Æmilia's image remains unimpaired, significantly independent of any outside stimulus. Hence there is nothing fortuitous in Æmilia's two reappearances on stage after we have been led to believe her dead. "Beyond time," Hugnet observes in his *Petite Anthologie poétique*, "a force is perpetuated through the rational and the irrational which suddenly consents to putting in a haunting, phantasmal appearance" (p. 12).

Hugnet raises no objection in his *Petite Anthologie* to the use of interpretable symbolic elements, either in writing or in painting. He contends, rather, that these put us in direct contact with the mode of cognition advocated in surrealism. He evidently considers them especially appropriate to the task he has set himself as a surrealist writer—"to *disclose* where each of us has passed by without seeing, where man always has been his own victim" (p. 28). For this reason, while the young man in *Le Muet* fills his Orphic role, Æmilia personifies an atemporal force to which supreme importance attaches in the play. And she does so without losing her vitality as a real woman, even while representing an ideal to which the young man aspires. According to Hugnet's *Petite Anthologie poétique*, the role of dreams as *"living reality"* is self-evident, since they dominate us and belong to us at the same time, because "they are us" (p. 20). Upon this basis, Hugnet argues that surrealist activity escapes censure from reason and the real, "not to flee from thought and reality, but to take them as they are, beautiful and mysterious as an egg, as a butterfly" (p. 25). And so this is why he rules out rational explanations when the young man questions Æmilia:

THE YOUNG MAN
You have never lived with a sailor?

ÆMILIA
No. *A pause.*
I met a sailor just now on the road. When he saw me, he fell forward, he cried my name and he fell down senseless, his nose in the grass.

THE YOUNG MAN
That's just what I thought.

Throughout the third tableau reasonable explanations are set aside, patently inadequate to the task of accounting for what goes on. Thus, for instance, hardly has the young man informed Æmilia that, by tearing up her photograph, he has brought about the death of the sailor than three strollers appear, determined to arrest the sailor for murder. They leave in confusion after finding Æmilia alive, although they saw her dead earlier.

ÆMILIA
Well, then, did he kill, yes or no?

THE YOUNG MAN
We shall never know. To be a murderer he should have killed you.

ÆMILIA
Why me?

THE YOUNG MAN
I don't know. Not everyone who wants to be a murderer is one. You have to know how to pick your victims.

Our only guidance, then, is this remark by the simpleton, Jean-Marie: "everything lies in admitting, and understanding has less importance. You understand because you admit."

Continuity is established between the third and fourth tableaux by the presence of Æmilia, convalescing in the latter, after being wounded accidentally by the hunter in the former. We find the young man reviewing his activities with several friends. He is particularly concerned, as the new tableau opens, with plans for an unspecified crime to be carried out at once, in some house (presumably the Mute's) in a forest. Later we learn that, for the young man, who has told his accomplices that he cannot take part in the crime, the purpose of his plan—which includes setting a trap for his friends—is to "tear from life its secrets." He explains, "One must *dupe* life, take it by surprise, catch it out, if one wants to know its secrets."

On the one hand, Hugnet accumulates melodramatic elements in Tableau Four. On the other, he takes full advantage of coincidence and chance occurrences, of contradiction and ambiguity.

The unidentified cloaked visitor with whom he contracts to have his associates in crime killed and photographed ("Death," Hugnet's hero insists, "must be photographed like an obscene film") warns the young man against showing himself at the window. A little later, a girl who claims to have saved his life in the past comes to ask him to pay a last call on a dying woman, Gabrielle. The young man stoutly denies ever having met her, even though he knows the girl has posed for obscene photos and we have heard him mention Gabrielle's name. No sooner has the girl left than someone enters by the window, revolver in hand. Contrary to appearances, this is not a burglar but a somnambulist with suicidal impulses. Hearing a knock on the door, the young man advises his uninvited guest to hide behind the drapes. Now he is confronted by a well-wisher who warns him his house is under surveillance, sees Æmilia's likeness to his sister, and begs for one of the photos of Æmilia delivered earlier by the cloaked man, on behalf of a dealer in obscene photographs. Finally, to the young man's amazement, the Mute arrives. While the most recent visitor falls to his death from the window, attempting to make his escape, the Mute tells the young man, "I survived the massacre because I am ignorant of none of the secrets on earth. You are not responsible."

As agreed, the man in the cloak returns to deliver a box, as well as the first proofs of the photos requested:

THE YOUNG MAN
The mystery remains the same. These photographs teach me nothing. *He opens the casket and takes out of it the dead bird from the third tableau.*

And what auguries are to be taken from a dead bird! *He picks up a revolver, aims at Æmilia and fires at her.*

Nothing. Nothing. I thought I might find her dream by her side like a dead bird. Nothing.

When the police arrive, the young man promptly confesses to killing Æmilia. The policemen turn to question the Mute about the dead man beneath the window and about what has occurred in the forest. The Mute opens his mouth to show he has no tongue and indicates that he cannot communicate by writing. After taking a picture, a news photographer finds on the table a photo like the one on the body outside: "The affair is becoming involved and yet there is a thread running through it all," he observes. "Perhaps we shall soon have a new lead." On cue, the somnambulist, who has fallen asleep behind the drapes, emerges, still carrying his revolver. Everyone except the young man follows him off stage.

To criticize Hugnet for using "outworn conceptions of dramatic art," as Henri Béhar does,[9] is to miss the important point that the playwright rescues these conceptions in *Le Muet* by applying them, against the sophisticated taste of twentieth-century theatregoers, for his own purposes, to ends that give them new meaning in the light of surrealism. The dramatist's effort is directed toward exploitation of the inexplicable. The effect he obtains is to deny his audience the reasonably satisfying resolution of mystery to which they feel entitled. This is why the dominant presence in his play remains to the end the enigmatic figure of the Mute, whom we hardly see at all and who seems to have a largely inactive role. This man can speak or literally lose his tongue, when it suits his obscure purpose to do so. His unexplained omniscience permits us to measure the ludicrous faith in circumstantial evidence that leads the representatives of law and order, a journalist, and a news photographer to follow the false lead provided by a sleepwalker. It also permits us to account for the failure of the young man at the end of Hugnet's play.

The young man is successful in possessing his heart's desire only so long as he does not attempt to achieve his ends by rationally approved means. The last tableau of *Le Muet* is by far the most conventional, by standards of melodrama. Significantly, this is the tableau that shows us

9. Henri Béhar, *Etude sur le Théâtre dada et surréaliste* (Gallimard, 1967), p. 291.

the collapse of the young man's dream. In the most realistic section of Hugnet's play the hero fails signally to "tear from life its secrets." Seeking tangible evidence, when he should be content with what he already has, he pays the heaviest of penalties: loss of his ineffable ideal.

In Georges Hugnet's first play surrealism finds an outlet in situation, more than in language, particularly in deviation from the natural course of events, brought about by chance and by coincidence. *Le Muet* gives weight to the statement of another surrealist, Robert Desnos: "There exist coincidences which, without stirring feelings in landscapes, still have more importance than the dykes and lighthouses, than peace on the frontier and the calm of nature in the solitude of the desert at the hour when explorers pass."[10] And so does *Le Droit de Varech*.

On an island he calls Prediction, King Gualbert has set his astronomer-physician-alchemist, Didier Laroque, the task of inventing Magic Balls. Laroque has been asked to find the secret to revealing past and future "without concern for time, depth, space, perspectives, and conventions."

As the play opens we learn that a special kind of granite apparently attracts ships to the island, causing them to pile up on the coastline. The Marine Museum already has three thousand five hundred wrecks in its collection when the yacht *Zélie* runs aground with only one man, Frédéric, on board. Almost at once comes the news of a second wreck, the yacht *Frédéric* on which the only survivor is a woman, wrapped like Frédéric in her national flag. He name is Zélie. Each is armed with a magnifying glass that they use to set the granite alight before committing suicide by "carbonization of the heart."

From the beginning, Hugnet emphasizes improbability of plot in *Le Droit de Varech* and exaggerates its theatrical nature in a manner bound to weaken its claims to realistic representation. The phrases "The coincidence is strange" and "Yes, Your Majesty, the drama seems to be coming to life" take ironical effect. So does Gualbert's remark, when Didier Laroque arrives at the very moment that his presence is needed: "Everything happens here as in the theatre." Statements of this

10. Robert Desnos, *La Liberté ou l'Amour!* (Aux Editions du Sagittaire, chez Simon Kra, 1927), p. 26.

kind, designed to stress that the illusion of the stage is no more than an illusion, are balanced by Gualbert's firm assurance, "My imagination will do the rest," and Laroque's revelation that he is conducting research into Magic Balls "according to the chance of [his] imagination."

The first tableau ends with Gualbert's announcement that slavery is to be reestablished on the island and that Wreck Rights will be operative. By his edict, all ships running aground on Prediction belong to him by Wreck Rights and are to be placed in the Marine Museum.

In Tableau Two, Gualbert comes to the beach where the bodies of Frédéric and Zélie lie, to see for himself "that adventure in which death, surprise, mystery, or powerful secret, fire and water clash for first place, a kingdom belonging to death alone." Concluding that Frédéric and Zélie were spies, the king resolves to find out the secret of Prediction before others do.

In the course of the third tableau, Didier Laroque shows the sovereign his first attempt at creating a Magic Ball. It is capable of revealing the past. Looking into it, Gualbert sees a woman holding a glass bell being shut up inside a statute—the very statute before which he and Laroque are standing. Legend has it that the woman, Adrienne Suplice, speaks from within the statue of her mother, Antoinette-la-Parricide, by ringing her bell. Gualbert is not slow to suggest that Adrienne personifies Destiny, Prediction, the ringing of her bell being brought about, he argues, by earthquakes. "And what if Adrienne Suplice personified just as much the attraction exercised by our island, which furnishes our Marine Museum?" What makes this apparently "reasonable and scientific hypothesis" interesting is that Gualbert gives it no credence: "To me, the statue and Adrienne Suplice signify nothing other than a tomb in which a young girl was shut up alive and in which she is perhaps still alive. To the devil with Destiny and its crystal bell!" As the king takes a position that not only reveals his responsiveness to irrational explanations but also denies the role of destiny in human affairs, so he repudiates the fatalistic influences exercised over the life of the young man in *Le Muet* by the enigmatic personage whose name gave the play its title. It remains only for Gualbert to pronounce the words "Be majestic," inscribed on a ring he finds buried at the foot of the statue, to free Adrienne Suplice who emerges when the statue opens to release her.[11]

During the fourth tableau, Adrienne gives the monarch to under-

11. In Tableau Four, Gualbert comments, "Out of pure speculation of the mind,

stand that spies like Frédéric and Zélie are drawn to the island by the legend she embodies. She does not specify however the nature or significance of that legend. Remarking that he does not yet possess the secret that fascinates him, Gualbert explains, "I love in you the freedom of the city." Even without this clear statement, we should have no difficulty recognizing that Adrienne plays in *Le Droit de Varech* the mediative role that so frequently in their writings surrealists reserve for woman. Just like Breton's *L'Amour fou* and *Les Vases communicants*, like Benjamin Péret's *Anthologie de l'Amour sublime* (1956), like the poems of Eluard, Hugnet's *Le Droit de Varech* pays tribute to the mediative function of woman, which makes it possible for man to pass from the depressing world of the known into the exciting universe of the unknown, where his hopes and aspirations are no longer denied. Breton's *Arcane 17* (1944) speaks of "the revelation you brought me," adding, "even before knowing what it might consist in, I knew it was a revelation," while Trost in his *Visible et Invisible* (1953) declares, "And more than ever it rests with *woman* to make it possible for us to find that conciliation of the visible world with the invisible world." As Gualbert puts it, in *Le Droit de Varech*, "Know this, one doesn't die of love; one lives because of it."

Gualbert tells Adrienne she belongs to him by Wreck Rights, "even though not having been thrown up on my coast by the sea, but thrown into my arms by my imagination and your love." He can do this, apparently, because, reviving the age-old Wreck Rights, he has extended their application to every domain—"love, imagination, life, mystery, liberty"—domains that never cease to hold the strongest appeal for surrealists. As for Didier Laroque, in the fifth tableau we find Adrienne criticizing his method of investigation into the secret of the Magic Ball, which he has now succeeded in inventing: "You are not even capable of caressing my body when I offer it to you. You live with inventions, images invented by reality." To perfect his Magic Ball, she assures him, he would need the sound and transparency of her crystal bell, the "drop of maternal blood that steeps the whole island in blood," the secret that she alone knows and that, in his madness, Gualbert holds in contempt.

While Gualbert satisfies his need to make himself a wrecker, order-

---

I formulated the hypothesis of a symbol in which I didn't believe; and I was right not to believe. Didier, you are a dreamer. Doesn't Adrienne live, isn't she among us, a reality more powerful than legend, than dream even."

ing that fires be lit along the coastline and lighthouses be darkened, Laroque begins to doubt the validity of his scientific pretensions:

> My hands can no longer sleep, nor can my head. In which direction to pursue you, Adrienne, now that my plans have collapsed, that nothing is invented, that veils and veils fall and that there always remains one veil to lift, that all my calculations are inaccurate, you lost, my mind chasing after fabulous despairs, now that only you remain like a door which is closed to me?

Adrienne takes advantage of Didier's self-doubt to persuade him to surrender his revolver to her. With this weapon she shoots a shadow she claims to be her father. When Gualbert returns with his entourage, Adrienne orders a guard to walk in the direction she indicates until he comes upon a dead man. On the body Gualbert discovers a ring like the one he found earlier in the sand, with the same inscription: "Be majestic." He discovers also a paper identical with the one carried by Zélie, Frédéric, and a merchant arrested as a spy. He finds in addition a drawing of a siren, together with a plan. The latter indicates that a secret is hidden in the left breast of a siren forming the figurehead of a galleon in the Maritime Museum.

According to legend, the spectre of Adrienne's mother is separated from the world by a wall of glass. Hearing this, in Tableau Four, Gualbert expressed approval, stressing that the wall of glass was not a symbol. Didier Laroque, on the other hand, denied that "legendary and human image" any reality. Yet he is the one present in Tableau Five when Adrienne shoots the shadow and the sound of broken glass is audible as she exclaims, "I am free." Didier is made an uncomprehending witness, while the playwright shows chance beginning to operate beyond the reasonable limits of theatrical coincidence and as a reliable source of beneficent revelation. Thus we see Laroque in a tavern, at the beginning of the sixth tableau, remarking how events fit together like a Chinese puzzle:

> And in the middle there is something I don't see and which is the real countryside, in place of this décor elaborated by life, something I cannot say and which is the word, the Word, that order after which every tongue is loosened or babbles, every forest opens up, every irony crumbles, before which love for a woman cannot resist.

While circumstances allow Didier to do no more than measure his inadequacies, Gualbert can boast, "I have found again the order of the code thanks to which all plans are legible, all languages familiar, all cataclysms simple toys." His special gift of penetration enables him to see that two persons posing as conjurers are the spies Frédéric and Zélie who, he announces, only feigned death earlier so as to accomplish their mission. Meanwhile all Adrienne needs do is ring her crystal bell, and everyone in the tavern except Gualbert, Didier, Zélie, and Frédéric is immobilized so as to facilitate Gualbert's search for the paper he seeks. As the curtain falls, Adrienne observes, "Magic, you see, Didier, is more than a little crystal ball, more even than a crystal bell, more . . ."

Magic is not confined to objects. In *Le Droit de Varech* it finds expression through events. More exactly, it operates through the chance links that lead from one event to the next. So we find ourselves at the beginning of the seventh tableau in the Maritime Museum, otherwise known as the Palace of Navigation, where there are now more than four thousand ships, increasing in number at the rate of fifty a day. Here, following the plan and drawing of a siren tatooed on his chest, a sailor attempts to extract the secret hidden in the siren on the bow of a galleon. He ignores the warning, inscribed with the plan, against touching the figurehead's breasts and stomach and against looking into its eyes. As a result, he discovers in the siren the warmth of a human body and a resemblance to Adrienne. In a struggle during which his companion, a sea captain, stabs two night-watchmen, the ladder bearing the sailor topples, throwing him to the ground, where he is found by Gualbert, Adrienne, and Didier Laroque.

Realizing that it was she whom the sailor was seeking, Adrienne breathes life back into his body. Meanwhile she has only to ring her crystal bell to recall the captain. The latter is really an escaped prisoner, he confesses, condemned to a twenty-year sentence for a crime committed out of love for Adrienne. As the tableau comes to an end, the siren's breast is about to be removed upon Gualbert's orders, even though he and Adrienne doubt the usefulness of searching for the secret it supposedly contains.

In Tableau Eight Gualbert is unperturbed by warnings that the Palace of Navigation is expanding at such a rate as to threaten to extend over the whole island. "Well," says the king to his advisors, "know that if heaven has its plan and the earth also its own, and the stars, and the sea, and conspirators, and regicides, and you yourselves, I also have mine and it is my policy. [. . .] To all ills, if ills you judge them to be, I have my remedy." Meanwhile Gualbert, who earlier affirmed, "One has the right to do anything if one has the power to do it," confides in Adrienne, "I have admitted everything that love, thought, dream, habit, insouciance, madness, liberty, sadism, revolt . . . have thrown up in my head and in my hands, as the earth admits the tree and as it throws to men bread, anguish, night, poison, ennui, life. I have accepted everything: ships, conspiracies, passion, royalty, mystery, Magic Ball, incomprehensible deaths, pink seas, magnetic depths, languages in code . . ."—and Adrienne, to whom he remarks, "I find only in you and in me that incessant miracle of movement, that imperceptible movement that makes towers lean and volcanoes emit a lurid glow."

Reviewing what has happened, Gualbert is impressed to see how often he has come upon "the same language foreign to the life of others." This is the language spoken by statues, written on papers carried by spies, tatooed on a sailor's chest, hidden "like a heart in an allegorical wooden siren, mistress of a crew searching for gold," and engraved on a ring found by chance: "the language spoken also by our love, our vices, our ships, our magnificent ignorance." Having accepted and invited so many mysteries, he feels himself surrounded and even menaced by them. As for Didier Laroque, he has at last recognized "the uselessness of the future," has given up seeing symbolism in things, and has lost faith in his Magic Ball. Yet he cannot penetrate the enigma of the inscription "Be majestic," which Frédéric, disappointed to learn that the siren's breast contained the same paper as he and Zélie carried when coming to Prediction, now claims to understand.

Gualbert's major advantage over Laroque is revealed in Tableau Nine. Here Adrienne refers to the king in the following terms: "Gualbert pretends to search, searches to amuse himself, to know how one ought to find me, normally, in foreseen ways, with preconceived perseverance, but he has found me by instinct, by pleasure, by love, by chance . . ." Thus, as Adrienne intimates when calling him "a mysterious searcher for gold," Gualbert, not Didier, is really the alchemist in Le Droit de Varech, exerting his power inadvertently, through the use of words, as when he released Adrienne from the statue of her mother by reading aloud the inscription "Be majestic," without realizing the consequences of doing so.

Now detesting Gualbert, Didier Laroque kills Zélie and Frédéric, burns all the secret papers, and the sailor's body: "No more trace . . .

Like a bad dream . . . I shall search alone now." Gualbert is less concerned about this action than about the effects of the Wreck Rights edict upon the population, divided at this point into revolutionaries, who oppose his policy, and patriots who support him. It is out of hate for the latter that Gualbert revokes the edict, announcing the release of all ships and prisoners. The island is to be evacuated, leaving Gualbert and Adrienne alone on Prediction.

Questioned by Didier Laroque about the secret of the island, the king indicates that it is Adrienne. Didier leaves the stage, declaring, "I know what remains for me to do." Trying to halt an evacuation in which he senses impending catastrophe, he stirs the royal guard to revolt: "The Guard is with us," he tells Gualbert, "Here is a revolver: treat yourself as you deserve." Taking the weapon, the king cries, "Innocent! Treating ourselves as we deserve has never meant anything. Here everything changes." He fires and Laroque falls mortally wounded, exclaiming, "Forgive me." Gualbert is overpowered and bound. But Adrienne rings her crystal bell, causing a volcanic eruption that sets the fleet of ships on fire. Left alone on Prediction, she and Gualbert watch the holocaust.

It would take no more than ringing her bell for Adrienne to silence the volcano. Similarly, all Gualbert would have to do is throw his ring into the sea in order to calm the waters, give them back their natural color, and restore their salinity. By mutual agreement, neither exercises his power. "People speak of the last cigarette of a condemned man and never of the first kiss of a murderer," remarks the king as the walls cave in and the curtain comes down for the last time.

Part fairy tale, part science fiction, part spy drama, *Le Droit de Varech* is none of these with any degree of consistency. It amalgamates a variety of theatrical elements, brought together without regard for reasonable sequence or sustained credibility. Hugnet employs techniques which reveal that for this playwright surprise and chance are not merely convenient methods of sustaining dramatic interest. They are, rather, to be taken as clear indications that, beneath the surface of life, even where life assumes strangely exotic forms, certain inexplicable forces exert an irresistible influence. It is to these mysterious forces that *Le Droit de Varech* and *Le Muet* direct our attention.

In seeking to make his audience aware of undercurrents at which his text hints repeatedly, Hugnet wishes to use the drama presented before our eyes as allusive to underlying impulses and conflicts that constitute the real subject matter of his plays. In this respect his writing for the stage is entirely consistent with the ambitions of surrealism, as Breton characterizes these in *Les Vases communicants*, where he says of surrealism, "I wish that it will be credited with nothing better than throwing a *clew* between the all-too-dissociated worlds of waking and dreaming, of outer and inner reality, of reason and madness, of the calm of knowledge and of love, of life for life's sake and of revolution, etc." (p. 116).

When Hugnet talks in his *Petite Anthologie poétique du Surréalisme* of "the suppression of the artistic mentality and the advent of the spirit that emits waves" (p. 22) he simply reaffirms his agreement with Breton, evidenced in plays where dramatic unity, characterization, and credibility of plot come second to the depiction of the marvelous, "heart and nervous system of all poetry," as Benjamin Péret once called it.[12] In his single-minded pursuit of invigorating manifestations of the marvelous, Hugnet makes a valid contribution through theatre to that "action of discovery and re-creation of the world of realities" mentioned in his *Petite Anthologie* (p. 12). As Gualbert insists, it is less life than the way life is lived that counts: "But what of the way we see life?" asks Hugnet, speaking through him. As one of the nightwatchmen remarks in *Le Droit de Varech*, "You know, one has to expect everything." More than this, one must actively cooperate in making things happen, as Gualbert does when he provokes wrecks and when he clears an immense airfield, which anticipates the *Jardin gobeavions* (*Airplane-Swallowing Garden*) painted by Max Ernst in 1934.

Because he is not content to let events take their course in the submissive fashion of the young man in *Le Muet*, but instead turns chance benefits to account without pausing to judge whether or not they are founded in reality, Gualbert participates actively and profitably in the realization of his desires, in reconciling imagined and lived experience. In so doing, he sets aside moral values that could exert an adverse influence upon the fulfillment of his deepest and least reasonable needs. But in the process, he redefines ethical values upon surrealist principles

12. Benjamin Péret, "La Pensée est UNE et indivisible," *VVV* (New York), No. 4 (February 1944), p. 10.

chat give his life meaning and direction. For this reason, his behavior foreshadows the conduct of two apparently dissimilar heroes who typify surrealist attitudes: Gordogane in Radovan Ivsic's play *Le Roi Gordogane*, and Perceval in Julien Gracq's *Le Roi pêcheur*.

Radovan Ivsic

It's going to begin. I'm not obliged
to explain everything to you.[1]

DETECTING PARALLELS between the plays of Georges Hugnet and a
variety of works by other surrealist writers in the twenties and early
thirties is no difficult task. The existence of affinities that Hugnet himself has helped bring to public notice attests clearly to one fact: when
writing for the stage, he was conscious of working in a favorable *climate,* and of belonging to what may fairly be termed an already established tradition. Points of reference are therefore easy to locate by
which to situate his theatre exactly where he wished it to be viewed
and where its underlying forces might most readily make their influence felt.

The situation of a Parisian surrealist in 1930, with access to all the
published material he could possibly need and in contact with persons
from whom he might draw precious stimulation for his writings, was
very different from that of Radovan Ivsic in Yugoslavia around 1940.

In 1939, at the age of eighteen, Ivsic acquired Breton's surrealist
manifestoes, the twelfth number only of *La Révolution surréaliste,*
Hugnet's *Petite Anthologie poétique du Surréalisme,* René Crevel's *Le
Clavecin de Diderot* (1932), Eluard's *Capitale de la Douleur* (1926),
together with books and magazines by the Yugoslav surrealists, and the
works of Lautréamont, Rimbaud, and Mallarmé.[2] The influence of
some of these writings is immediately visible when we open his first
play, *Airia,*[3] written in the early forties.

1. Radovan Ivsic, *Le Roi Gordogane* (Editions surréalistes, 1968).
2. Information supplied in a letter to the author, January 10, 1971. Subsequent
details from the same source will be asterisked in the text.
3. Radovan Ivsic, *Airia* (Jean-Jacques Pauvert, 1960). *Airia* was published in a

The first act of *Airia* begins with a soliloquy. Confiding in us his love for Airia, Crilice makes this statement:

> Sometimes, when I am alone and I contemplate something for a long time, or half asleep, when my thought founders, submerged by dream, I hear myself pronounce aloud: "I love Airia" at the very moment when it seems to me I have thought of her least. This message which recurs often, always unexpected and yet so simple, seems to me to have a meaning but it remains obscure. I know nothing. I have loved her so much, I love her so much, that it is another who speaks through me, and he says, "I love Airia."

As surrealists have done so often before him, Ivsic links love with a discovery that engenders an exciting feeling of dissociation. Moreover, in alluding to a precious revelation experienced on the threshold of sleep, he plainly echoes the following lines from the *Manifeste du Sur-réalisme*, where Breton speaks of a strange incident that was to orient the inquiry from which surrealism originally took form:

> One evening then, before falling asleep, I perceived, clearly articulated to the point where it was impossible to change a word in it, but separated however from the sound of any voice, a rather bizarre phrase which came to me bearing no trace of the events in which, by consent of my consciousness, I found myself involved at that instant, a phrase which appeared to me *insistent*, a phrase I shall go so far as to say *which rapped on the window pane*. (p. 34)

True, Crilice does not hear, as Breton did, a phrase that makes no sense to him. All the same, the manner in which an unsummoned thought commands his attention, forcing itself upon him, indicates that surrealism was a potent influence on the composition of *Airia*.

Ivsic reveals also how deeply he has been impressed by Arthur Rimbaud. Specifically, in *Airia* he finds inspiration in the celebrated Rimbaud dictum, "For *I* is another"[4] to which, from the first, surrealists paid deep respect. Doing so, he explores its implications from a standpoint that is truer to surrealism, no doubt, than to Rimbaud: linking the wonder of dissociation with the miracle of love. "When you are near me," Crilice tells Airia, "I become another." Hence under two

series called "Le Lycanthrope," funded in part by Robert Benayoun out of royalties earned from his *Le Dessin animé après Walt Disney*, Jean-Jacques Pauvert, 1961 (letter from Robert Benayoun to the author).

4. "Car JE est un autre." See Rimbaud's letter to Paul Demeny, May 15, 1871.

confluent influences Ivsic expresses unquestioning trust in the mediative role of woman when he has Crilice explain to Airia, "When I was without you, I imagined, I was waiting. But now I love you. Near you it is necessary to imagine. You are near. That which I could invent is nothing next to what you are, beside the place where you are leading me."

Significant as elements of this kind are in revealing how readily Ivsic gives *Airia* a thematic development entirely in keeping with that of works he feels moved to imitate, these are not the aspects of his play that impress us as most noteworthy. What strikes us above all is how faithful *Airia* is to some of the fundamental and most distinctive features of theatre in surrealism, despite its author's complete ignorance of trends in surrealist play-writing in France from the early twenties onward.

In *Airia* Ivsic follows practices that one might well think he has learned from the example of predecessors whose writings, in fact, he has had no opportunity to read. His first essay in theatre is expressive of an instinct to decentralize drama by means of that very form of poetic interference used by French-language Dada and surrealist dramatists to turn attention away from plot. We see at once that this instinct has two direct consequences for the form and substance of theatre: erosion of the concept of character and use of dialogue evocatively, rather than informatively.

Ivsic shows he has grasped the principles of surrealist dialogue, as sketched in Breton's first *Manifesto*. He constructs the most inventive verbal exchanges in *Airia* as parallel monologues. Dialogue here takes the form of a lyrical development in which two voices are implicated without actually being attuned to one another. Early in the first act Airia sees coming toward her a man whom Crilice identifies as Noiral:

> CRILICE
> He is as handsome as if he had never used his reason. Now he's turning away. He's going off.
> AIRIA
> And yet I would have wished him to come.
> CRILICE
> But he's coming back toward us.

This demonstration of the irresistible power of desire is succeeded by a scene beginning as follows:

NOIRAL

Red of undulating fern . . .

AIRIA

The somnolent color of death burgeons in me . . .

NOIRAL

Swirling in the panic of a lightning's eclipse . . .

AIRIA

To approach and the black rocks would change into light water . . .

Earlier, Crilice said to Airia, "When you speak, it is a soft murmur, and to anything that is not your murmur I cannot listen, but I do not distinguish your words. All you say to me must be staggering, only I don't grasp it. Oh, if only I could know which are the words you pronounce in my presence!" Now, as he listens to Airia and Noiral talk, apparently without hearing one another, he comments, "Even if I yelled, Noiral, you would not hear my cries. And my words would not come to you, I know, except to render your mirages more present." Bearing out what Crilice has said, Noiral soon after makes a few of the former's words the starting point for a characteristic utterance:

> You say "lugubriously" and "dread of cliffs" but you speak quietly and you are but a clearing, clover in the blue, however there is crafty silence streaming down on the back and on closing hands, so long only as rapid nails do not reach your hair, so long as you can wake up in the direction of lairs and breathe behind the bloodied ponds.

The scene ends on an interrogative note. Seeing that his presence means nothing to Airia or Noiral, Crilice wonders whether he may not be invisible. Noiral asks Airia, "Why speak to me?" Her only reply is the question, "Where am I?" Crilice's departure now goes unnoticed. Its effect is simply to leave Noiral and Airia face to face. Noiral begins to circle slowly around Airia. Yet he is unable to make contact with her through words. Asked if he is Noiral, he says he does not know. When Airia seeks his help in identifying herself—"Am I that little fish without fins before which immense mountains of water suddenly rise up?"—his only response is "A white oak or a fire-fly." Now, much to Airia's distress, he announces his intention of leaving. The first act comes to a close as he goes off, saying, "If I come back . . ."

From the beginning, *Airia* takes its elusive quality largely from indifference on its author's part to developing a dramatic situation by conventional means. Ivsic makes no effort to use dialogue as a means of communicating essential facts, calculated to engage the public's interest in what those on stage are doing, and why they behave as they do. The audience does not take long to realize that the playwright is denying words their elementary and supposedly essential dramatic function. Evidently, his purpose is something other than weaving a plot. For this reason, he is released from the traditional dramatist's obligation to delineate character and to probe motivation. He is under no constraint to create the illusion that those whose voices we hear are "real" people. Instead, he emphasizes the falsity of such an illusion. Even before he brings Noiral on stage, he has Crilice tell Airia, "He never speaks. He is always somewhere else." When Noiral does arrive, it is to demonstrate his peculiarly nondramatic quality of *absence* through an ability to speak that shows no dependence upon a sustained consecutive verbal exchange with others. This is to say that Noiral's absence in no way distinguishes him from Airia, whose statements are equally self-sufficient. Thus the comment she makes to Noiral applies just as well to Airia herself: "You are still here, but you are already gone." And so does Ivsic's description of Noiral at the end of Act I: "Still somewhere else [. . .]."

In *Airia* Ivsic's disinterest in placing substantial characters before his audience is most clearly reflected in someone we meet at the beginning of the second act. She introduces herself to Noiral in these terms: "You want to know my name? I have none . . . I have just been born . . . You want to see my breasts? . . . Or something else? . . . As you wish! . . ." Being nameless and without tangible identity, she is called !? . . . . From Noiral she elicits the admission, "When I look at you, I perceive nothing." A little later, Crilice, who feels divested of his being while Airia is not near, confesses to !? . . ., "Everything would be easier for me if I could give you a name." Informed that this is impossible, he confides, "Without your name, I lose you time after time," receiving this response: "I am more naked this way. And if one day I desert your arms, I shall not leave you an empty name." Asked who she is by Airia, in the third act, !? . . . says with greater frankness, "I don't know."

At first the obviously peculiar nature of !? . . . leads us to consider her as an oddity in Ivsic's play. Little by little, though, we come to realize she is much less exceptional a character than we have assumed. When Crilice ask Noiral where Airia is, in the second act, Noiral's reply is, "Who is Airia?" Airia, then, is without identity to the man she loves. As for Crilice, he feels stripped of his being by Airia's indifference and preference for Noiral. "I am no more, Noiral," he explains in the third act. "[. . .] with Airia everything went away and there is no more me." When he asks, "Why do I still have hands?" Noiral's reply, "You haven't any," brings to mind Crilice's opening soliloquy in which he said, "My hands move away from me."

One may feel inclined to dismiss Noiral's remark as irrelevant because one of Crilice's comments in Act II still rings in our ears: "There are words that kill, but to you, Noiral, one cannot speak." However the fact remains that identity is precarious in *Airia*. This is why nomination is a sign of conquest. In the third act, significantly, Crilice confides in Noiral that a certain hidden word has enclosed him in silence. The word itself—"birds"—is innocuous. Yet being able to use it at last permits Crilice to qualify it with numerous adjectives and then to progress to a whole list of exotic varieties of birds: "And I'll not name the butterflies," he concludes with a pride we understand all the better after hearing the troubled interrogatives: "Who are you?" "What is your name?" "Have I been a conch up to now?"

The last line of Act II is uttered by !? . . ., who asks, "When then will the echo speak first?" To put it another way, when will the *logos* be truly revelatory, ceasing to repeat thoughts previously formulated? A similar question underlies a remark at the beginning of the third act, in which Airia too displays longing for the inexpressible. "Why speak to you this way?" she says to !? . . ., "Even if I told you what color my waiting was and how I drowsed and where I hid the cries, even if I tried to be close to you, murmuring to you in the language of the reeds the sandy words of death, what would you do with my mute appeals floating toward what I had glimpsed in the direction of the shadows and had thought I could reach outside the dreams themselves, perhaps?"

Although evidently an immature work in which the author is more conscious of the models that inspire him than of what their example can enable him to attempt, *Airia* is still an interesting experiment in bending the theatre to surrealist purposes. Here the essential dramatic element is not the confrontation of clearly defined characters in a moment of crisis. Drama is located in language, in its adequacies and inadequacies. When Crilice talks to Airia of her "grass-in-the-wind language," the young woman's response has a Biblical ring: "I said to myself: 'Water in the dream. Water that is the dream.' And water was the dream." The real difference between !? . . . and the three other people on stage lies in her frivolous approach to love. It lies just as much in her frivolity when confronting language.

"Who is the one I shall love? . . .," she says to Noiral at the beginning of Act II, "Perhaps you . . ." Now she proposes a game: "I remember that one must imagine something . . . hide one's hands and proffer the word in a rush. Yes . . . You are going to imagine what I want. I'm going to move away and I shall think. And then I'm going to come back to you and tell you what I have imagined. If we imagine the same thing, we shall love one another." The game does not work out satisfactorily on this occasion, her word ("thunder") not matching his ("water"). By the third act !? . . . apparently has learned her lesson. Inviting Crilice to play the same game, she modifies the rules slightly, to her own advantage. This time she has the other player voice his thought first. Then when Crilice says he is thinking of water, she replies, "Me too, I've thought of water. Therefore we are in love with one another," while the stage directions specify, "*Obviously she is lying.*"

Refusal to take language and love seriously sets !? . . . apart from those among whom she finds herself. She admits in the second act, "I don't know how to talk." Indirectly, she confesses also to the disability of which she accuses the others at the end of the play: being unable to love. We hear her crying, "I love you" to someone we cannot see and whom she has probably imagined, Ivsic assures us.

When the words spoken by Airia, Crilice, and Noiral are not following independent courses in a manner that indicates how difficult it is for them to make verbal contact intentionally, they concentrate upon what is unattainable through language. Thus we hear Airia telling Noiral, "What you are saying now . . . Your words that flee toward the fragile distant shores for which I, at one time, would have liked to leave. I believed, when I had turned away the showers, and when bruised by a lull in the weather and fearful, alone and open, after my waiting, I believed that I would find not the dragon-flies' wings but perhaps . . ." Like the play that bears her name, Airia hesitates on the brink of saying something too fragile to encompass with words.

In the fifth scene of the third act, Airia and Noiral engage once again in the kind of conversation that the rational mind must reject as noncommunicative:

AIRIA

I have lost my way. I am a nebula.

NOIRAL

Or the lairs with dishevelled lakes.

AIRIA

I am but grass.

NOIRAL

The indivisible ravines or the vertiginous spring.

AIRIA

I am fear. Kill me.   *Slowly, menacingly, Noiral approaches Airia. He stops. He begins to move again and his steps describe a big circle around Airia, in the opposite direction from that of Act One.*

Noiral's circular movement in Act III does not explain his circular movement in Act I. All that these actions do is cancel one another out, disposing of the impression that there is symbolism here that the spectator can expect to penetrate reasonably. In *Airia* the public is faced with a challenge: how to bridge the gap between statement and response; how to complete declarations like the one by Airia that peters out before total comprehension has dawned in the listener's mind? Under the conditions Ivsic has created in his first play, audience participation must take a special form. It cannot complete the text satisfactorily for the spectator unless he is willing and able to prolong the statements he hears in the direction favored by the author, unless he recognizes the necessity to eschew reason and the deductive principle and gives free rein to imaginative play unrestricted by rational prejudice.

On the evening of April 18, 1956, the French radio broadcast a play written thirteen years before, which was to remain unpublished for a dozen years more: Radovan Ivsic's *Le Roi Gordogane*. Reading the text at the end of 1954, André Breton had invited Ivsic to join the surrealist movement.* It was only natural, therefore, that performance of the play should be marked by an interview with the author, conducted in the latest surrealist magazine.[5]

5. Charles Flamand, "A Propos du 'Roi Gordogane': Interview de Radovan Ivsic," *Le Surréalisme, même*, No. 1 (1956), pp. 155–56.

Asked to explain the circumstances of *Le Roi Gordogane's* composition, Ivsic recalled how in February 1943, during the German occupation of Yugoslavia, he was indulging in "that gratuitous activity, or, if you prefer, in that monstrous perversity which consists in coupling words."

Ivsic's allusion to the coupling of words is significant. Ever since Breton wrote his essay "Les Mots sans Rides" ("Words without Wrinkles," in *Les Pas perdus* [1924]), ending with the declaration, "Words make love," surrealists have continued to be fascinated by the generative qualities of language.[6] This is why we find Ivsic reporting that he wrote down the word "black" next to the word "hump," adding, "The world of oaths, imprecations and proverbs opened up before me: *May a black hump swell up on your back!* I held the key: the birth of an oath corresponded to the springing forth of an image—or, more precisely, of a poetic crux. *Bear with a beak! May scabies ride you!* It came to me that these proverbial expressions would lend themselves admirably to theatrical language, which demands the highest condensation. At that very moment, I began to write a dialogue. It was the first scene of *King Gordogane.*"

Two things call for notice at once. *Le Roi Gordogane* was not written because its author wished to practice the playwright's art, but because dialogue form promised to set off to best advantage a number of expressions in which Ivsic detected poetic virtue. The expressions he began to write down in 1943 were not without precedent, either. They were, he insisted in response to a question by Flamand, "but a new aspect of an experience lived previously." As early as 1940, in fact, he found pleasure in bringing together two common words whose "coupling" fascinated him. In the phrase "red rails," he explained, "something new, unknown to me was born, a poetic image in its simplest form." Rejecting realism, Ivsic confided in Flamand, "Indeed the theatre that can arouse my enthusiasm is inseparable from poetry."

Affirming, "Thus, for me, poetry and theatre technique become one," Ivsic's interview provides an essential basis for evaluating his undertaking in *Le Roi Gordogane.* Yet it leaves many things unsaid.

First, although Radovan Ivsic was obviously not motivated by an

6. In borrowing the Japanese *tanka* form for certain of his poems, Ivsic hoped to find in it, he told Flamand, "a catalyzer to remove from words that carapace of their parasitic and routine environment and to prepare for them a rendezvous of unexpected love."

ambition to succeed in the theatre, he did foresee the staging of *Le Roi Gordogane,* "not by an official theatre but by a small theatrical company in Zagreb which had broken with the theatre of that time and of which [he] was one of the promoters."* Second, the play was written only a few months after the authorities had seized Ivsic's *Narcis,* issued in a privately printed edition of one hundred copies.* Its composition coincided with a period when, as its author reminded Flamand, "everything was denied us, even walking by moonlight and touching the bare night." During a time of coercion and severe controls, *Le Roi Gordogane* came as a cry of revolt and a plea for liberty.

It is in this sense that we must interpret Ivsic's reply to an inquiry regarding his knowledge of the work of Alfred Jarry when he wrote *Le Roi Gordogane:* "I knew UBU-ROI of course at that time. I say 'of course' because I wanted this to be noticed and wanted it to be a sort of tribute to Jarry."* Ivsic's indebtedness to Jarry is manifest in at least three aspects of his play: in the behavior of his characters, in the incidents in which they are involved, and in the atmosphere of the drama. Of course, one can classify the areas where Ivsic's debt is revealed only by arbitrarily separating elements of *Le Roi Gordogane* that are essentially interdependent and combine to communicate a general impression that provides conclusive evidence of the influence exerted by *Ubu Roi* over Ivsic's play. Hence plot parallelism—like Ubu, for instance, Gordogane, who has just executed all his financiers, goes out to collect taxes for himself—is used to emphasize how much the character and conduct of Ivsic's king owes to Jarry's. Accompanied by the Royal-Ear-Severer and the Royal-Eye-Gouger, Gordogane confronts one of his subjects:

> GORDOGANE
> Let him pay! I'll strangle him later on. Let him be brought here! No. Stay here. I'm going to let you see how terrible I am, how I am feared and how the whole world is afraid of me! I'm going to fasten my eyes on him, like a viper on a frog, and out of terror he'll jump into my mouth, or rather I'm going to strangle him! Come little one, little one, little one. *Louna, as though under a spell, advances step by step toward Gordogane. And arriving near him, bows to him calmly, then goes by him singing:*
> > LOUNA
> > Gordogane, oh dear king
> > You are our bread and faith!

GORDOGANE

Let him be arrested, may his faith braid his legs, so that I can strangle him straight away.—Why did you sing?

LOUNA

Who would not sing, King, in your happy kingdom!

GORDOGANE

Now *that*'s well said, and I feel a little less furious. But even so I am still in such a rage that I am going to strangle you at once.

THE ROYAL-EAR-SEVERER

Sire, the taxes.

GORDOGANE

The taxes. It's good that you reminded me. I'll strangle him in a little while.

Just like Ubu, Gordogane is a grotesque unprincipled despot, at the same time horrible and a figure of fun. Louna escapes by farcical means the fate his sovereign lord reserves for him. In return for his life, he presents Gordogane with a miraculous cheese, guaranteed to make him invisible, provided the king and his henchmen follow a preposterous ritual that involves face-slapping to the accompaniment of the magic words, "The more I slap you/The more you become invisible." The first act of Ivsic's play ends with the king, the Royal-Ear-Severer, and the Royal-Eye-Gouger all slapping one another.

When Ivsic spoke to him of his passion for a theatre that is inseparable from poetry, Charles Flamand interjected, "and from humor, I suppose?" Ivsic agreed without hesitation: "Of course, but humor is also poetry." The humor of the scene during which Gordogane meets Louna is of the kind for which a precedent may be found in *Ubu Roi*. Yet in its humorous aspects Ivsic's play does not fall entirely within the framework established by Jarry, any more than the drama as a whole is limited in scope to repetition of effects originating in *Ubu Roi*. "It would be a mistake," Ivsic has pointed out, when speaking of *Le Roi Gordogane* as a tribute to Jarry, "to see only this aspect of *King Gordogane*, and one of Breton's fears was that the French critics would see only this facet."* He has added, "In certain other respects, *King Gordogane* is a 'tribute' to Sade."*

The only work by Sade known to Ivsic at the time he wrote *Le Roi Gordogane* was *Aline et Valcour ou Le Roman philisophique*, for which he exchanged almost the whole of his library.* In this epistolary novel, Aline's father, President de Blamont, "attests through crime his monstrous grandeur."[7] He is described on the second page of Sade's text in terms which show that he was surely just as much a model for the character of Gordogane as Jarry's Ubu:

> As for M. de Blamont, as for that unworthy husband of too worthy a wife, he was peremptory, systematic, and churlish as if he were seated on fleurs-de-lis; he stormed at tolerance, defended torture, spoke to us with a sort of sensual enjoyment of a wretch whom he and his colleagues were going to break on the wheel next day; assured us that man is wicked by nature, that there is nothing which should not be done to fetter him; that fear was the most potent resort of monarchy, and that a tribunal charged with hearing denunciations was a masterpiece of politics.[8]

After the example of Sade, in *Le Roi Gordogane* Ivsic celebrates the unbridled triumph of wickedness. For, like Breton, he has recognized in the work of Sade "ground which lends itself to the mutation of life."[9] Thus we understand Gordogane better after reflecting upon a letter written by Blamont to his henchman Dolbourg, whose physical characteristics (he is all belly) vividly recall those of Ubu: "Am I not happier than you, refining *everything*, as I do, never arranging for myself *physical* pleasures without their being accompanied by a little *moral* disorder?" (V, 280).

Exemplary of Sade's influence upon Ivsic's conception of Gordogane's character, in this regard, is the king's behavior toward his son. Out of love for Blanche, daughter of King Blanc, whose throne his father has usurped, Tinatine rebels against the new regime. As a punishment, Gordogane proposes to hang Tinatine:

> My faithful subjects, I am today in a good humor. For a long time I haven't felt so pleased as today. By my crown, son, I shall hang you well. How do you feel? Why do you remain silent? By its silence we recognize a fish, and by its roar, the lion! Tell me what happened in prison. How did you lose your eyesight? (V, 12)

7. Jean Fabre, "Préface," *Aline et Valcour ou Le Roman philosophique, Œuvres complètes du Marquis de Sade*, Vol. IV (Au Cercle du Livre précieux, 1966), p. xviii.
8. Readers interested in revelations of Blamont's character to be found in his own letters should read Letter IX (pp. 34–35) and Letter XXVI (pp. 130–32) in Sade's *Œuvres complètes*, Vol. IV (1966), together with Letters XXXVII (pp. 12–16), XLIV (pp. 278–82), LII (pp. 317–19), and LXIV (pp. 351–53), in Vol. V (1966).
9. André Breton, *Anthologie de l'Humour noir* [1940], rev. ed. (Jean-Jacques Pauvert, 1966), p. 64.

When Louna urges him to get the hanging over quickly, Gordogane objects to having his "finest day" spoiled.

The moral disorder accompanying the physical pleasure Gordogane anticipates as he looks forward to his son's execution permeates the whole of Ivsic's play. This is why Blanche appears no more admirable a character than the king. In fact, she deliberately uses Tinatine's love to her advantage ("Kill Gordogane?" he exclaims in horror, "But he's my father. That's forbidden!"), and for reasons she does not even bother to conceal. Speaking of Gordogane in the second act, she remarks:

> He reigns in my place and—he's told me so—it isn't easy to reign, it isn't as it was in the time of my father, King Blanc. To-day, to maintain order in the kingdom, he has to strangle with his own hands some ten thousand subjects a day. Just think a moment, what a lot of work, if I were queen! By the time I was strangling my fifth, my white hands would be numb with fatigue. And how many more would I have to strangle? Ten thousand less five! Count for yourself, I've forgotten mathematics. (II, 4)

Small wonder, then, that she wants Tinatine to declare himself king and do the strangling in her place.

The more we read *Le Roi Gordogane*, the more our attention is diverted from conventional moral standards thanks to a humorous note audible in scene after scene. Ivsic asserts that it was not until 1947 that he saw Breton's *Anthologie de l'Humour noir* (originally published in 1940). The surrealist concept of *black humor* was, he says, no more familiar to him, at the time of *Le Roi Gordogane*, than Breton's anthology.* In the circumstances, we must conclude that it was the dual influence of Jarry and Sade that inclined Ivsic to use comic effects that typify black humor, as surrealists speak of it.

The truth is that Breton's preface to the *Anthologie de l'Humour noir* does not define black humor very precisely. Indeed it comes no closer than asserting that black humor is "par excellence the mortal enemy of sentimentality that seems perpetually at bay" (p. 21). It is not so much by theorizing about his subject as by presentation of illuminating examples that Breton seeks to make his point. Thus, among other extracts, Jarry is represented by "La Chanson du Décervelage" ("The Song of Disembraining") from *Ubu Roi*.[10] As for Sade, the

10. The text of "La Chanson du Décervelage" is omitted from the translation of *Ubu Roi* by Michael Benedikt and George Wellwarth in their *Modern French Theatre: The Avant-Garde, Dada, and Surrealism* (New York: Dutton, 1964).

black humorous aspect of his writing is exemplified in two texts: a letter to his wife and an extract from *Juliette ou Les Prospérités du Vice*, describing the cave home of the giant Minski.[11] A glance at the latter will bring us closer to an understanding of black humor, in the surrealist sense of the term. It lets us see Minski proudly showing off his living furniture: chairs and tables composed of "groups of young girls artistically arranged," on whose backs hot plates will rest during a meal that, he promises his guests, will give them the opportunity to taste human flesh only:

> "We will try it," said Sbrigani; "repugnance is absurd; it comes only from a fault of habit; all meats are made to sustain man, all are offered us to this end by nature and there is nothing more extraordinary about eating a man than a chicken."
> So saying, my husband dug a fork into a quarter of boy which seemed to him well done, and having put at least two pounds on his plate, devoured it. I followed his example. (VIII, 563)[12]

Even though Breton does not transcribe any of the more violently obscene details figuring in Sade's description, he provides a faithful enough impression to authenticate his accompanying observations, where he appositely highlights Sade's "deliberate transgression of the real and the plausible," giving it as his opinion that one of Sade's greatest poetic virtues is that he situates the depiction of social iniquities and human perversions "in the light of the phantasmagoria and terror of childhood" (p. 53).

It is precisely that quality of poetry for which the wondrous nature of childhood imagination provides passage into the world of dull reality that is to be detected in the curses studding the text of *Le Roi Gordogane*. Their exoticism is a protest against the natural order of things, giving the keynote to this drama from the opening scene. Here we cannot miss the discrepancy between Louna's crime (stealing Odan's gourd and drinking up the wine in it) and the extreme forms

---

An English version is to be found, however, in Barbara Wright's translation of *Ubu Roi* (London: Gaberbocchus Press, 1951).

11. Breton, *Anthologie de l'Humour noir*, pp. 57–64. Breton abbreviates Sade's text, which is to be found in *Œuvres complètes*, Vol. VIII (1966), pp. 555–63. Needless to say, Sade prolongs the scene to the end of the volume (p. 576) and continues it into volume IX (1967). In Austryn Wainhouse's translation (New York: Grove Press, 1968), the passage Breton uses covers pp. 578–85.

12. When an independent touring company staged *Le Roi Gordogane* in August and September 1970, they began their tour, by pure coincidence, at La Coste, site of the Marquis de Sade's country estate.

of punishment that Odan calls down on his head: "May your carcass undulate," for instance. It is no mere coincidence, therefore, that when we first see Gordogane he is mouthing imprecations: "May spiders weave fog before their eyes! May a rusty arrow pierce their ears! May their tongues hang down to the ground, may they be like pears, *fff! fff!*" (I, 5).

Implementing a policy of social injustice in the name of justice, imagining and imposing cruel physical punishments that express his instinct for moral disorder, King Gordogane issues an edict announcing a per capita tax system that, he assures his subjects, will eliminate poverty by imposing six times the tax burden on the poor, while the rich will be exempt from taxation. "So that we, Gordogane, the Glorious and Royal Sovereign, can see immediately which head has paid the tax, and which has not, an ear will be severed from the head that has paid the tax. The ear will be severed by the Royal-Ear-Severer. From the head that does not pay—may poisonous thunder reduce it to pulp! —from the head that does not pay, an eye will be gouged. The eye will be gouged by the Royal-Eye-Gouger."

Evidencing a grasp of the underlying principle of black humor as profoundly anti-sentimental, Ivsic has the Royal-Eye-Gouger make the following doleful report on his day's work: "Only twelve, oh king, by my sad mother! And also five blind men, five one-eyed and two cock-eyed people." Introducing as he does here humorous elements in which surrealists detect a most welcome scandalous note, Ivsic succeeds in making *Le Roi Gordogane* something more than an imitation of a violently cruel play like Webster's *The Duchess of Malfi*, even while being aware of feeling the influence of the Elizabethan theatre.*

From what we have seen already—Ivsic's contempt for realism in the theatre, his wish to pay tribute to Jarry, Sade, and the Elizabethan dramatists—it is clear that, if his play is possessed of dramatic unity, this is thanks to the coincidence of various influences, rather than because the playwright has aimed to achieve this effect. Indeed, speaking of his drama, he has declared, "One must not forget that *Le Roi Gordogane* is also a *collage* (not solely)."* The name of its hero typifies this aspect of Ivsic's method: "Gordogane" is a collage combining "Gordon's Gin" and "Gordon Craig."*

The fundamental contribution of collage in surrealism is to juxtapose elements torn from their normal context and placed in unexpected relationship to one another. We see its operation when, examining the plot of *Le Roi Gordogane,* we discover that, not content to bring together dramatic elements characterized by unity of tone, Ivsic has also undertaken to pay tribute to Maurice Maeterlinck,* by way of a theme to which no reference has been made so far.

Usurping King Blanc's throne, Gordogane has had Princess Blanche shut up in a White Tower, built in a dark forest by seven masons working for seven days. When the play opens, on the three-hundredth day of Gordogane's reign, the Jester asks Odan to bring him the rarest of all herbs, the herb of forgetfulness, gathered on the night of the full moon, when Joline haunts the forest. Currently very angry, because of the arrival in his domain of a strange knight who cannot be killed by anyone having already committed murder, Gordogane intends to use the herb on the knight, so avoiding the trouble a prediction has warned him to expect from the young man. These fairy-tale elements are set aside while Gordogane is shown collecting taxes. But they are taken up again in the second act, where Blanche meets the knight, who arrives in shining armor on a black horse.

Blanche asks the knight his name and is warned that one must not pose this question: whether he finally divulges his name or not (depending upon whether or not he likes her), he will inevitably leave after she has asked it three times. The knight knows all about her but cannot recall where he gained his information ("Who told me? Nobody. And yet I know. That's strange."). He tells her that, madly in love, Tinatine is seeking her, and then duly leaves when Blanche questions him a third time about his identity. In a soliloquy delivered just after the knight's departure, Tinatine confirms that he has fallen in love with Blanche, even though she has never seen him. When they meet at last, Blanche admits, "I knew that one day you would come, and I was waiting only for you."

The second act ends with Blanche encouraging Tinatine, who has agreed to attempt parricide: "Make a good job of killing him, my love." Early in the third act the knight loses his memory, after accepting Gordogane's invitation to drink a potion derived from the herb of forgetfulness. Gordogane celebrates the knight's departure by killing the last three peasants in the realm. Tinatine bemoans the fate to which love has committed him. Reluctant to assassinate his own father, he appeals for clemency in Blanche's behalf. But Gordogane throws him into a dark prison where moisture will render him blind.

By the end of the third act, Ivsic has amalgamated the fairy-tale thread of his plot with that of senseless cruelty. One might say, at this stage, that, while the unqualified success of Gordogane parallels that of Sade's Juliette, whose adventures are subtitled "The Prosperities of Vice," the unjust fate that has befallen his son is reminiscent of the experience of Juliette's sister Justine, whose life history Sade subtitles "The Misfortunes of Virtue." Ironical elements henceforth predominating in *Le Roi Gordogane* support this impression.

Searching at night for a herb that will provide an antidote to the philtre derived from the herb of forgetfulness Odan encounters the fairy, Joline. The latter subsequently meets the knight. He has no recollection of the mission that brought him to Gordogane's kingdom, but she promises him the bitter herb that will bring back his memory. Meanwhile, despairing of seeing Tinatine return to her, Blanche has left the White Tower and is wandering through the forest. By this time Louna has become the Royal Executioner. Still seeking revenge on Louna for the theft of the wine at the beginning of the play, Odan agrees, at the Jester's suggestion, to alert the knight to Tinatine's imminent execution and runs off to fetch him.

As Gordogane is urging Louna to carry out the sentence on Tinatine ("To work, our Royal Executioner! Stick your tongue right out, my dear son!"), Blanche arrives. She miraculously restores her lover's sight, yet is unable to do anything to prevent the Executioner from putting a rope around her own neck as well as Tinatine's. Dramatic suspense is present as Tinatine repeatedly asks the Jester, who has posted himself on the roof, if the knight is coming. Before the knight arrives the good Jester falls to his death, the Executioner hangs Blanche, and Gordogane hangs his son, crying, "Ha, ha! They are wriggling! they are wriggling!"

Only now does the irony of the fifth act strike us with full force. When the knight finally comes on the scene, we perceive that he has fallen hopelessly in love with Joline, who evidently had no intention of helping him recover his memory. Thus the well-intentioned Jester has died in vain, and Tinatine can be seen to have been deluded, in pinning his hopes on the knight as an emissary of justice capable of restoring law and order.

At the end of *Aline et Valcour*, M. de Blamont escapes the legal consequences of his crimes by taking flight. He will go unpunished. *Ubu Roi* closes upon Ubu's anticipation of being appointed Master of Finance in Paris. Gordogane, too, looks to the future with optimism.

Having murdered almost everyone in the realm, he is exultant. Watching the knight and Joline go off, he exclaims:

> He has gone. *fff!* I am still alive. A mountain does not attack a mountain. He didn't even see me, may death see him! And that monster with him: hi, hi, hi! Hi, hi, hi! And what to do now? *fff!* I can bind the wind with a ribbon. Jester! Jester! There is no more Jester! Do you see anyone coming? Everything is empty and deserted. May a tail sprout on my forehead if I know what I am going to do! *fff!* Oh, I know! I am going to go into the forest, and tree after tree: *tsaf, tsaf, tsaf, tsaf, tsaf, tsaf, tsaf!*

True to his destructive nature, unrepentant for a series of murderous acts that have left him with no one to rule over, Gordogane sets off to cut down forest trees just as he has cut down his subjects. As we last see him, he gives frightful meaning to the boastful cry of the romantic hero of Victor Hugo's play *Hernani,* "*Je suis une force qui va*" ("I am a force going its way") (III, 4). For Gordogane gives a totally new significance to Hernani's definition of himself as "Blind and deaf agent of funereal mysteries." Commenting upon *Le Roi Gordogane*, Philippe Audoin remarks appositely, "One cannot see the King without laughing, and if one laughs, *tsaf*, you know!: this isn't a card game."[13]

Who does escape Gordogane? Only the fairy, Joline, and the knight to whom forgetfulness has brought a supreme blessing: it has made it possible for him to emulate the achievement of the hero in Buñuel's film *L'Age d'Or*—the ability to place love before duty.[14] In *Le Roi Gordogane* those only prove worthy to survive who, avoiding confusion of goodness and imposed obligation with responsibility, personify aspects of surrealism's protest against conventional ethical values.

---

13. See Philippe Audoin's "Ouverture" to *Le Roi Gordogane*, entitled "Au Miroir miré," p. 12.

14. On *L'Age d'Or* in the perspective of surrealism see André Breton, *L'Amour fou* (Gallimard, 1937), pp. 113–16; Adonis Kyrou, "*L'Age d'Or:* Centre et Tremplin du Cinéma surréaliste," *L'Age du Cinéma*, Nos. 4–5 (August–November 1951); Kyrou, *Le Surréalisme au Cinéma* [1953] (Le Terrain Vague, édition mise à jour, 1963), passim; Kyrou, *Amour-Erotisme et Cinéma* [1957] (Le Terrain Vague, édition mise à jour, 1966), passim; J. H. Matthews, *Surrealism and Film* Ann Arbor: University of Michigan Press, 1971), pp. 90–105.

Julien Gracq

Desire is always disturbing, Perceval.[1]

JULIEN GRACQ wrote his first novel, *Au Château d'Argol* (1938), under the double influence of the Gothic mode and surrealism. His narrative immediatedly attracted the attention of André Breton, whose mistrust of the novel form made his interest in Gracq all the more noteworthy.[2] Ten years later, Gracq published two works, one a study of Breton, and the other a play on the theme of the Fisher King, *Le Roi pêcheur*.

In his *André Breton* Gracq insisted, "We are less athirst for truth than for *revelation*. It is not displeasing to us, very far from it even—and perhaps the fascination is bought at this price—that a certain fringe of intellectual darkness should float irremediably for us about a few attractive positions, points of view which in other respects beckon to us, which appear to call to us."[3] He continued, "In the last resort, it is always to a lure, to an unconditional *appeal* to the imaginative affinities, to the motive schemata that we must address ourselves solely, in order to make people take the plunge, to 'carry conviction away'" (p. 75). Two years later, in a note appended to his *La Littérature à l'Estomac*, he stated, "It is not—I do not even think the idea could have gone this far—and never has been a question of returning to restful literature, to literature considered 'as an art of embellishing, however little, other people's leisure.' "[4] The same note makes his viewpoint quite clear:

1. Julien Gracq, *Le Roi pêcheur* (José Corti, 1948).
2. On *Au Château d'Argol* in the light of surrealism see Michel Guiomar, "Le Roman moderne et le Surréalisme," in Ferdinand Alquié, ed., *Entretiens sur le Surréalisme* (Paris and The Hague: Mouton, 1968), pp. 70–98; J. H. Matthews, *Surrealism and the Novel* (University Park: Pennsylvania State University Press, 1965), pp. 91–106.
3. Julien Gracq, *André Breton: Quelques Aspects de l'Ecrivain* (José Corti, 1948), p. 19.
4. Julien Gracq, *La Littérature à l'Estomac* (José Corti, 1950), p. 73.

"When I say that literature has for some years been the victim of a formidable maneuver of intimidation on the part of the nonliterary—and of the most aggressive nonliterary—elements, I wish to recall only that an irrevocable commitment of thought in *form* lends breath from day to day to literature: in the domain of feeling this commitment is the very condition of poetry; in the domain of ideas, it is called *tone*" (p. 74).

It is true that, quite consistently, Gracq speaks in his *André Breton* of a "climate" of surrealism (p. 26). All the same, one may feel there is some discrepancy between the emphasis upon literature in the note following *La Littérature à l'Estomac* and the firm declaration made by the surrealists in Paris on January 27, 1925: "We have nothing to do with literature; but we are quite capable, if need be, of making use of it like everyone else." The temptation is to set aside this declaration when we concern ourselves with the writings of Gracq. Yet if we do this, we risk the false assumption that his attitude is at variance with surrealism, that his preoccupation with myth is of purely literary origin and consequence. Discussing the recent history of the theatre, Gracq talks in his foreword to *Le Roi pêcheur* of an "effort toward sublimization by myth as insistent as that of the lung of someone suffocating toward oxygen" (p. 9). Yet an examination of his own work makes plain that he is not seeking to effect an adaptation designed to demonstrate the relevance of mythical themes to a literary fashion very much in evidence during the thirties and forties, in the French theatre especially. He is engaged in a search for a myth, expressive of desire, that will give life both meaning and direction, as these are conceived and pursued in the light of surrealist imperatives. As Breton affirmed pertinently, when introducing the 1947 International Exhibition of Surrealism, "The fragmentary and scattered forms of collective desire, which remains a secret to every human being, tend toward one point of convergence and [. . .] at their intersection a new myth awaits us."[5]

The deep interest in legends and folklore so consistently displayed by participants in the surrealist movement is sustained and directed by an urgently felt need to discover a myth suited to our time, going with a firm conviction that such a myth inevitably must be revealed. Antonin Artaud, for example, has expressed his belief that "There have not been, for a long time in Europe, myths in which collective groups can

5. André Breton, "Comète surréaliste," reprinted in his *La Clé des Champs* (Editions du Sagitarraire, 1955), p. 100.

believe. We have reached the point of being on the lookout for the birth of a valid collective Myth." Persuaded that such a myth might be found in Mexico, Artaud wrote, "And I think that Mexico as it is being reborn will be able to teach us again how to bring Myths to life. For that country too is on the lookout for the Myths that are returning to life."[6] As for Benjamin Péret, observing that "all Myths reflect the ambivalence resulting in its turn from the profound feeling of dissociation experienced by man and inherent in his nature,"[7] this surrealist poet followed a path of exploration parallel to Artaud's, seeking guidance in the *Livre de Chilám Balám de Chumayel,* and subsequently assembling an *Anthologie des Mythes, Légenedes et Contes populaires d'Amérique.*[8]

While Artaud looked to Mexico and Péret to Latin America, Jean-Louis Bédouin has shown himself fascinated by myths in primitive societies. Bédouin's examination of one of a number of cultural elements "of which we had lost the significance, mistaken the importance" —the use of masks—leaves him asking, "We ourselves, what are we if not precisely us *and* ourselves—the two faces of a double mask? We shall not know perhaps which of these faces is the true one, and which is but an illusory and misleading appearance."[9] Bédouin's *Les Masques* confirms that the enigma of human identity and self-identification, which guarantees the image of Oedipus' encounter with the Sphinx and that of confrontation with the Minotaur their special value in surrealism,[10] has helped also direct the surrealists' search for a new myth, in accord with their needs.

Like the ethnographer and the anthropologist to whom on occasion

6. Antonin Artaud, *Vie et Mort de Satan le Feu* suivi de *Textes mexicains pour un nouveau Mythe* (Editions Arcanes, 1953), p. 53.

7. Benjamin Péret, *Anthologie de l'Amour sublime* (Editions Albin Michel, 1959), p. 19.

8. Benjamin Péret, *Livre de Chilám Balám de Chumayel* (Denoël, 1955); *Anthologie des Mythes, Légendes et Contes populaires d'Amérique* (Editions Albin Michel, 1959). A translation of the *Book of Chilám Balám of Chumayel* by Ralph L. Roys appeared with the University of Oklahoma Press (Norman) in 1968.

9. Jean-Louis Bédouin, *Les Masques* (Presses Universitaires de France, 1961), p. 127; Bédouin collaborated with another surrealist, Michel Zimbacca, on a surrealist documentary on primitive art, *L'Invention du Monde* (1952), for which Péret wrote the commentary. See Bédouin and Zimbacca, *L'invenzione del mondo* (Milan: Schwarz, 1959); J. H. Matthews, *Surrealism and Film* (Ann Arbor: University of Michigan Press, 1971), pp. 116–19.

10. The theme of masked identity is of central significance in Maurice Fourré's novel *Tête-de-Nègre* (1960) and is one of the elements that combine to give this text its surrealist orientation. See Matthews, *Surrealism and the Novel,* pp. 141–57. The most lavishly produced of all surrealist magazines was *Minotaure* (1935–38).

they have readily accorded space in their magazines, the surrealists recognize man's innate need for myth. Beginning an essay on the marvelous, written in Mexico in 1944, Pierre Mabille spoke of man as "to himself a conscious frontier erected between two worlds: that of the interior, the indivisible self which is the real life, directly unknowable; that of the exterior, the limitless universe, endlessly multiplied and divided."[11] Mabille soon detected in man's relations with the universe a form of alchemy of which he wrote as follows: "The self, an alembic where air, water, strange pabulum is made flesh, a flesh similar to that of all living creatures and at the same time so personal that it reflects a particular formula, a unique equation. Bursting forth from this mysterious alchemist's furnace, the rockets of desire (thrusts of total violence, eruptions of flames), needs, appetites and also disgust and denial" (p. 11). With such aspirations as these, man experiences also an instinct for resistance in this universe that Mabille calls "the domain of the Other" and "a world of forces each of which is a moving interrogation," hence a "source of terror and also of joy, the origin of all questions and also of all the answers, the field of action for what we produce" (p. 12).

Yet one cannot treat the surrealists' preoccupation with myths as simply analogous to the ethnographer's and the anthropologist's. Speaking for surrealism, Péret confides in his *Anthologie de l'Amour sublime*, "The important thing, with myths, resides in the aspiration to happiness which rises up between man and his desire. In short, they express the feeling of a duality in nature, in which man participates and to which he sees no possible solution in his existence" (pp. 19–20). If, as one should, we accept Péret's outlook as typical of surrealism, then from the outset we must accept too that the surrealist approach to myth-making reflects a distinctive and significant orientation.

We notice that Péret talks of aspirations toward happiness and, in his *Anthologie de l'Amour sublime*, clearly identifies the instinct to formulate myths with an urge fundamental to man: "Desire proposes to fill the void, inherent in man's fate, by means of the being who will permit man to form an harmonious whole" (p. 61). Breton, also, stresses not literature but desire and its satisfaction. In support of the conclusion to which their insistence seems to point comes Péret's reference to "the present of man's fate, without issue and without perspective, which calls for the consolation of a myth to demands impossible

11. Pierre Mabille, *Le Merveilleux* (Les Editions des Quatre Vents, 1946), pp. 9–10.

to satisfy in the current conditions of our world" (p. 29). Pierre Mabille accurately summarizes the surrealist attitude: "Now the marvelous on the human scale finds its origin in the permanent conflict which opposes the heart's desire and the means we dispose of to satisfy this desire."[12]

Mabille's words illuminate the situation in which the surrealist finds himself. Keenly aware of all that separates him from what he desires, yet eager to throw off restraints, he remains confident that the experience of the marvelous will enable him to achieve his goal. In the surrealists' eyes, the marvelous permits man to conceive of solutions to the pressing problems with which the universe confronts him, for the very reason that, as Mabille remarks in *Le Merveilleux*, it is "even less the extreme tension of a being than the coming together of desire with exterior reality" (p. 69). As it is, in Mabille's phrase, "probably the only reality that preserves hope in man and in the future" (p. 20), the marvelous fosters trust in a myth to which surrealist ambitions lend special pertinence: that of the Grail.

The surrealists have shown themselves to be responsive to what Gracq, introducing *Le Roi pêcheur*, calls "the treasure, neglected up to now and used too little, of the myths of the Middle Ages" (p. 10). On August 11, 1954, Breton took the opportunity to speak in the newspaper *Arts* of the "Rediscovery of the Art of Gaul." In the following January Adrien Dax was to write of "The Topicality of Celtic Art." The anti-classical emphasis discernible in these texts is self-apparent. Greek forms, Dax asserted, take their origin in a static vision of the world, while Celtic forms stress something he calls "expressive rhythm."[13] The distinction made by Dax assumes considerable importance if we wish to establish clearly the reasons for the surrealists' disrespect for classical myths and their preference for medieval myth patterns. Dax felt constrained to emphasize that Greek art was founded on a point of view with which surrealists can have nothing in common, "that of the idealization of the concrete," resulting, he would have us believe, in the promotion of conventional aesthetic creations to the detriment of the natural world and with this inevitable consequence:

12. Pierre Mabille, *Le Miroir du Merveilleux* (Editions de Minuit, 1962), p. 258.
13. Adrien Dax, "Actualité de l'Art celtique," *Médium: Communication surréaliste*, Nouvelle Série, No. 4 (January 1955), p. 6. The forms of which Dax speaks are those figuring on Greek and Celtic coins. His article was occasioned by the appearance of Lancelot Lengyel's book *L'Art gaulois dans les Médailles* (Editions Corvina, 1954).

"Here, let us not doubt this, beauty is situated outside life and art is nothing more than an illusory refuge."

While Dax's reasoning is too tendentious not to demand an examination that would be irrelevant in the present context, it does reveal plainly enough how much separates surrealism from the classical view of things.[14] If we still doubted this fact, we should have only to read the introduction to *Le Roi pêcheur*, where Gracq argues that classical mythology is all too readily assimilable to the Christian outlook. "We are easily convinced," Gracq declares, "that the punishment of the Greek tragic hero, with the distance we are given by Christianity, is basically hardly anything more than ersatz original sin" (p. 9). Hence classical myths tend to become, for Gracq, "those closed myths, those implacable police reports of failure [. . .] for the most part 'infernal machines' set up by the gods for the mathematical reduction of a mortal to nothingness" (p. 10). No more than for Dax and Mabille can classical mythology represent for the author of *Le Roi pêcheur* something that Dax finds in Celtic art: "the first signs of an expressive tendency whose Cause has always remained that of Liberty itself" (p. 6). Gracq is categorical when he asserts, "The Myths of the Middle Ages are not tragic myths, but 'open' stories—they tell not of gratuitous punishment, but of permanent recompensed temptations [. . .] seen from a certain angle, they are an instrument forged to ideally break down certain *limits*" (pp. 10–11).

In *Le Miroir du Merveilleux* Mabille attaches considerable importance to the theme of the Grail. His final chapter, "La Quête du Graal," provides ample proof of the care the surrealists have taken to select and give expression to myths suited to the purposes to which they are dedicated. "The Quest for the Grail" exemplifies their willingness to adopt and modify to their own ends certain myths long established in literature.

As presented in *Le Miroir du Merveilleux*, the Grail epitomizes man's search for happiness through the marvelous experience of love. In this respect it is identified with a theme that has exerted a powerful attraction over the surrealist imagination, that of *l'amour-passion*, the twinning of spirits in resistance to oppressive social and moral pressures. The Quest, as Mabille interprets it, thus becomes man's search

14. Those interested in further expressions of the point of view defended by Dax are referred to Lancelot Lengyel's article "La Découverte de l'Art celtique bouleverse l'Histoire de l'Art occidental," *Médium*, Nouvelle Série, No. 4 (January 1955), pp. 11–14.

for "the being promised his heart," in conformity with the surrealist belief that, to find, one has only to seek: "And man pursues the quest for the Grail; he moves perilously through space searching for the golden chalice, thanks to which the rite can be celebrated. He comes up against invisible obstacles, is bruised in fruitless attempts; he knocks on closed doors; his trembling effort reaches out toward unknown beauty, toward the woman whose presence alone will at last reveal to him the aim that is his, will give him true knowledge of the world and will forever break, by virtue of love, sterile solitude" (p. 261).

Evidently, Mabille sees the theme of the Grail as linked with and drawing strength from the Tristan theme, of which Lancelot Lengyel has remarked, "What is expressed is not so much love as its mystery; not happiness but tension, not repose but movement, that is to say the very essence of the Celtic conception."[15] Just like Mabille, Lengyel has in mind an element that the former has called *la magie* and equated with the marvelous, "the operations as a whole by which can be brought together those beings separated by hostile space or by the malevolence of men." According to Mabille's *Le Miroir du Merveilleux*, the magic in question "permits the one who bears desires within to attract the Other, the predestined companion. Thanks to secret rites, all resistance will be vanquished" (p. 261). In surrealism, Breton comments appositely, "love unique, entirely given to one being, is considered, also, a state of grace."[16]

Noteworthy here is the stress placed upon predestination, viewed in its most optimistic perspective, and presented as "the inner certainty of meeting the being of our dream."[17] In the first act of *Le Roi pêcheur*, Kundry speaks of a person whom all in the Castle of Montsalvage are awaiting, and whom she calls "The Pure One": "He comes as a conqueror. He has killed Méliant. He is coming. Whatever stops him he breaks. He goes straight ahead, marvelous, and the accomplishment of his desire is the measure of his day." In *Le Roi pêcheur*, "The Pure One" is Perceval, "the predestined," "the Chosen One," to whom the hermit Trévrizent says, "You have brought with you that fascinating thing—a desire limitless and innocent." In other words, Perceval is pos-

15. Lancelot Lengyel, "Le Moment historique de la Prise de Conscience de l'Amour-Passion et le Symbolisme dans les Sources celtiques du Mythe de Tristan," *Le Surréalisme, même*, No. 2 (1957), p. 24.
16. André Breton, *Arcane 17 enté d'Ajours* (Sagittaire, 1947), pp. 204–5.
17. Mabille, *Le Miroir du Merveilleux*, p. 270.

sessed of the certainty about which Mabille wrote, "A certainty as un-shakable as it is impossible to explain logically." In this case, as always in surrealism, dismissal of logical processes is simply a tribute to the beneficence of destiny, which, "acting as if it had a concerted plan, scatters along our path very disturbing indications."

While Gracq admits that certain classical echoes can be detected in the Grail theme (the image of the garden of Hesperides and the journey of the Argonauts, notably), he will not accept these as evidence sufficient to diminish the value he seeks to attach to the Grail: "Nothing takes precedence over my private feelings: the air I breathe is no longer the same, *the direction* has changed inexplicably—out on the open sea, the sails suddenly bow to some auspicious trade-wind" (p. 10). To Gracq, consequently, Tristan represents "the temptation of absolute love," while Perceval embodies "the temptation to possess the divine in this world." Suffering neither the inertia of the Fisher King, Amfortas, nor the wretchedness that Clingsor feels at being rejected by the Grail, Gracq's Perceval affirms, "I will deliver the Grail in this world or in no other, forever."

When examined in the perspective of surrealism, the limits against which certain medieval myths exemplify protest become the very ones that the surrealists have set themselves the task of breaking down. And so Gracq sees these legends as relating "the glorious exploits of block-ade-runner heroes." They "in the end blaze a trail for the road to victory: perfect love, Tristan and Iseult see it through, against its force even death does not prevail: the brambles born of their bones intertwine over their graves—Galahad conquers the Grail" (pp. 10–11). Identification of the hero of medieval romance with the surrealist hero becomes permissible once man is seen to be "made erect once again by a singular pride, armed with limitless ambition," innocent of that sense of the tragic which Gracq condemns in classical mythology and for which the counterpart in the Middle Ages was, in his estimation, Christianity.

Just as Gracq's interpretation of the meaning of the Grail myth takes up Louis Aragon's famous cry, "Temptation alone is divine," so it carries forward the characteristically surrealist resistance to Christianity implicit in Mabille's reading of the legend. Returning to the theme of the Grail in its pre-Christian, Celtic form,[18] Gracq voices more

18. See, in this connection, Jean Markale, "Mystères et Enchantements des Lit-tératures celtiques," *Médium*, Nouvelle Série, No. 4 (January 1955), pp. 7–10.

Theatre in Dada and Surrealism

openly in his introduction to *Le Roi pêcheur* than does *Le Miroir du Merveilleux* the protest expressed by Mabille in his *Thérèse de Lisieux*, "The first stage undertaken in the direction of love owes it to itself to suppress the existence of a supernatural, immaterial, and divine love. The presence of the Christic myth must be abolished."[19]

Considered from the angle of surrealist love, the violent antipathy felt in surrealism for Christian religion is not difficult to explain. The Church, declares Péret in his *Anthologie de l'Amour sublime*, "canalizes the sexual impulse without trying to go beyond it on the affective plane and limits itself to directing toward divinity the spiritual forces which used to tend dimly toward the metamorphosis of love" (p 33). Péret continues, "In this religion, man is endowed with blinders which reduce his horizon to the shadow of the cross" (p. 34). Once one appreciates that, in surrealism, Christianity can be seen only as "a religion of repression like no other," then one understands how important it is for Gracq, when writing *Le Roi pêcheur*, to liberate the theme of the quest for the Grail from Christian associations. As early as 1938, in fact, in a prefatory note to his novel *Au Château d'Argol*, he emphasized that he regarded the Christian interpretation of the Grail legend as a deformation, and specifically condemned Nietzsche for classifying Wagner's *Parsifal* too hastily as of Christian inspiration.[20] Similarly, when presenting *Le Roi pêcheur* he does not omit to remark that neither the Tristan theme nor the Grail is Christian in significance, and adds, "The concessions of which their plot so often bears traces cannot put us off the scent of their essential function as alibis" (p. 11). His own version of the Quest is one in which all elements that betray the influence of Christian thought are shown to be irrelevant.

It is not that *Le Roi pêcheur* appears to have been written in order to propose an anti-Christian interpretation of the Grail legend. Rather, Gracq demonstrates that the features of the Grail story introduced in concession to Christianity cannot conceal the significance of Perceval's adventures, as surrealism teaches us to regard them. Asked by Perceval, "Have you heard of Arthur?" the hermit Trévrizent replies, "Like everyone else, I know him to be an old madman who is still looking for the promised land here on earth, [. . .]." Trévrizent's reply offends

19. *Thérèse de Lisieux* (José Corti, 1937), cited by Paul Eluard in *Donner à Voir* (Editions de la N.R.F., 1939), p. 155.
20. Julien Gracq, *Au Château d'Argol* [1938] (Librairie José Corti, 1961), pp. 8–9.

Perceval, who ripostes, "Do not blaspheme. The Grail received the blood of Christ on the cross. There is no more noble task in the world than its deliverance, you should know this" (Act II).

At first glance, this response might seem to suggest that Perceval's motivation in Gracq's play is acceptably Christian. But the subsequent dialogue permits us to understand that this is far from being the case:

> TREVRIZENT
>
> You asked me your way a moment ago and I tell you this: leave this path which is not the straight path and listen to the word of the Christ from the mouth of his servant.
>
> PERCEVAL
>
> He cannot go back on his word who is dedicated only to His glory.
>
> TREVRIZENT
>
> His glory is not entrusted to your hands, whoever you are, Perceval. He commands everyone to find his own salvation, humbly, in the place where destiny has put him, in prayer and submission. He has taken charge of everyone's destiny with His arms spread on the cross. This was not so that the first adventurer to come along should give in to the imaginings of his empty head, and believe himself personally charged with making the sun rise upon humanity.
>
> PERCEVAL
>
> What then do you believe? I want to be only the very humble servant of the Grail.
>
> TREVRIZENT
>
> But you designated yourself for this service with great presumption, and that is already too much.

Something that appears initially to be no more than the confrontation of the contemplative ideal with the militant becomes an accusation and, finally, temptation, as Trévrizent seeks to persuade Perceval to abandon his quest and to resign himself to an imposed destiny. In accusing Perceval of the sin of pride, Trévrizent is inviting him to commit what is, to the surrealist, the much greater sin of acceptance. Pride, Perceval's example indicates, is necessary: "But there is a task to be done, and that only one man can do, and tasks have to be completed. And who will do this if the one designated for it does not undertake it alone?"

When Trévrizent asserts, "The Church disapproves as I do of these confused adventures, and this pagan desire for triumph and for deliverance which is deep in your heart," the veneer of religious responsibility is stripped away, and Perceval's true situation is revealed. We not only discover that his motives draw strength from surrealist ambitions, rather than from Christian teaching, but we comprehend also that religion, in his case, could only be an impediment:

> TREVRIZENT
> So much has not been asked of you. You could have grown old between your father and your mother, exactly rendering justice to your people, standing up for the poor, honoring the Church.
> PERCEVAL
> Yes. Only, for me that was not possible. The Grail was mentioned to me, and at once the world dried up before my eyes. I no longer had father, mother, brother, or people.

Trévrizent accuses Perceval of having been prompted to take up his quest by a demon, and once again seeks to persuade him that "The Lord has established a simple law for us: to be just and charitable, to serve in his place." The hermit believes that, "*Here* is renunciation, submission to the common rule, and salvation." Yet the virtues surrealism acknowledges are those that incite man to rejection of submissiveness, and to refusal to accept a line of conduct imposed by any authority outside himself. Indeed, Gracq allows us to hear Trévrizent argue, unwittingly, against the attitude he must defend:

> TREVRIZENT
> I belong with those who have renounced . . .
> PERCEVAL
> What have you chosen?
> TREVRIZENT
> I have chosen tranquil death—certainty.
> PERCEVAL
> And what is the other choice?
> TREVRIZENT
> Life.

As for Perceval, he can explain himself quite simply: "That is what life is: to desire to satisfy in an embrace like the mouth in the air, like the fingers of one's hand on the hilt of one's sword."

Here surely lies a partial explanation of the significance of the Grail in *Le Roi pêcheur*. At least one may say that we come close to an explanation. For Gracq is far from being concerned to present a drama that will render up its meaning without resistance, even though it follows a simple narrative pattern. Act One lets us see how Amfortas' sin—allowing love for Kundry to take his mind off the Grail—has brought down upon him retribution in the form of a grievous incurable wound. It shows us, moreover, that the Fisher King enjoys his role as outcast and takes pleasure in the suffering visited upon him. This is because, we understand, he accepts the justice of his present situation. Hence inertia weighs upon the Castle of Montsalvage, where everyone awaits the arrival of the predestined individual designated to break the spell that binds them. When Perceval comes to his hermit's cottage at the beginning of Act Two, Trévrizent makes a confession that reveals his state of mind to be no different from that of Amfortas. Asked by the young knight—Perceval, who has been searching for the Grail for a year already, is still only sixteen—if the Grail really exists, Trévrizent replies, "I neither desire nor wish ever to know." While Amfortas feels grateful for being rejected, because he no longer has to take any positive action, the hermit makes it very clear that he has no wish to be involved. In both cases, we note, religious sentiment fosters inactivity and unprotesting acceptance. In contrast, Perceval asserts that the Grail is "the recompense of the bravest." This, obviously, is why he boasts, "I live for the Grail. I will find it." For his is, as Trévrizent observes, a "Heart of desire, where the word of God takes up very little space."

While Perceval's motives are magnificently stripped of complexity —"My destiny is the Grail, and I have no other"—the plot of Le Roi pêcheur has no need of intricate embellishments. On the contrary, its use of unadorned coincidence bears witness to the role of predestination that Gracq is intent upon bringing to our attention. Thus the meeting between Perceval and Amfortas is placed under the auspices of beneficent chance, and they are both aware of this.

Introducing his own translation of a play by H. von Kleist, Gracq commented in 1954, "Like all truly symbolic works Penthesilea does not signify anything precisely: you would waste your time trying to encompass its 'message'; rather it raises to the level of significance, it recharges with power, with nostalgia and with depth everything that is magnetized in its magnetic field, everything which rises from the shadows—from our shadows—to burn up in a spellbinding nocturnal spinning movement, in its molten-metal heat."[21] The hints given here regarding Gracq's aspirations in *Le Roi pêcheur* are not difficult to detect. Nor are they hard to grasp in the response he made to Nora Mitrani's inquiry about the fascination *Penthesilea* held for him: "I admired this play perhaps in the degree that its characters remain more or less foreigners to me. [. . .] they are unleashed after the fashion of *natural* forces. Completely natural, yes, indeed. No contradiction, no incoherence weighs them down—any attempt at *justification* is perfectly indifferent to them."[22] Evidently, it is in the light of these remarks that we are to evaluate the character and conduct of Perceval in *Le Roi pêcheur*.

Commenting on the dramatic form to which he inclined, Gracq wrote in introduction to his play of the need to "remagnetize life" and to introduce "an indispensable *lubricant*" into the workings of a social machinery whose complexity at every moment is in danger of making it "jam" (pp. 8–9). This is not to say that Gracq was trying to do with his version of the legend of the Fisher King and of Perceval's quest something analogous to Jean Anouilh's adaptation of *Antigone*. What counts in *Le Roi pêcheur* is the need felt by its author to effect a transposition of the remagnetization of myth to the remagnetization of life itself. For this is as characteristic of the surrealist purpose giving Gracq's writing its vitality as is the image of magnetism that he so often uses when speaking of surrealism.

Discussing the cycle of the Round Table in his introduction to *Le Roi pêcheur*, Gracq uses the phrase, "the indefinitely renewable capacity of pure poetry—the most magic kind" (p. 15). In his view, the cycle of Arthurian legends "belongs to the highest form of myths: it is in essence one of those crossroads of which I spoke above where, for the traveler, moving about just a little corresponds each time to abundance of new perspectives." What is more, he continues, the cycle "provides the archetype of the ideal 'Bund'—of elective community" (p. 15).

Jules Monnerot has made it unnecessary to return to the significance of the group in surrealist activities.[23] We can, however, take the

21. Julien Gracq, "Le Printemps de Mars," in Heinrich von Kleist, *Penthésilée* (Libraire José Corti, 1954), p. 13.
22. From an interview by Nora Mitrani, conducted in *Médium*, Nouvelle Série, No. 2 (Feburary 1954), p. 15.
23. Jules Monnerot, *La Poésie moderne et le Sacré* (Gallimard, 1945), pp. 72–77.

opportunity to remind ourselves of the appropriateness of the theme of companionship that runs through the Arthurian legends. Gracq, certainly, does not wish us to forget it. Presenting *Le Roi pêcheur*, he writes, "The companionship of the Round Table, the passionate quest for an ideal treasure which, however obstinately it eludes us, is still represented as *within grasp*, these figure for example very easily as a background reference—an indefinite reverberation—for certain of the most typical aspects of contemporary phenomena, among which is surrealism" (p. 12). He elaborates for a whole page, drawing attention to the close parallel the legendary tales offer to the activities of the surrealist group, from the moment of the latter's inception. Particularly noteworthy at this point is the stress Gracq places upon "the almost hypnotic obsession with imminent discovery." This, beyond doubt, is the source of the energy that makes it possible for Perceval to resist the temptation personified in Trévrizent, just as it enables him to avoid defeat at the end of the play.

In Perceval's conversation with the hermit, Gracq has already hinted at what he and the surrealists believe—that religious acceptance means a resignation that limits man's capacity to act and to achieve for himself what everything and everyone about him conspire to deny him. Perceval is being asked to pay the price for something that in his *André Breton*, Gracq calls "a deep-seated feeling of being chosen, in the person predestined for discovery" (p. 103). Without aspiring to paradox, one may say, therefore, that through his account of Perceval's adventures, Gracq offers a definition of the divine that is entirely withdrawn from Christian context. In *Le Roi pêcheur* we witness the individual's confrontation with the self, through a quest that finds impetus in man's need to uncover the divine within himself. As Gracq notes in *André Breton*, our conception of adventure has changed because, "with the end of exploration of the planet (exploration of matter does not have the same imaginative reverberation) has ended the era of diffuse and aimless adventure: that of the Round Table novels just like that of Robinson Crusoe." But this does not mean that the Round Table can no longer supply a fitting image for the quest in which man, and especially surrealist man, is engaged. Speaking of adventure, Gracq points out that "the only survival we can assure it consists in imagining this coagulated world, *solid* today to the point of suffocation, as though cut

---

Monnerot prefers the word "set" to "Bund," but his conclusions are no less valid for his somewhat fanciful interpretation of the English word.

across by 'faults,' by veins along which, with open hands, adventure could still persist in following a path as narrow as a tunnel" (pp. 105–6). The idea expressed here is similar to that of Breton, in *Arcane 17*: "The great enemy of man is opacity. This opacity is outside him and it is above all within him, where it is maintained by conventional opinions and all sorts of suspect interdictions" (p. 52). This, then, is why Perceval speaks as he does of the Grail: "The Grail is sufficiency, ecstasy and a better life. It is thirst and the slaking of thirst, deprivation and repletion, possession and ravishment."

At the beginning of the third act Perceval admits to feeling ill at ease in the castle of Montsalvage, where he is Amfortas' guest. Here, it seems to him, procrastination appears to be the rule. At once sensitive to the timeless atmosphere that infects the place, he likens the castle to a clock that has stopped. Amfortas makes no attempt to dispel this impression. Indeed he speaks of Montsalvage as "petrified" and of himself as "a Medusa head." As for Kundry, she refers openly to "this limbo." Perceval admits to fearing the Fisher King who casts nets and Montsalvage "which takes you in a trap," and where he is beginning to feel infected by the same sickness as everyone else. To rid himself of the troublesome knight, who disturbs the even tenor of existence in the castle, Amfortas destroys the youth's illusions about Kundry with whom the boy has fallen in love. It looks as though the Fisher King has achieved his aim: Perceval announces that he will leave Montsalvage before evening, when his continued presence would have made the Grail visible to all in the castle.

Amfortas recognizes that, thanks to Perceval, "Montsalvage could have flourished anew." And yet he confesses that, despite his love for Perceval, he prefers the "repose of Montsalvage" to the young man whom Kundry loves also. In contrast, Kundry says to the king, "I know that seeing the Grail has its price. I know that when it shines here, I shall live no more." All the same, she continues, "But even at that price, do you understand, I want it! Even at the price of suffering, —even at the price of death! Let it destroy me, but let me see it—but let my thirst be quenched!" Responding to her entreaties, Perceval agrees to spend the night at the castle. His final words at the end of Act Three, uttered as he falls asleep, are "The Grail."

The fourth and final act of *Le Roi pêcheur* brings a last on-stage confrontation between Perceval and Amfortas, who assures the youth that he can be king of the Grail, shortly, if he so chooses. "You will put off the old man. You will put off man altogether." Behind these phrases, to which the Bible lends a note of authority, lies the ultimate temptation for Perceval: that of conformity, to which are added the attractions of security.

Pierre Mabille has described unequivocally the dangers a surrealist associates with security. In his *Le Miroir du Merveilleux* he wrote, "If danger presents itself to woman in the form of an agreeable seduction, if it is invested in her eyes with false luxurious attractions, for man it takes on the mask of security. The hero dreams of resting from his labors, a deadly inertia takes possession of him, compromising the results of a long period of courageous effort" (p. 301). Mabille refers pointedly to "our heart's questioning" (p. 270), which, we infer, will find answers only so long as we continue to inquire. Once man has surrendered his right to interrogate the universe, he falls back, like the Fisher King, into hopeless inactivity, insidiously inviting. Like the other inhabitants of Montsalvage, Amfortas has lost the ability to act purposefully and independently, because he has entrusted his destiny to someone else, to a savior figure. In contrast, while in the castle, Perceval has no hesitation in saying, "I do not like this dreaming somnolence." His is a state described in *Le Miroir du Merveilleux:* "And not to be able to sleep, not to want to sleep, to refuse oneself the voluptuous plunge into anonymous cosmic irresponsibility" (p. 192).

If, as Judith Reigl asserts, "the foundation of any creative advance is the desperate desire to destroy the contradictions and limits of personal, human, and universal existence, and to expand through permanent revolt,"[24] then in the closing scenes of Gracq's play Perceval is faced with the prospect of ceasing to be the creator of his own destiny:

> PERCEVAL
> Shall I see you no more?
>
> AMFORTAS
> With those eyes that are still questioning, no—never more. You will bathe in certainty, and that is something which dispenses with looking.
>
> PERCEVAL
> I shall fight for the Grail. I shall win for it. My life henceforth will be nothing but an adventure of light—in full daylight—in splendor . . .

24. Cited in *Médium*, Nouvelle Série, No. 4 (January 1955), p. 45.

AMFORTAS

You will have no more adventures. There is no more for someone who possesses everything. Your adventure ends tonight, Perceval! You will see how strange a thing it is to outlive adventure.

PERCEVAL

My life will be about me like a harvested field. My task will be
done.

AMFORTAS

You will be at peace with yourself, for always. I hope you will
enjoy sleeping well.

Offered possession of the Grail, Perceval in the end declines. He
resists the final temptation of repose, with the fateful extinction of the
spirit of interrogation that must accompany repose. His last act of
withdrawal is therefore to be expected, even though it may be misunderstood by those who have criticized surrealism for proposing for
itself unattainable goals, and who have concluded, as a result, that the
surrealists have doomed themselves to failure. Such critics remain indifferent to the fact that it has always been in the nature of surrealism
to leave its ultimate aims ill-defined. They fail to notice that surrealists concentrate instead upon methods capable of bringing man into
closer proximity with these goals, without necessarily achieving them.
The true image of surrealist aspiration is not that of a point in time or
space that all surrealists are intent upon reaching. It is the image of the
horizon, tantalizingly present but continually receding before us; it
draws us forward and gives us direction—justification enough for the
effort required of all who seek to advance under its attraction.

Surrealists are acutely aware of the world as enigma, "A world," as
Mabille puts it in *Le Merveilleux*, "which some call reality but which
is only incessant discovery; a mystery reborn indefinitely, which imagination, armed with calculation and precision instruments, shows us
differently from the way our senses perceived it on first contact; a
universe about which it is permissible to wonder whether it is not altogether other than we conceive it habitually" (p. 17). The essential
elements of surrealist protest are here: a challenge offered the rational-
ist perspective, as much as to the acquiescence of routine acceptance,
the conviction that the transformation demanded by desire will be
brought about by the use of forces liberated in imaginative play; in
short, the world as conception, not as acceptance. In surrealism, therefore, man's interrogation of the universe surrounding him and his need

to comprehend do not direct his attention to reason and are indeed very far from inculcating faith in the mind's faculties. Instinct, or more accurately intuitive insight supplies the key to meanings, and makes possible perception of what Mabille calls "the hidden rule."

For the very reason that it lends itself so easily to an adaptation in keeping with the surrealist conception of man's search for the meaning of existence, the Grail provides in surrealism a symbol of evocative power. To a group of men and women permanently opposed to something Gracq's *André Breton* calls "the fetishistic cult of logical intelligence" (p. 114), there can be no question of following Descartes, "that French knight who sets off at such a good pace," as Charles Péguy called him. Thus Nora Mitrani has spoken for all surrealists when announcing, "But to the French knight Descartes we prefer the Percevals who, with heart full of anguish, plunge into the dark wood, searching for the impossible."[25] So, as Gracq treats it in *Le Roi pêcheur,* the Grail serves to make us recognize something mentioned in his *André Breton:* "upheaval intact, in the modern mentality, of the same effervescent feelings which could *move* the *epic* hero of old and showed themselves to be capable of 'transmitting the current' to those listening to the ancient poems: the feeling of 'being led,' the sense of being entrusted to supernatural (or surreal) forces and the overflowing, lived, feeling of miraculous *possibility*" (p. 104). While Amfortas' "Fault" has separated him from God and left him unable to act—the last lines of *Le Roi pêcheur* repeat the religious invocation of the first, and suggest a full circle of pessimism—Perceval escapes "this malady of languor," and fully appreciates the necessity for independent action: "the rule of the quest is solitude." Hence the significance of surrealism's rejection of Christian values is made clear to those watching Gracq's play.

In surrealism man is the center of the universe, agonizingly placed under the stress of time, and face to face with the inevitability of death. Likening man's existence to "the match one lights in opaque darkness," in *Le Merveilleux* (p. 42) Mabille intimates that man must be his own light in this world, since he is able to look nowhere outside himself for help and guidance. He must therefore fend for himself as best he can. "The 'word of light' must indeed be preserved in a place unknown to learned and sage old men . . . and here begins the quest for the Grail,

25. Nora Mitrani, "Le Congrès s'amuse." *Médium,* Nouvelle Série, No. 1 (November 1953), p. 16.

the conquest of the Golden Fleece, the search for the Philosopher's Stone" (p. 27). Thus it is the impulse to seek the light of illumination which constitutes that form of predestination acknowledged in surrealism's name by Mabille's *Le Miroir du Merveilleux:* "The individual, man or woman, who carries in him the inner mark of election, possesses, throughout discouragement and failure, an unshakable certainty which obliges him to persevere" (p. 231). Gracq's Perceval bears this "inner mark." Hence the designation that qualifies him for the title of "Pure One" serves merely to mask self-designation. This, then, is why he declines the role for which he was thought to be predestined, electing instead to continue on his way.

Perceval eventually leaves Montsalvage: clear proof that Gracq considers medieval myths to be "open" myths. Those that tend to exert most appeal for the surrealist's imagination are the myths that, beyond the confines of reasonable conjecture, permit him to envisage solutions where none seem rationally permissible, in situations that current conditions oblige him to accept as insoluble. Here the anti-rational emphasis that is fundamental to surrealism brings its finest rewards. Conjecture, liberated from the constraint that the reasoning mind must accept, is free to project a sense of affranchisement that ensures the myth of the Grail its special merit in the surrealists' estimation. It is the distinction of the Round Table cycle that it represents, as Gracq explains when introducing *Le Roi pêcheur,* "at the heart of the myth and as though its kernel, this panting face-to-face encounter, this unbearable hand-to-hand struggle—here and always now—between man and the divine immortalized in 'Parsifal' [. . .]" (p. 15). It depicts the destiny of man who, "alone of all beings endowed with life, secretes something irrespirable, is condemned to this face-to-face encounter with the purest elements he has drawn from himself"; man, whose fate it is to find himself repeating, "I can live neither with nor without you" (p. 16). Thus the Grail is a myth that inspires in surrealists confidence, not despair. It is permanently linked in their minds with the marvelous, which, as Mabille makes plain in *Le Merveilleux,* "expresses the need to go beyond imposed limits, imposed by our structure, the need to attain greater beauty, greater power, greater pleasure, the need to endure longer" (p. 68). For Julien Gracq, the myth of the Grail, epitomizing faith in man's capacity to pursue the coincidence of desire and lived experience, is invested with a timeless vitality, exerting a fascination to which *Le Roi pêcheur* pays grateful tribute.

Jean-Pierre Duprey

APART FROM THAT, once again, I warn the
spectators that what they will be able
to see bears only a distant relationship
to what really happens behind our eyes.[1]

OUR DISCUSSION of the work of Radovan Ivsic left out consideration of
a one-act play, named after its hero, called Vané.[2] It is time to mention
this unpretentious work in relation to a noteworthy trend in surrealist
writing in dramatic format.

When we first see him, Vané is flying a kite. From behind a cloud
passing across the sun emerges a flower. It floats gently down to the
young man, appealing ambiguously, "Take me, take me, Vané." Later, in
response to Vané's request, the Flower makes his parents' house fly
away, his mother and father hanging to the structure, "flapping like
flags." At the end of the sketch, Vané clambers up the string of his
kite and is carried off while the Flower, temporarily changed earlier
into a young woman, becomes a flower once again.

What makes this brief text deserving of attention is the fact that, in
it, Ivsic bothers little with the practicalities of staging. Here his treatment of theatre betrays indifference to the technical difficulties such
a work would present a director. Thus *Vané* brings into focus a question that, until now, we have not had occasion to consider, even though
it could not be ignored entirely by anyone wondering about the dramatic potential of a number of the plays considered so far.

Jean-Claude Barbé has written plays that he himself describes as
unperformable. They are works, incidentally, that he has not made
public. Leonora Carrington has put together a sketch called *The Invention of Molé*. Here one of the characters, Moctezuma, speaks "in
Nahuatl naturally." Another, Tlaxcluhuichiloquitle, the Great Witch
of Imperial Mexico, performs a miracle beneath the Archbishop of

1. Jean-Pierre Duprey, *La Forêt sacrilège* (Le Soleil noir, 1970).
2. Radovan Ivsic, *Vané*, in *Phases*, No. 8 (January 1963), pp. 50–55.

Canterbury's clothing: "suddenly bands of short-haired dogs and quetzales come cascading out from under the clergyman's cassock. They begin a battle to the death; they kill one another and change respectively into garments of silver and of plush."[3] As for Robert Benayoun, in the perspective that concerns us now, his publications in dramatic form are especially interesting.

In 1959 Jean-Jacques Pauvert published a volume of four plays by Benayoun, *La Science met bas, Les Jumeaux, Un Acte de Naissance*, and *La Vente aux Enchères*.[4] The subject matter of these texts need not detain us. More important is a remark their author has made about them: "My short plays are going to be staged soon, in a small, shall I say *off-boulevard* theatre, in alternance [*sic*] with a play by Arrabal, who is now a great friend of ours. I'm surprised, since I didn't write them to be played, but simply as a poetic form of pamphlet."[5] Benayoun's outlook upon the theatre, prior to 1960, is clear enough to anyone prepared to accept this statement as sincere. But what if he were only posing when expressing surprise at the prospect of seeing his work produced? Would he not then have been willing to give at least a little more attention to his medium, upon seeing the possibility of a career as a playwright opening up before him? This suspicion is laid to rest as soon as we read Benayoun's *Trop c'est Trop (Too Much is Too Much)*, published in the seventh number of *La Brèche: Action surréaliste* in December 1964. In fact, the special importance of *Trop c'est Trop* lies here. It appeared at the very time when its author might have been tempted to place the cause of surrealism second to the demands of the theatre.

Trop c'est Trop is subtitled "unperformable play." It is set in King Arthur's palace at Camelot "as this can be imagined by a color-blind Demi-Sikki pygmy." We are to see "refrigerators, birds made out of folded paper, and sibyls in dungarees." Varech enters. He appears to be dressed for force-feeding asparagus, but "one realizes at first glance that he is really a shoe magnate in his breakfast Sunday-go-to-meeting clothes." His sits down, "giving us to understand that he is thinking of the future." Played by an hepatic in chimpanzee costume, his dog

3. Leonora Carrington, *L'Invention du Molé*, trans. A. Adelmann, in *Phases*, No. 9 (April 1964), pp. 20–23. Molé is a sort of Mexican stew. Quetzales are Mexican birds.
4. Robert Benayoun, *La Science met bas* (Jean-Jacques Pauvert, 1959), Collection "Le Lycanthrope."
5. Letter to the author, 1963.

Tricot crouches at his side, giving itself a manicure, "with a foppish air." After Tricot has asked and been denied permission to scratch its left ear, both characters lose themselves in thought: "Obviously, Varech has just reached the irrevocable decision to stop the allowance of his son Rroyce, a landscape painter from Cévennes whom he adores, but whose painting aggravates Tricot. The latter, hired by Metro Goldwyn Mayer to play the role of *A Dog of Flanders* under Dreyer's direction, clearly has not learned its lines, and is thinking over a nervous breakdown."

True enough, Benayoun comments that "these two brainstorms" can be "exploited in a discreet bit of stage business." But he offers no hint on how the latter may be prolonged for the forty minutes he foresees this section of his play occupying "in complete silence hardly punctuated by timid requests for explanation from a melomaniac lady in the audience who thinks she is in the Salle Pleyel." Even if a director could see a way around the difficulties facing him at this point, how could he hope to follow Benayoun's next instructions to the effect that Tricot must be seen dozing while the Nice–San Francisco express passes across the front of the stage, where its lights have a hypnotic effect on the prompter?

Benayoun's play calls for a cyclone from the Azores to make spherical objects of bronze and lead revolve above the orchestra stalls. The author concedes that these objects may be made of papier-mâché, but insists that they have the correct weight. He reserves half an hour for critics to speak up from the front three rows of seats, but specifies that each must be silenced the moment he attempts to open his mouth. The participation of a varied collection of well-known figures is required, each playing himself: Fidel Castro, Frank Sinatra, François Mauriac, Jayne Mansfield, etc. "If the manager refuses to hire these prestigious names, he will have to give up the idea of putting on *Trop c'est Trop*. He gives it up."

THE DIRECTOR
Ladies and gentlemen, to our great regret we are not able to put on for you *Trop c'est Trop*. We remind you that it is, by the author's own admission, an unperformable play. [. . .] Kindly be so good as to leave without protest, with the firm assurance that the ticket money not refunded will be devoted entirely to the cause of the Drop of Gin.

When a spectator makes a contribution—it takes the from of a bottle of gin, hardly touched, intended for his grandmother—the whole audience rises to its feet and applauds. At this very moment, spring arrives with blossoming flowers, darting swallows, and snow "melting with the sound of marmalade." This, Benayoun informs us, is why *Trop c'est Trop* will be particularly appreciated in winter, and why it should be staged only when the temperature drops to at least five degrees centigrade below zero.

Irony and humor prove that *Trop c'est Trop* was composed in a provocative frame of mind. Benayoun evidently wrote not to challenge a director's skill so much as to defy professionals of the theatre to transpose his text to the stage, or even to believe that doing so would be worth the effort. In this sense, his sketch is typical of a number of works in theatrical form conceived under the influence of surrealism. Comparable to the unperformable film scenario advocated by Benjamin Fondane, the unperformable play stands for a distinctive conception of the theatre in its relation to surrealism.[6]

The approach to drama exemplified in *Trop c'est Trop* impresses us as extremist, even to the point where it may be taken as calling for a parting of the ways for surrealism and theatre. Actually, its significance is best appreciated somewhat differently. The unperformable play voices a determination to emancipate surrealist expression in the theatre from all obligation to respect the contingencies of dramatic presentation. To this extent, it interests us as an assertion, in unusually aggressive terms, of imaginative independence for surrealist theatrical dialogue and situation, at the expense of confining limitations customarily associated with stagecraft. As such, it renders explicit an attitude that, elsewhere, may be far less conscious than is the case with Benayoun or Barbé, but that nevertheless invariably resolves any conflict that may seem to exist between surrealist and dramatic concerns to the detriment of the latter. We are talking now of surrealist writers to whom adoption of a dramatic framework for their writings by no means implies concern for the practical demands of stage presentation. If the possibility for production presents itself, well and good. But there is no chance that the writer will make a special effort to facilitate stage adaptation, when doing this entails the risk of infringing upon

6. On the *scénario injouable* see Benjamin Fondane, *Trois Scénarii* (Brussels: Les Documents internationaux de l'Esprit nouveau, 1928); J. H. Matthews, *Surrealism and Film* (Ann Arbor: University of Michigan Press, 1971), pp. 74–75.

the liberties granted him by surrealism. Such a writer is Jean-Pierre Duprey.

Duprey's *Derrière son Double* (*Behind One's Double*) and *La Forêt sacrilège* (*The Sacrilegious Forest*) date from 1948 and 1949, a period of intense creative effort by an author who, only three years later, decided to concentrate mainly upon sculpture and who, from 1951 to 1952, was an apprentice ironsmith. Returning to poetry in 1959, Duprey wrote his last text, *La Fin et la Manière* (*The End and the Means*), mailing the manuscript to André Breton just before committing suicide at the age of twenty-nine.[7]

Generally speaking, in the texts he has left behind, regularity of form and exact literary classification are the least of Duprey's preoccupations. One section of *Derrière son Double* is headed "Act One and Only." It is followed by five other sections where dialogue quite frequently recurs. Yet only in the third section does the author again designate a passage of his text theatrical. If, then, we first concentrate upon those areas of *Derrière son Double* where Duprey speaks of theatre, this is not to suggest that the stage has priority here. It is, more pertinently, to examine how he integrates theatre in a remarkable endeavor that caused Breton to write, "You are certainly a great poet who has as a double [*doublé de*] someone else who intrigues me."[8]

At the beginning of *Derrière son Double* adoption of dramatized format is much more a matter of convenience than the expression of confidence in theatre as a means of communicating the author's intentions with special efficiency. This is brought home to us as soon as we read Duprey's version of the stage directions. The latter set the scene as follows: "The earth, the sky, the air, the sea, the void (sometimes filled with air), or nothing." From the very beginning we are struck most by the vagueness displayed by the playwright. Yet acquaintance with his text will teach us that, in *Derrière son Double*, the role of the

7. The first edition of *Derrière son Double* was published under the imprint Le Soleil noir in 1950. A second edition, somewhat expanded, appeared with Le Soleil noir in 1964. The other works of Duprey were also published by Le Soleil noir: *La Fin et la Manière* (1965), and *La Forêt sacrilège* (1970).
8. Letter dated January 18, 1949, reproduced in *Derrière son Double*.

void is as central as that of the double.[9] Had his instincts been those of a man of the theatre, Duprey would surely have felt obliged to address himself to the problems this raises. But, significantly, the difficulty of how to convey on stage the dramatic force of the void does not give Duprey pause for one instant.

A direct consequence of Duprey's fixation upon the void seems to be the peculiar nature of dialogue throughout the opening phase of *Derrière son Double*. Someone called Monsieur H is presumably of special importance. Not only does he take part in the first act, but he also is the author of a series of letters and diary extracts making up the second section of the text. Yet it is difficult to trace any reasonably progressive sequence in what he has to say in Part One: "A hole is a very good thing, you understand! It makes a very good telescope to see all black to the end; it is even used as a magnifying glass to look into the details of the place Nothing where Nobody lives." What he has to say is comprehensible, of course. But replying to such a statement would present a problem. Duprey skirts this by allowing Monsieur H's interlocutor to make no response at all. Instead, he has Monsieur H take out of a drawer two birds made of folded paper. Pushing its head through a hole in one of these, Body A engages Body B in conversation of a kind quite familiar to those who know surrealist drama:

BODY A
Listen: there is a sea in the earth, like a great tide that is undressing the tombs, and the dead are flames without a candle, lost to us. But whence comes this limitless joy that has killed us?

BODY B
Our inhuman night has rolled us together to the deep depths, and that which animates us is called the joy of the abyss. Are you dead or alive? Is your name Nosferatu?

Questions hang in the air, either going unanswered or eliciting no other response than more questions, to which answers are not forthcoming. The first scene ends with Body A stabbed by thunder: "However, the gleaming of his blood, changed into blue flames, dances with the lice [listed among the characters in the scene] around the other

9. See J. H. Matthews, "Jean-Pierre Duprey vu de loin," *Phases*, No. 11 (May 1967), pp. 83–85.

characters who draw back, swallowed up by fire, like dummies made of chalk quickly swallowed up, for, the set never changing, the scene must change . . ."

This ironical note at the close of Scene 1 confirms that dialogue is featured at the beginning of *Derrière son Double* not so much because the author attaches particular value to drama and to theatrical representation as because dialogue seems to him a practical means for bringing doubles together. As Scene 1 has Body A and Body B, so Scene 2 has The Spirit Within and Spirit II, while Scene 4 will show Monsieur H and his double (announced at the end of Scene 3 as "the multiple bodies of Monsieur H").

Subsequently, Monsieur H describes himself in a letter-preface to the second part of *Derrière son Double:* "P. S. Desiring above all to remain anonymous, I will not, either, push lack of tact so far as to reveal to you the surname and first names and profession of a character me, who, in fact, does not exist. Let's imagine for a moment that he is called Monsieur Other. Perfect. It could be Monsieur Everybody, but, if you will allow, I prefer Monsieur Nobody or better still and more simply Monsieur H." Providing a double for a nonexistent person is hardly likely to make for clear character definition in the fourth and last scene of the First and Only Act that opens *Derrière son Double.* The fact that Duprey does just this is proof enough of one thing, anyway: bringing distinctive characters on stage is not his purpose, when he takes advantage of dramatic structure so as to set *Derrière son Double* in motion and devote himself to contemplating "the Nothing place where no one lives."

Essential to Duprey's undertaking here is suppression of those elements by which characterization of people and things is generally taken to be possible in the theatre. This is why Monsieur H speaks of "the point H" of his body, "where I did not know myself yet [or "still," or "again": all three interpretations are ambiguously permissible in this context]." This is why he writes a long letter to himself, admitting to "having very little the honor of knowing you." And this, surely, is why he is brought face to face with his double in the closing scene of the first section.

If one may describe the conversation between The Spirit Within and Spirit II as informative, in the second scene, this is only in a very restricted way, rationally speaking. Each in turn evokes a strange spectacle, situated in "the other room," that other side of reality that is so different from the face of the real we are accustomed to see:

THE SPIRIT WITHIN
Have you seen, in the other room, the woman-spider with hard and hairy limbs like barbed wire scratching the floor, and do you know what monster lives there?
SPIRIT II
In the room, there is, hooked by its bleeding eyes, a cat's head ending in woman's hair; I saw no spider, unless it was caught within the hair which is perhaps its legs, thinned down.
On the wall I touch the devil's horn.

In however limited a sense, what we have just heard momentarily seems to promise to lead somewhere, since Spirit II's reply does have some bearing upon The Spirit Within's previous statement. But this illusion collapses at once. Duprey prolongs his scene without a trace of nostalgia for conventional dialogue. A Subterranean Chorus brings Scene 2 to a close with the comment, "And the Spirit not replying to the Spirit, there followed the fall of the sky like the sputtering cough of a world beyond the frontier."

As we read the dialogue of *Derrière son Double*, our difficulties are directly related to the all-important fact that dialogue here is posited upon the concept of failure. Duprey uses words as unsatisfactory substitutes for the inexpressible. He entrusts them, moreover, to characters who, indistinct as they appear before us, are still crudely substantial representatives of the ineffable creatures with whom the author is really concerned but who are too elusive to be brought on stage. The figures we see are, so to speak, the distorted shadows cast before our eyes by entities whose nature may only be inferred from what we see, as their thoughts find a muffled echo in the words we hear. This is why throughout Scene 3 the stage is empty and only the distant voice of the Subterranean Chorus is audible, informing us, among other things, that "The reality of a void appeared on the screen whitened by powdered bone."

Setting the scene for Monsieur H's encounter with his double, Duprey reveals himself more than willing to jettison the real. They have met, he tells us, "facing the seas which resemble at a lower level the hair of a tree suddenly rolling branches that a wind from afar propagated in the direction of depth." Nowhere more strongly than in Scene 4 does the reader of *Derrière son Double* feel excluded, kept at an irreducible distance by the characters Duprey has assembled. Here, being permitted to eavesdrop, as do all spectators in a theatre, is really to be granted nothing more than the opportunity to measure one's incapacity to cross a barrier by the well-tried means of rational comprehension or emotional empathy. And this barrier is far more formidable than that conventionally presented by the footlights. Only on the surface—externally, so to speak—does the conversation between Monsieur H and his double follow statement with response, question with answer:

> MONSIEUR H
> When your head speaks to you, I feel something like a great clap of thunder tearing a scarlet robe. Do you believe that our heads are books of chance bound in bone?
> THE DOUBLE
> If there are books, I know a finer one; in it I have read between the lines the plan of the weather. There is a path; if you take it, you find yourself in the direction of fire.
> MONSIEUR H
> Do you remember the void in the solidified stone?
> THE DOUBLE
> I have seen somewhere a cannon opening the mouth of a statue.
> MONSIEUR H
> As for me, I have seen you somewhere where you were not; it was at the agreed time, without an appointment at night.

In the letter-preface to Part Three of *Derrière son Double*, Monsieur H speaks of a "journey with which I shall not omit to keep you up to date by means of the diary that will follow." This is a curious journey into a "country newly discovered or, if you prefer, invented by us." The country in question defies description, however, "for reasons of which the main one is that I have no knowledge of it." It is a country which, he suspects, does not exist. "Heavenly captain of the mystery ship," Monsieur H offers us "the schematic vision of a globe decked out for the main scene." Yet he never evokes the dramatic situation he allows us to anticipate; at least he does not do so with enough clarity to give us a distinct impression of it. Instead, in Part

Two he communicates an apocalyptic description of strange sights seen while "following our course upside down." In Part Three elements without which the concept of theatrical representation becomes inconceivable are eliminated: "And it was in the same order that things occurred, after the sea had been drowned, the earth buried, and fire burned up, the air disappeared in the smoke of the new fire re-engendered by all that."

Given such radical changes in the universe, it is no surprise to find that the "First and Only Scene" that figures in Part Three dispenses with an evocation of the setting and, losing its autonomy, shades off into a "letter-conclusion" culminating in the reminder, "And for those who would be ignorant of it, I recall my name: Monsieur H or Nobody." The whole scene, we are told in advance, is conjured up by Monsieur H, "sorcerer without sorcery," whom we are watching "navigate in the film without actors." He projects it on "the imaginary screen," which is nothing other than the top of the peaked cap belonging to a decapitated general. Now Duprey does not even pretend to involve his characters, three clowns, in conversation. Each in turn utters a statement having no bearing upon what the others say. Then, as though losing patience with them, Duprey interjects: "Etc . . . Etc . . . As for the rest, Monsieur H, his journey taking place upside down or not taking place at all, could communicate only the final scene of the last act, a scene then reduced to its minimum [. . .]." That minimum is the single word "END."

The fourth section of *Derrière son Double* is entirely dialogued. But this does not mean that Duprey now seeks to make his peace with the conventional theatre. The opening scene is set in a field of nettles at the bottom of the sea. "Vegetable men" are mentioned, as are a girl, called Ague, and The Eye, enlarged a hundred times and "round like a globe that is not the earth." None of the statements following one another here is clearly attributed to anyone. Meanwhile what is said makes it in no way easier for us to distinguish one voice from another. Identity has been erased or has not yet been attained. At best one can speak of identity as something to which the speaker still aspires. At worst it is something he has already lost: "We lived right enough when we were not!" Without knowing who is the aggressor and who the victim, we learn that the former takes away the latter's head, teeth, and body, before everyone "empties himself." Now our only contact with the elusive creatures whom we have heard talking—their voices—

becomes "the creaking of a gateway opening onto the Foreign Domain."

Set "outside time," the second scene allows us to hear two of the characters from Scene 1 in conversation. Learning their names gives us little help. We still do not know who they are. Talamède's questions elicit no comprehensible response from Quicri-Kirat. What is more, there is reason to believe that the latter's responses would hold little significance for the former, even if they were meaningful. Talamède recalls a strange dream: "I was in a sort of manor house where everything—furniture, walls, lights, clocks (especially the clocks)—where everything was changed into crows. They spoke to me. I was indifferent."

On the dramatic level, the third episode in Part Four does nothing to redeem the second. Talamède and Philîme simply indulge in speculation of a kind that reason must condemn as unproductive. Nor does the epilogue bring about a reconciliation between Duprey's text and the theatre. It just makes us witnesses to a discussion between Talamède and Philîme (now called Salex). Here no explanations are forthcoming before Part Four closes on a pistol shot and a flashing firecracker, while Salex, Talamède, and Quicri-Kirat "become the heirs of the property owners of Death."

Duprey locates in the next section a "Conversation Talmède-Dalmète." The name of the second character being merely the first name (itself a contraction of Talamède) rearranged, it implies that Dalmète is entitled to no distinct personality. In other words, Talmède is in conversation with himself—with his double. When he falls to the ground, breathing his last, "THE OTHER no longer exists [. . .]." It is time for a first postscript "in which speak without head or sex the changed characters of doubles in their intermingled bodies." Now, preparing to jump "into Nowhere," Monsieur Lorc, "who is perhaps Dalmète," talks to someone called Amabol-Dalmète. Predictably, we find the latter impossible to differentiate in attitude or speech from Dalmète's other double. As Lorc says to Amabol, "However, I swallowed myself in your mouth." They are, as Lorc remarks in the second postscript (or "Second Tableau of Death Within"), "Siamese brothers" in "a world of depth-surfaces."

Nowhere in *Derrière son Double* does dialogue express a need on the author's part to communicate by way of consecutive statement and response, appealing to reason and taking effect on the plane of rationality. Duprey's natural inclination is one to which surrealism offers every encouragement and is reflected throughout his text. In the second postscript, for instance, Amabol replies to a remark by Lorc far less relevantly than his first words imply: "I remember! At that time I was inside you for as long as a birth lasts, but I was born very much further on . . . You appeared to be black like teeth submitted, with ashes, to the test of fire and I called you Fantomâte. Then, after being a soft automaton, you became a wheel and, thus traversed by a double-horizontal member, you approached me to teach me the torture of the wheel and the way to use it . . ." Obviously, reasonable thought has surrendered control over the progress of this statement. What Amabol says can be explained best, in other words, if one is attentive to sound associations, exerting an influence that eludes the supervision of common sense. Thus *Fantomâte* suggests *automate*, and *mou* ("soft") engenders *roue* ("wheel"). For Lorc another world (*un autre monde*) is "the shadow of a wave" because reason does not detain him when he thinks to associate *monde* with *un ombre d'onde*.

Long before it is over, *Derrière son Double* has made clear that it will induce nothing but frustration in readers whose firm convictions about the autonomy of drama must give rise to protest against the liberties Duprey feels entitled to take with the theatre. Jean-Pierre Duprey makes no apology in *Derrière son Double* for bending dramatic convention to purposes before which he demands their total surrender. His cause is fundamentally nondramatic. It is in the nature of his undertaking to complicate his approach to drama in a way that leaves an important question in our minds. Is abuse of virtually every traditional feature of stagecraft the expression of necessity in *Derrière son Double*, imposed here by the special requirements obtaining in a text where dramatic elements are utilized only intermittently; or is it, more significantly, representative of a basically skeptical attitude toward theatre that *La Forêt sacrilège* will confirm?

It is evident that the subject matter of Duprey's three-act drama, written only a few months after *Derrière son Double* (it bears the date August 1949), places it in a category very close, to say the least, to the one where his earlier text belongs. It would be wrong to look here for widely divergent themes, necessarily calling for different treatment. And this is just as well since, otherwise, we should find ourselves left to choose between two incompatible modes of theatrical experimentation, without having any reason to believe Duprey thought one more acceptable than the other. The special value of *La Forêt sacrilège* is this. It allows us to see how Duprey elects to handle theatre when he is at liberty to concentrate exclusively upon drama.

In comparison with those parts of *Derrière son Double* that are dramatized, *La Forêt sacrilège* appears to demonstrate more serious concern for plot continuity. At all events, we feel more sure of ourselves in tracing a theme through the later work. There are two reasons for this. First, Duprey is no longer using dramatization from time to time, in a way that incidentally casts light upon subject matter which appears obsessive, rather than clearly focused. Second, we take confidence in identifying a narrative thread in *La Forêt sacrilège* because we can detect here some elements palpably more traditional than those we glimpsed fleetingly in *Derrière son Double*.

La Forêt sacrilège deals with the triumphant love of Ueline and Estern, whose story is one at which no surrealist would look askance. It conforms to the surrealist view of love as a marvelous regenerative experience, well suited to presentation in the magic forest where the scandalous nature of amorous passion fully justifies the dramatist's insistence upon an element of sacrilege. For the latter has always appeared to surrealists as a token of the authenticity of Love. But we do Duprey a disservice if we limit his text, as we inescapably must do when devoting ourselves in this fashion to skimming sense from the surface of a play that runs deep. In *La Forêt sacrilège* the creative impulse is both too powerful and too complex to yield before reason's appeals for continuity and elimination of ambiguity.

Ambiguity marks *La Forêt sacrilège* indelibly, as it does *Derrière son Double*, making its influence felt on both texts in similar ways. Thus, as in his earlier work, Duprey uses doubles in his three-act play and does this in a manner that makes identification of unified personalities difficult, even when we concentrate solely upon his hero and heroine. Estern is listed among the characters of the drama as The Stranger, as well as under his own name. Meanwhile Ueline is not only La Noire too, but she is also No. 4. Duprey's preoccupation with this kind of *dédoublement* is given, at best, only indirect and partial explanation, as when Ueline announces that she is also La Noire and speaks of searching for herself "in the dark of her life" ("*dans le noir de sa vie*").

Ueline first sees Estern as he is crawling among stones: "If you are a snake, get up, for I make you a man! But who are you? I know and recognize you, since I have never seen you. I shall suck your blood, and, if your name is Estern, we can drink the sea together . . ." Estern, we notice, wears a mask at this point. He ought to be less easy to recognize for this reason—but only to someone who knows him, of course. Meanwhile he fails to recognize Ueline, who is unmasked: "Where have I seen you, except when myself upside down?" As before, Duprey introduces inversion in *La Forêt sacrilège* and once again invokes the dialectical principle of Hegel, which has never ceased to hold the surrealists' imagination. Significantly, then, Duprey's version of the recognition scene departs strikingly from dramatic norms. Ueline advises Estern, "Don't talk or talk to death! That then becomes the same thing, since we do not exist . . . Make yourself then!" However, the need for self-identification alone is not enough to account for Duprey's treatment of character in *La Forêt sacrilège*. When next we see Estern and La Noire, the latter is "present more in her shadow than in herself." Addressing himself to The Limping Man, Estern muses, "Are *we* really present?" Speaking subsequently to Estern, Ueline proposes that they meet the next day, "AFTER YOUR DEATH." Then the first act comes to a close on this clear warning, delivered by a blind Sorceress: "APART FROM THAT, once again, I warn the spectators that what they will be able to see bears only a distant relationship to what really happens behind our eyes."

Of the two shadowy figures to be seen meeting marauders in the forest, at the beginning of Act II, one is Estern in the guise of The Stranger. He explains that the other "is but a double of my appearance here"—Estern's second double, then, who remains silent. When struck by a stone thrown by the marauder chief, the overcoat worn by the second double falls to the ground, "empty of body as of smoke."

At first, in the beginning of Act II, Scene 2, "like the dream of an appeal that exists," Estern's voice is heard while the stage is still bare. It poses questions that neither Estern nor anyone else answers about the love binding him and Ueline. Estern concludes, "This said, you can go on stage or trace to its source the flow of this mirror that holds us, for the die is cast." Followed by Estern, Ueline now appears. Each of them wears a mask shaped like a dog's head. Ueline sheds some light upon what we have seen and heard so far, as she defines their purpose as "the conquest of the physical." She promises "The Sacrilege will be carried out according to the laws in force . . ." But from this point onward her statements become increasingly difficult to understand. The masks, meanwhile, have been set aside. Estern cries out cryptically, "In a moment or two, and henceforth for all the hours possible, I shall violate my own body until death follows; and I shall violate it by the very strength of my Ueline, my Noire."

In this scene we are struck particularly by the way in which verbal ambiguity intrudes between us and sure knowledge of the playwright's intentions. Ueline says, "We shall finish at the beginning, or rather at THE END IN VIEW which I married, thus committing incest since it was my father." Evidently what Duprey has done here is extract *BUT* ("END IN VIEW") from *début* ("beginning"), so establishing linguistic relationships where no rational connection is possible. A moment later he has Estern comment, "But a suicide does not have the importance of a torch burning on me," justifying this assertion with the ambivalent explanation, "puisque JE N'Y SUIS PAS"—which can be read both as "since I AM NOT IN IT" and as "since I DON'T UN-DERSTAND IT," but on the level of reasonable discourse, does not illuminate what Estern has said.

As Scene 3 opens, Estern is talking of "an endless fall to the bottom of a chasm THE BOTTOM OF WHICH is in us only!" If it measures up to his demands, the love uniting Ueline and himself will become self-sufficient: "And the Order thus reversed, we shall perhaps find a possible world scaled to our greatness!" Henceforth, Ueline declares, they are cut off from other mortals. Without making an effort to introduce systematic alternation between relatively straightforward statements of this sort and impenetrable passages of the kind figuring in the previous scene, Duprey does allow his drama to oscillate vertiginously between clarity and obscurity, obviously unwilling to give the former precedence over the latter.

The Sorceress' mention of "this world and its projection into the the OTHER" at the end of the fourth scene introduces the fifth. This shows Estern "identified with his Eternity, possible and absolute, finite or infinite," and lets us hear him declare, "My sought-after Form is the lost Formula" as well as express the following wish in the face of death: "I want myself alive then and erect in my Two-Faced-Being." Once more Duprey, whose Monsieur H is an alchemist after his fashion, alludes to alchemy when, bringing on Estern's double, he has the latter say, "Face to face with myself, I then want to communicate a secret to you, ESTERN, to make you the master and guardian of what I want to lose . . ."

The scene does not change as, in the darkened forest, two men await a new dawn, to be announced by a spider, not a rooster: "When the spider has spat three times, when she has spun her voice of web thickened by her crutches of trumpets, the world will have changed meaning and the earth changed its name." These two men, No 1 and No 2, Estern's servants, are joined by No 3, who declares that his companion No 4 has a great announcement to make: the arrival of a knight called Sagittarius. No 4 tears off her dog mask and is identifiable as La Noire. Temporarily immobilized, her companions regain the power of speech and movement in the final scene of Act II, after Ueline has left, so giving us the opportunity to discover that No 1 is The Limping Man who appeared briefly in Act I.

Whereas Act I and Act II are situated in the forest, the third act of *La Forêt sacrilège* is set indoors, in a room of which we have some idea thanks to Estern's description: "An endless waiting room . . . Is it a square or a circle? . . . And the walls are false. [. . .] It is very dark and almost pitch black, for the windows are false . . . or rather the walls are false and the windows do not exist, as the doors do not exist . . . like the walls . . ." In this limbo locale, Estern cries, "I divine [*je devine*] everything; or rather, I deviate [*je dévie*] between two lives [*deux vies*]." He goes on to make a reference to The Sorcery Sagittarius (*Le Sagittaire sortilège*). Then he falls senseless to the ground. His double appears, explaining, "*Estern knows*. His body has preceded him before his shadow." We infer that Estern has gone ahead to Castle Sacrilege (*le Château sacrilège*). For this is where we see him as The Stranger, in Scene 2, where we learn that the Sagittarian figure is but another projection of Duprey's hero. Informing himself (as Estern) that he is enchanted by his love (*Ton amour te sortilège*), The Stranger expresses the hope that Estern will be able to penetrate "the Sagittarian wall behind which, behind which . . . But the secret will be able to divine you!" Only when Ueline has been credited with having "accomplished all the RITES by the magic of love" do Estern and she appear.

While Ueline talks of wishing to die in his arms, "after having caressed you with all the enigma of life," preferring to see "True Life" with him beyond death, Estern voices this hope: "And may your form always be my Sagittarian formula." As though these words have conjured him up, the Knight Sagittarius appears, to make just one statement: "Your shadows' shadows are becoming impatient. Your men are beckoning." Outside time, Estern predicts, he and Ueline will love one another forever: "The Sagittarian Norm will be achieved." The play comes to an end in Castle Sacrilege, on a scene in which Ueline exclaims, "Our love creates the pathway of the Solitary Sagittarian. Let us follow it!" Both Estern ("But our love is killing me!") and she ("Your breathing will kill me . . .") recognize that their passion can lead only to death, the gateway to "unlimited life." As total darkness descends, we hear Estern and Ueline without seeing them. Ueline says, "I read your name: you are MYSELF! And the interdiction being raised, may the castle be struck with ruins like smoke, for here rises the Sorcery Spectre!" A clap of thunder is heard. Then a distant but strong voice closes the play with the three words, "THE SAGITTARIAN SHADOW."

Duprey takes up the phrase on which La Forêt sacrilège stops and makes of it the title for a fragmentary text, L'Ombre sagittaire. The latter is not relevant to a study of his treatment of theatre, however. Of greater interest, then, is Duprey's use of the word "interdiction." The phrase where it occurs continues to be vague, of course, so long as we do not recognize one important thing. It is a sign that the motivating force of Duprey's drama owes less to theatrical ambition than to surrealist aspiration. Specifically, the author of La Forêt sacrilège invites us, at the very end, to measure his achievement in the light of André Breton's conviction that imagination offers us the prospect of "raising the terrible interdiction just a little."[10]

From the second act onward we become aware of an undertow of meaning in La Forêt sacrilège. We cannot be quite sure where it is to take us, because Duprey never speaks out openly. The clearest allusion to the direction the play is following comes in the fifth scene of Act II. In the background we see ("but perhaps this is only an impression," the playwright remarks) "the male and female Armor, visor down, legs and lower abdomen in shadow, that is to say uncertain about their existence." Stage directions identify this figure as The Sorcery

10. André Breton, Manifestes du Surréalisme (Jean-Jacques Pauvert, n. d. [1962]), Premier Manifeste, p. 17.

Spectre, otherwise called Knight Sagittarius. Duprey is referring to the Centaur Chiron, who was educated by Apollo, god of divination and prophecy, and by that other deity of sudden death, Artemis, goddess of the forest. Recalling that Chiron, suffering an incurable wound, exchanged his immortality for the mortality of Prometheus, we are free to draw suggestive conclusions. These relate to the development of Duprey's drama of life and death, in which Estern is called by one of his servants a "doctor of esternity." But they also may be seen to cast light upon the mind of a man to whom self-destruction finally appeared the logical answer to the problems of living.

"With the unstageable 'plays for reading' by Salacrou—as well as by Daumal and Gilbert-Lecomte—," Michael Benedikt has asserted, "the Dadaist and Surrealist drama reached what might be regarded as an aesthetic impasse."[11] Benedikt lays his argument upon certain assumptions that are, to say the least, questionable: that while first experimenting with theatre, somewhat under surrealist influence, Armand Salacrou made a significant contribution to surrealism on the stage; that, before they found limited and short-lived notoriety as surrealist dissidents of the Grand Jeu group, René Daumal and Roger Gilbert-Lecomte produced skits worth taking into account, when dominant trends in surrealist treatment of the theatre are being assessed. But whether or not we agree with Benedikt on these matters, it is quite another thing to condone confusing Dada and surrealism with aestheticism.

If it teaches us nothing else, Jean-Pierre Duprey's use of drama demonstrates that when we raise the question of aesthetic preoccupations, in connection with theatre as practiced in surrealism, we must end up following a false lead. The way in which Duprey handles theatrical elements is especially instructive. It shows how wrong it is to speak of surrealism in the theatre as falling under the temptation to succumb to attractions to which no true surrealist has ever submitted, whether writing for the stage or not. Furthermore, the special demands made upon language in all Duprey's work—whether he borrows the framework of drama or not—leaves no doubt on one score. Duprey

11. Michael Benedikt and George Wellwarth, *Modern French Theatre: The Avant-Garde, Dada, and Surrealism* (New York: Dutton, 1964), p. xxvii.

was more obedient to poetic demands, as these magnetize surrealist writing, than to dramatic convention. Whatever students of the art of the theatre may think of *La Forêt sacrilège*, no surrealist would have anything but approval to express for the choice its author unhesitatingly made.

José Pierre

just imagining the liberties
We shall take is enough to make our breeches bristle.[1]

ALONE among the French surrealist writers whose work was published for the first time in the sixties, José Pierre, who joined their ranks in 1952, has evidenced sustained interest in the theatre. His *D'Autres Chats à fouetter (Other Fish to Fry)* contains two short texts in dramatic form, *Ubu-la-Trinité* and *Le Dernier Métro*,[2] as well as several short stories. And he has authored three plays substantial enough to fill a sizeable volume. Grouping these three dramas together and accompanying them with interrelated prefatory notes, Pierre encourages thematic study of his plays. These reflect a concept of theatre upon which several influences make themselves felt.

Publishing his *Théâtre*, José Pierre admits openly to admiring Jean Genet, Alfred Jarry, a play by Christian Dietrich Grabbe translated by Jarry as *Les Silènes*,[3] Oscar Panizza's *The Council of Love*,[4] and Radovan Ivsic's *Le Roi Gordogane*. Indebtedness to certain predecessors does not preclude originality in Pierre's work, however. On the contrary, what these writers have accomplished simply provides him with a point of departure for a noteworthy contribution to surrealism in the theatre. It is a contribution that can be assessed best when examined under a number of headings: plot, the author's attitude to something he calls "the natural," his use of verse in his plays, his use of music and dialogue, of scatology and vulgarity.

1. José Pierre, *Le Vaisseau amiral*, in his *Théâtre* (Denoël, 1969).
2. José Pierre, *D'Autres Chats à fouetter* (Eric Losfeld, 1968).
3. See André Breton's *Anthologie de l'Humour noir* (Jean-Jacques Pauvert, 1966), where a translation of Grabbe's *Scherz, Satire, Ironie und tiefere Bedeutung* is reproduced, pp. 124–36.
4. Translated from the German by Jean Bréjoux as *Le Concile d'Amour*, Panizza's play of 1895 appeared in France (Jean-Jacques Pauvert, ed.) in 1960, with an enthusiastic preface by André Breton. It was reprinted in 1964 in a more accessible edition, in Pauvert's series "Libertés."

If we have come to a performance of any of José Pierre's dramas feeling curious about what is going to take place on stage, we are likely to take away an impression which reading the text confirms: that his plays fall flat. In the first of them, *Le Vaisseau amiral* (*The Flagship*), completed on August 8, 1967, dramatic elements are obviously minimal. Moreover, the author's lack of interest in developing them is only too transparent. Pierre's introductory notes inform us that *Le Vaisseau amiral* was "born solely of a desire to write for the theatre." This play, we learn, "took form curiously out of the following phrase, noted during a stay in a nursing home, 'The general is looking for his collar stud,' a phrase which would become, for reasons of personal mythology, 'The admiral is looking for his collar stud' " (p. 9). By a process interestingly analogous to that of automatism as described in Breton's *Manifeste du Surréalisme*, Pierre's drama originated in a banal yet oddly mysterious phrase for which its author feels no embarrassment at being without an explanation. By the time the first act had been written, he tells us, the title "asserted itself, and there was no going back on it" (p. 10). Nevertheless, in the light of what occurs in this play it is hard for either readers or spectators to persuade themselves that compelling reasons underlay its composition.

As it begins to unfold in the first scene, the action of *Le Vaisseau amiral* offers little promise of excitement. To help keep his mistresses in jewelry and in his bed, the king of an unnamed country has been selling off his fleet, piecemeal; or, as the Admiral puts it characteristically, the monarch has been stuffing his ships between his pretty pussies' thighs. The naval commander's only recourse, now, is to conceal the whereabouts of his flagship by a ruse: he has it repainted and renamed daily.

We soon discover that the Admiral's sense of humor, like Gordogane's, makes his worthy of a place in the universe of Sade. He roars with laughter when recounting how he torpedoed the yacht belonging to the King of Greece (or Ireland; he is not sure which), during a state visit. The King is no more admirable a figure, morally speaking. In ruling his kingdom, his chief weapons are electrocution and castration. Although in the past seventeen years he has electrocuted a mere one hundred twenty-nine people, the King has resorted to castration one thousand three hundred-four times. In the course of the play, he indicates that he stands ready to make the Admiral the one thousand three hundred-fifth victim. He takes cruel pleasure in asserting that the sound of the flagship's siren, which we hear repeatedly, is no assurance that it has not been sold already. Indeed, he has made a profitable deal with the Portuguese who, before the drama is over, will have used their new acquisition to mount an attack upon his territory.

The plot proceeds at a leisurely pace, with no air of urgency. The King and the Admiral hold a press conference to make public the sale of the flagship and to explain:

THE KING
We have opted for an invisible navy.
THE ADMIRAL
An invisible but present navy.

But the consequences of this announcement receive no more than incidental development. While the kingdom falls to the Portuguese, the King and the Admiral devote themselves to making love, both at the same time, to someone called the Lady-who-has-lived.

When we turn to the longest of José Pierre's plays, *Bonjour Mon Œil* (*Good Morning, Eye*), written in August 1968, it would seem that we have a right to expect something more than in *Le Vaisseau amiral*. The second drama is to be considered a "didactic play in five acts," we learn. It should have a well-developed theme, then, carefully followed through. This it has indeed, and yet *Bonjour Mon Œil* will hardly prove enlightening to many reading or watching it.

Didactic purposes lead Pierre to include among his prefatory notes a section entitled "The Play's Message." Here he explains that he does not have a thesis to defend yet must warn actors and audiences alike that, while unaware of having anything to prove in *Le Vaisseau amiral*, he is conscious of several intentions underlying *Bonjour Mon Œil*. These lead him to borrow Eluard's distinctions between "involuntary" works (*Le Vaisseau amiral*) and "intentional" ones (*Bonjour Mon Œil*). Pierre is scrupulous enough to forewarn us that the subtitle of his second dramatic text, "Le Héros positif," is more important than the title itself. Like the literature of Social Realism, it gives us to understand, *Bonjour Mon Œil* will propose a "positive hero" whose conduct is designed to appear exemplary.

A glance at the text of *Bonjour Mon Œil* makes one thing clear without delay. Pierre has taken elaborate precautions to point out the obvious. Utilizing the framework of science fiction, he has granted his positive hero temporal disorientation (which, incidentally, the play-wright regards as advantageous). But the consequence is by no means such that spectators could remain in doubt about the writer's intentions. One can only conclude that Pierre's careful introduction to his play has an ironical function, insistence being intended to make the obvious only more so.

The reason why he acts in this fashion soon strikes us. He situates the action of his new play on Earth, in the capital of the Promethean Federation, around the year 2069. But he does not do so in order to indulge a taste for exotic stage sets. He sees no objection, for instance, to having the role of the omniscient, ever-present dictator played by a man confined in a cage above the stage, should it not be possible, when his drama is performed, to use cinematic or televisual means. Indeed, "A shabby picture of the twenty-first century certainly would not displease me," he confides. We appreciate that parodic elements do not displease him, either; the main characters are rescued in the final act, to the accompaniment of a bugle call that Western movies have taught us to associate with the welcome and opportune arrival of the U. S. Cavalry.

Dedicated to Daniel Cohn-Bendit, "the only *thinker* of our period," *Bonjour Mon Œil* has an explicit theme that its author summarizes before the action begins: "In which we see that sensual pleasure is in the final analysis more interesting than servile discipline." It opens in the office of Supervision over Mental Inclinations, First Section: Sexual Relations. Here a conversation between Angle Obtus (Obtuse Angle) and Angle Aigu (Acute Angle) proceeds according to the playwright's wishes to set off unrhymed versified statements, like those in *Le Vaisseau amiral*, against rhymed verse passages that are to be either recited or sung to music. A lamp lights up every time the dictator, Mon Œil, is cited.

Genetic control, we discover, has made it possible to predict the level that every person born in the Promethean Federation may attain in society. However, a margin of uncertainty remains: "bad social relationships" or "an anti-Promethean attitude" may prevent an individual from attaining the grade foreseen for him.

It is evident already that José Pierre makes no serious effort to be innovative in *Bonjour Mon Œil*. Indeed, he anticipates being criticized for having slavishly imitated books like *1984* (even though he claims not to have read George Orwell's novel). What matters is that he is content to work within stereotyped literary conventions when depicting oppressive society, projected into the future.

Fifteen-year-old Angle Aigu has been assigned to the Office of Sexual Relations, which, according to the department head, Angle Grave, "supervises in / What state of mind each individual uses / The ephemeral pleasure to which he has the right." This really means judging whether sexual pleasure makes an individual better suited or less well suited to fulfilling his role in Promethean society. As the play begins, the Brigade of Young Angles (classified as *vulviacées*) is to be assisted by the Brigade of Double Consonants (these men are *phallophores*) in an experiment. Three persons of each sex are to be paired off, so that they may "discover the mysteries" of ephemeral pleasure and "determine its hidden laws."

Double K gives it as his opinion that reprehensible moral conduct is attributable to the practice of ephemeral pleasure in contempt of the law. In appreciation, the dictator, Mon Œil, promotes Double K to the rank of positive hero, "cornerstone of Promethean dynamism" (that is, of revolution). However, at the end of the first act Double K confesses that his ambition is not so much advancement in the Promethean Hierarchy as "discovering / The secrets of human behavior / And the laws governing man."

As the experiment proceeds, Angle Aigu, Double K's partner, is distinguished from the other two women by her realization that sex is used in the Promethean Federation to satisfy the needs of the State by keeping the popuation in docile contentment. She also realizes that the practical sex education she has received was designed to "strip the body/ Of its mystery." Now, for the first time in her life, she enjoys making love, finding herself able to comprehend Double K's remark that, united in love beyond ephemeral pleasure, he and she will never be the same again. As Double K points an accusing finger at the portrait of Mon Œil dominating the stage, a lightning flash followed by a wink from the dictator's likeness indicates that the machinery which gives Mon Œil's voice its mechanical quality has broken down.

Act Three brings evaluation of the experiment in conjugal living, culminating in Angle Aigu's frank admission, "I think I have rediscovered love." The machinery activating Mon Œil's portrait breaks down once more, so for the second time releasing those on stage from supervision.

As the fourth act begins, Mon Œil is speaking of sabotage. His remarks lead the characters before us to conclude that they indeed have been guilty of wishing to release themselves from uninterrupted surveillance. In his rage, Mon Œil threatens all six with extermination, admitting that their discussion has been heard all over Earth, where it is fostering revolt. However, he agrees to punish only the person guilty of releasing the group from his control. This turns out to be Double K, who has come from another planet to study the means used on Earth for enjoying ephemeral pleasure. Now, while Earth is torn by insurrection, seven of Double K's companions arrive to liberate him. Their planet delivers an ultimatum to Mon Œil, but Double K decides against asking for military assistance from his own people, since "one never liberates / Anyone but oneself." As the fall of Mon Œil's régime is announced, a new order is established: "We decree the revolution of sensual pleasure."

In *Bonjour Mon Œil* José Pierre's use of some of the commonplaces of science fiction literature show perfectly clearly that he has made no effort to give his play even the semblance of originality. Meanwhile, his complete fidelity to surrealist attitudes regarding love and its revolutionary role in society precludes any departure from a plot line that is quite predictable to anyone acquainted with surrealist writing. Thus no more than in his first play does he evidence real concern for plot in his second drama. What then of his third play?

The subtitle of *Hara Kiri*, written in December 1968, is "The Laws of Advertising." To demonstrate these laws, Pierre represents the experiences of a young man recently hired by the Pigeonville Publicity Agency, initiated into the secrets of his chosen profession by the Agency's director. Presented in musical comedy format, *Hara Kiri* reaches its climax in the performance by which young Hector proves his worth as an advertising man, miming clues that the television audience has the opportunity to identify. His skill is such that these clues are soon successfully interpreted: "Use Hara-Kiri bottle-openers." Hector's performance reaches its high point when, providing the clue to the brand of bottle-openers he is promoting, he efficiently disembowels himself, on camera.

In treating *Hara Kiri* as a musical comedy, José Pierre has in mind Hollywood movies (his play is dedicated to Cyd Charisse), well insulated against the oppressive realities of everyday existence. So the secretary, Brigitte, whom the director has shot in rage when pursuing the chorus line off stage in the second act, returns in the third as the cameraman in the television studios where Hector puts on his performance. And Hector, whom we see fall dead after committing ritual suicide, revives to take part in the final song-and-dance routine that brings the curtain down. Thus, while at first sight *Hara Kiri* stands quite apart from Pierre's earlier dramas in showing greater inventiveness than they, it is firmly and significantly linked with both of them in one respect that we have not had occasion to notice yet. *Hara Kiri* is very definitely anti-naturalistic, or, to use the language its author prefers, it makes no attempt to be "natural."

In the third act, a stretcher is carried on stage. It bears an armature upon which are visible a red wig, articles of feminine underwear, and high-heel shoes—all used to represent Brigitte, "victim of the profit motive." The remaining actors make their farewells, singing ridiculous songs in praise of the dead secretary, during a scene that ends with a French Can-Can chorus line singing the theme song of the Agence Pigeonville:

> Ah the Agence Pigeonville
> It's a fine necropolis
> At the Agence Pigeonville
> When you kick the bucket
>   we all have a good time.

It is plain that in this play José Pierre remains faithful to the intentions expressed in his preface: mounting an attack upon "consumer society" by "turning the weapons of advertising against the profit-motivated society which employs them" (p. 182). It is not the intention so much as the method that takes us by surprise. Why does the author of *Hara Kiri*, who takes his subject so seriously, treat it in such a frivolous manner? To answer this question, we have to consider other aspects of the playwright's technique, to be observed in the first two dramas of Pierre's *Théâtre* as well as in the last.

As we watch plot downgraded in the theatre of José Pierre, as we see him use material so well worn as to appear quite threadbare, it is not difficult to infer that we are expected to interest ourselves in something other than the events taking place before our eyes. To find satisfaction in one of his dramas, one must look beyond plot. But in which direction? The playwright offers a most useful hint when remarking that, writing *Le Vaisseau amiral*, he was determined to disobey "a sort of sacrosanct law of nature." This meant avoiding any reference to real people and real places in his first play. But it meant also something far more significant: use of a rhythmic pattern of dialogue that the author felt constrained to term versification, but that "would at least have the advantage of discouraging efforts to read it, of making these almost impossible" (pp. 12–13).

Pierre's method consists in "diluting the phrase within a framework indifferent to syntactical order." That is, it aims to "drive out the natural." For example, in the fourth scene of the first act of *Le Vaisseau amiral*, the lines, "Are you kidding there are at least it can't / Be boring for you a good twenty of them if anyway I don't," correspond to the following statement, arbitrarily arranged as two lines of verse: "Are you kidding! There are at least (it can't be boring for you) a good twenty of them. If . . . Anyway . . . I don't . . ." Pierre demands that each line of his drama be delivered as though it terminated with a period and, furthermore, without any attempt on the actor's part to restore a sense sequence that has slipped out of sight along with the punctuation. Instead, those playing in his first drama are encouaged to bring to their roles diction that is as personal—and that means as fanciful—as they can make it. Diction must help the spectator, "but up to a certain point only." Delivery of each line must reflect more attention to "the weight of the words taken individually" than to general meaning: "The latter will emerge or will not emerge" (p. 9).

The verse form adopted throughout *Le Vaisseau amiral* is anything but a guarantee that we are going to hear a succession of rhythmically unified phrases, pleasant to the ear. Dated December 26, 1968, the introduction to *Bonjour Mon Œil* explains, "So far as the diction of the nonrhymed text goes [. . .] there is no difference from what has been said with regard to *The Flagship*. I know this is not poetry (of the latter I have too noble an ideal), but I cannot bring myself to use stupid prose with its periods, its commas, and its cloddish way of obstructing the whole page, while I wish for nothing so much as taking in air, breathing, and silences and hesitations of all sorts" (p. 88).

Stage directions make clear that those to whom we are asked to listen in both *Le Vaisseau amiral* and *Bonjour Mon Œil* are expected to react at all times as if they were engaged in a conversation proceeding normally. Meanwhile, whenever they speak they are required to resist the temptation to reconstruct the original sense of the unpunctuated phrases they utter. So long as they do this, José Pierre contends, acting and diction will shed light on the meaning of both his didactic second play and *Le Vaisseau amiral*, "histrionics in two acts." With regard to the latter, he adds the significant comment, "If, that is, there *is* a meaning, which it is not my place to decide" (p. 14). Hence, in conformity with a long-established principle of surrealism laid down by André Breton, the author of *Le Vaisseau amiral* and of *Bonjour Mon Œil* draws a distinction between the manifest content of his dramas and their latent content. It is when referring to the latter, obviously, that he concedes he understands nothing about his first play (p. 18).

Pierre's first two dramas offer the spectator an experience of a special kind. They offer readers an experience of another but related sort. Trained by reason to follow the sense of the printed page, the eye makes an effort to trace the thread of reasonable meaning running through both *Le Vaisseau amiral* and *Bonjour Mon Œil*. Restoring punctuation certainly facilitates detection of this thread. It therefore seems to suggest that the way to understand Pierre's theatre is to turn its verse back into prose. Yet, as we have seen, the plot uncovered by this method tends to be of questionable interest. As a result, those who sit down with a copy of the text and set out to discover "what happens" in one of his plays in the end fail to comprehend the real meaning of what they have read. In fact, Pierre sets a trap for such readers when he asserts, against reason, "It would not be absurd to present the Admiral as twice the age of the King, who is nevertheless said to be an ex-school-friend of his," adding, "In the same way, the Lady-who-has-lived can be seventeen or sixty" (p. 20).

As *Le Vaisseau amiral* opens, the stage is bare. The author specifies that the necessary furnishings will be brought on little by little, as they are needed. Meanwhile he thinks of entrusting to stagehands the task of displaying placards announcing the theme of each successive scene (I, 1 "The admiral is looking for his collar stud"; I, 2 "The ruler's craft," etc.). If this were to be done, it would be of course at the expense of realism, judged by present-day standards, although in accordance with a respectable theatrical tradition. However, this tradition would be invoked in *Le Vaisseau amiral* in a manner consistent with the exaggerated style of performance recommended in place of natural acting. In other words, Pierre would be using theatrical traditions to his own ends, turning it to account in a manner calculated to stress the unnatural atmosphere that he finds desirable.

The effect would be similar to the one produced as, about to recall the years when he and the King were in school together, the Admiral exclaims, "Projectionist run the film back will you as far as/The naked terraces of adolescence." No reenactment of the past is about to be staged, for the Admiral is content to reminisce briefly in the course of a soliloquy upon which he is already launched. So there is no need for a film projectionist's services at this point. Hence an appeal across the footlights for unneeded technical assistance is not merely superfluous; it undermines the illusion upon which theatrical presentation normally rests. A comparable effect of gratuitous intrusion by irrelevant elements is communicated during a press conference, when the King's press secretary wields a clapboard used on film sets to identify takes, crying, "Press conference number seven hundred thirty-four b/Object revolutionary organization of the royal fleet."

José Pierre's use of music takes on special value in relation to his distaste for natural drama. He confides that, even before he began writing *Bonjour Mon Œil*, he thought of an opera. This is interesting because, being, as he himself insists, a strictly conformist surrealist, he feels nothing but "amused indifference" to music in general. His reasons for using opera as a model, when planning his second play, emerge from his description of opera as "a play in which some actors, called the orchestra, are grouped in front of the stage to produce a racket intended to render the words exchanged by the others inaudible." The effect he describes in these terms is brought about all the more readily, he contends, by the fact that "responsibility for the text (the words exchanged) and responsibility for the music (the racket) are traditionally entrusted to two different people each of whom is persuaded that the other has no importance at all" (p. 82). What stimulates his imagination, then, is "the idea of a duel which would oppose two adversaries armed in ridiculously unequal fashion: one would have at his disposal a battleship and the other a cream tart."

The idea of conflict between the text itself and what it may suggest underlies Pierre's theatre from *Le Vaisseau amiral* onward. In *Bonjour Mon Œil*, he wishes to exploit the possibilities of duality from a rather special angle, however. Using words and music, he aims here at "enlarging the means of expression (that is, of action on the spectator)." In his second drama, the pretext of temporal dislocation, the author is convinced, justifies employing "a whole arsenal of audio-visual possibilities," used to evoke for the audience "a society, a way of life, and beliefs radically different from their own." The purpose in view is clear enough. Appealing at one and the same time to the eye and the ear, Pierre aims to address himself to the feelings and the intellect of his public, so as to make them "see and hear the unknown," immersing them in a future time period that will disorient them.

Whereas the role of music is distinctly accessory in *Le Vaisseau amiral,* where the Lady-who-has-lived opens the final scene with a song relating some of her experiences, in *Bonjour Mon Œil* it might have had "the lion's share," but for the dramatist's need to insist upon disorientation. This explains why, in the end, Pierre did not choose to write his second play in operatic form. Following a method tried out in his first drama, he sought instead to create a contrast between what was to be spoken and what was to be sung. The rhymed material set to music was to be sung "in a spirit of derision," being "the catechism in song form of the Promethean Federation," or *"that which is not thought* by the characters but imposed upon them." Right up to the end of the play, when liberative forces make themselves felt, music remains indicative of "deception, falsification, and inauthenticity" in *Bonjour Mon Œil.*

In one respect, José Pierre proceeds further with *Hara Kiri* in the direction to which *Bonjour Mon Œil* pointed. For he grants music and dance a larger share than ever in his third play, using these elements in a manner we shall have to examine shortly. Our first concern, however, is the danger to which he seemed to succumb gradually, imitating more and more willingly forms of entertainment that, though generally popular, hardly appear consistent with surrealist ambitions in the theatre.

Pierre reveals that he is keenly aware of this danger and has taken steps to avoid it when, prefacing *Hara Kiri,* he warns, "I don't write for school girls!" (p. 181). This bald statement proves his continued fidelity to the principles upon which he laid *Le Vaisseau amiral.*

No sooner had the phrase "The admiral is looking for his collar stud" claimed his attention than, according to the recollections he shares with us, Pierre realized what kind of language would be appropriate for his first play, "Or more exactly in what direction it tended, from which well it would decide to drink its water" (p. 10). The di-

rection Pierre deliberately chose led to coarseness of expression, to ob-
scenity even, gladly accepted as a means of defending *Le Vaisseau
amiral* from that process by which popular media like radio, television,
and the cinema assimilate everything. At once, it seemed to him that
the way to preserve his drama's independence was to employ pornog-
raphy or scatology.

As summarized in the introductory notes to his first play, Pierre's
motives permit of misinterpretation. Writing *Le Vaisseau amiral* and
the plays that followed, he had something quite different in mind from
the titillation usually associated with the use of pornographic and scatological elements. His interest in the authors to whom he acknowledges
a debt is thus of special significance. In them he salutes above all "a
lewd verve," inseparable in his mind from "basic refusal to come to
terms with established order" (p. 11). And so, just as Jarry notified the
public of his uncompromising opposition to accepted codes of social
behavior when he opened *Ubu Roi* with the novel expletive "Merdre!"
("Shittr!"), so Pierre begins *La Vaisseau amiral* on a note of violence
that reveals how close his Admiral stands to Jarry's hero:

> Son of a bitch son of a bitch shit
> Son of a bitch if I find you if I find the
> Find that collar stud fucked off
> Shit and shit if I find that
> Son of a bitch I shall flatten I shall flatten it.

Not the least striking aspect of these lines is the discrepancy between
the language used by the Admiral and the circumstances—his search for
a lost collar stud—that occasion its use, a discrepancy, we notice, that
helps give this play its unnatural quality.

While not expressed in such crude language, allusions to the me-
chanics of sexual intercourse are explicit in *Bonjour Mon Œil*, where
their role is central. In the playlet *Ubu-la-Trinité* (*Ubu the Trinity*),
Ubu's wife, son, and daughter all copulate on a table, hidden from sight
by a flag draped over them. The son, who is also the doctor (or
merdecin, as José Pierre calls him) who at the beginning of the play
delivered Ubu of the daughter, sired by Ubu's wife, then sings a song
ending, "What does puritanical morality matter to me/My conscience
is on my side!" As for *Hara Kiri*—at first glance the Pierre play most
likely to appeal to the public at large—this musical is infused with an
anti-conformist spirit that takes issue with established order in a number

of unmistakable ways. First, the publicity slogans that have made the Pigeonville company famous include some of the aggressively vulgar variety:

> To fart in silk,
> is good,
> To shit in mink,
> is better!

Then too some of its publicity stunts are, to say the least, ambiguous—for instance, releasing red ballons bearing the inscription "BAISER" (which means both "kiss" and "fuck"). Certain of the songs sung in this play are anything but faithful to the mood of Hollywood musicals. The director's first secretary, for example, sings of being the bitch that follows the guard dog, that protects the master . . . "The bitch that does its tricks for a lump of sugar/And opens its thighs for less than that." Meanwhile, in the second act, Hector's conduct at first is unexceptionable. His timidity in the company of a secretary to whom he feels attracted is in the best musical comedy tradition. Yet without warning he displays unexpected boldness. He takes such liberties with Hélène as to make her scream loudly enough to bring the other secretaries on stage, singing, miming, and dancing. The director, Hector, and his victim all join in the song-and-dance number.

Homosexual overtones are discernible in *Hara Kiri*, where the director points out that 71.6 percent of his employees are women, since "With the enjoyable I include the useful and vice versa." In *Le Vaisseau amiral* the King and the Admiral admire the physical attractions of the latter's Page, set off to advantage as he searches on all fours for the lost collar stud. Without reluctance, the Admiral confesses that his relations with the boy have a sexual aspect ("Oh yes in the early morning when he brings me/My coffee and my crescent rolls then"). The King's comment that there are one or two among the ladies of the Court who could accommodate the Admiral just as well elicits the reply, "Are you kidding there are at least it can't/Be boring for you a good twenty of them if anyway I don't."

One could go on, to consider perhaps the conversation between the Admiral and the little girl who remarks matter-of-factly that she allowed herself to be deflowered by the Page "because he is the prettiest of my brothers." But the role of vulgarity and erotic preoccupation, spiced with humor, is clear enough by now. Pierre uses these elements in every one of his plays, but never to stimulate the audience's interest in dramatic action. Use of scatological elements for their own sake would have been a betrayal of the spirit of surrealism as Breton understood it. If therefore they appear in the work of José Pierre, it is as a symptom of his ambition to divert the theatre from familiar paths. Seeking to close the door on generally accepted theatrical forms, he wishes to point to the necessity for opening a different door altogether, one previously kept closed. In other words, we do not have his true purpose in sight so long as we imagine Pierre to be concerned with the overt development of sexual themes, exploited for their shock value. Another look at the Admiral's words, reproduced above for the second time, will show better what is involved here.

Now that we can see where these words belong, we appreciate better than before how Pierre turns dialogue to account. Knowing the circumstances under which the Admiral delivers lines that seemed impenetrable earlier allows us to ascribe a precise meaning to them. But this is at the same time a limited meaning, imposed by the reader "making sense" of the words consigned to the printed page, yet resisted when the actor impersonating the Admiral recites them with unnatural emphasis and without regard for the limitations that, rationally speaking, give meaning to what he says. These are limitations imposed by something we have called, for want of a better designation, the plot of *Le Vaisseau amiral*.

Now we are able to grasp what Pierre had in mind when intimating that use of unpunctuated verse in his play was designed to make it almost impossible to read. To the author, the Admiral's reply when the King makes an explicit allusion to the sexual proclivities of certain ladies of the Court is imaginatively stimulating for the following reason. The former's response does not depend for justification or interpretation upon its place in some reasonable sequence of conversational exchange. The playwright's anti-conventional approach expresses a plea for theatrical liberation. Just as the King and the Admiral opt for an invisible but present navy, so Pierre elects to offer for our enjoyment a drama concealed behind the action on stage and behind the dialogue we hear between the actors before us.

When he denies knowing what *Le Vaisseau amiral* means, he gives fair warning that, whatever its significance, this cannot be circumscribed by the plot of his play. In this case, plot is no more than an excuse for setting down on paper words for which a special function is foreseen. Their function is not at all informational, since essentially the drama serves as a focal point for imaginative flights over which the dramatists takes precautions (leaving it to his actors to work out their own unnatural diction, for instance) to avoid exercising close control. José Pierre's ambition is fairly summarized in his own phrase: "constriction leading to enlargement."

Because he does not rely upon plot to give purpose to his drama, Pierre can find in a man's search for his lost collar stud as good a starting point as any for *Le Vaisseau amiral*. It is not where the play begins, he gives us to understand, but where it may lead that matters to him. On one level, to be sure, loss of the stud assumes easily recognizable meaning. The Admiral associates it with losing his dignity and with the degradation of being deprived of his command. No sooner has he embraced the Lady-who-has-lived than, raising his hand to his collar, he exclaims in wonderment, "My my my collar stud/ By what miracle madam is this dignity restored to me.'" The Lady replies cryptically, "Bah a woman who has lived has more than one trick up her sleeve." A more direct explanation comes from the words uttered a moment earlier by the King, questioning whether the Admiral, that "man without dignity," can find the strength to experience an erection. Some readers and spectators will be content to settle for an explanation that conforms to their interpretation of *Le Vaisseau amiral* as having been written to do no more than challenge good taste with vulgarity. They will be less sensitive than they should be, therefore, to one feature of the closing scene to which Pierre's aims lend special value.

Whereas all the scene titles provided so far have been descriptive in a manner that can easily be related to the themes they summarize, the one used for the closing section of Pierre's first drama is allusive: "The Trojan Horse." While the King and the Admiral are telling the Lady-who-has-lived why they love her, the Portugese take the city, some of their troops even appearing fleetingly on stage. Then, as the Lady reaches orgasm, lying between the King and the Admiral on the darkened stage, the backdrop opens. We see the flagship, all its lights burning. Its siren continues to blare, louder now that ever before, until not a single spectator remains in the auditorium.

When, earlier on, we heard the Admiral ask, "Why does this ship which no longer belongs to me / Continue to call me," accompanying stage directions revealed that he was to speak "as if in a dream." There was some reason, then, for dismissing his question without giving much consideration to its possible bearing upon the drama. But now, after we have heard its distress call throughout the play, the flagship appears before us. It is no longer permissible to treat the ship as present only in the Admiral's dreams. José Pierre comments as follows on its apparition: "As for the final vision of the flagship, which must extend if possible right across the back of the stage, it can be obtained equally well by *trompe l'œil* techniques or by cinematographic projection (cinemascope in color preferably), so long as its appearance at night can be preserved (a vessel foundering in the dark with all its lights burning) at the same time menacing and spectral. [. . .] The impression to be given is that the Flagship, announced by its pictorial representation, is itself coming on stage" (pp. 21–22). Full realization of the effect sought at this moment may well seem open to question. All the same, the ambition inspiring these notes cannot be ignored. Imposing itself upon our attention by means of the siren's recurrent wail, the inexplicable presides over *Le Vaisseau amiral*. Finally the flagship irrupts like the Trojan Horse, demolishing the barrier between the visible and the hitherto invisible. The effect is analogous to the one used at the end of *Le Dernier Métro* (*The Last Subway*), where an invisible train passes by, to the accompaniment of all the racket a real one would make.

Fundamental to *Le Vaisseau amiral* is the question of the playwright's responsibility to his public. By the criteria audiences are accustomed to see respected when attending a theatrical production, José Pierre seems to act irresponsibly. He brings on stage a few characters whose reasons for carrying on a conversation appear quite trivial. Their behavior lacks the air of purpose that would command attention and inspire interest. They cease altogether to convince us as we come to understand that it is not on the level of reason that we are supposed to listen to everything we hear. Only now can we appreciate that, by his own standards, Pierre is indeed fulfilling his obligations. He meets the responsibilities he has accepted, when setting about writing for the theatre, by undertaking to persuade his public that the purpose of drama is something more than to communicate merely what passes between people on stage in the form of rational dialogue. Instead, he bids us notice, drama as he conceives it becomes meaningful from the

moment when reason has proved ineffectual in delimiting its significance and the anti-reasonable has taken over.

Turning from *Le Vaisseau amiral* to *Bonjour Mon Œil*, we find a
noteworthy consistency in approach to dramatic presentation. As with
the former, José Pierre warns us that, writing the latter, he was not
responsible in the conventional sense. Agreement between two people,
he argues, rests upon "approximations" most of the time. "Therefore
I am going to undertake without too much hope (or despair either) to
cast as much light as I can on this play of which it seems that I am the
author (and what if it were the play that had written me?) . . ." (p.
81). Here, as in several other passages of his introductory notes, Pierre
adopts a light tone. This momentarily conceals how serious are his purposes in the theatre. Prefacing *Hara Kiri*, though, he remarks more directly, "It is to the honor of artists and writers worthy of the name to
be in fact always on the opposite side, even when power has become
revolutionary, never to accept anything as definitive, as revealed truth,
consecrated and henceforth immutable" (p. 187). Essentially, his aim is
to disorient his public without imposing upon them a new direction of
his own choosing; without, that is, imposing upon their response to his
dramas the restrictions that too precise a plan would entail. On the
face of it, then, *Bonjour Mon Œil* departs from the standards met in
Le Vaisseau amiral and *Hara Kiri*. And yet, significantly, Pierre does
not resolve the conflict between didactic intent and a mode of presentation that resists the communication of a rationally intelligible plot.
Thus he leaves himself open to charges of ambiguity. These in turn
seem to give grounds for objecting to his methods, until we grasp that
Pierre finds in ambiguity the condition that makes writing for the stage
appealing to him.

He tells us how one morning in 1968 he woke up to a magnificent
erection and to the thought, "Consumer society must be challenged"
(p. 182). He was prompted to attack publicity, he says, by the hand-
written commentaries (some ironical, some indecent) to be seen on advertising posters in the subway near his home. "But I should like also
not to hide my fundamental ambiguity on this point. Not only do I
appreciate how well founded are the demystifying commentaries by
which certain young people try to undermine the smug and sheeplike
habits of our contemporaries, but I have more than once admired their
percussive quality. [. . .] and yet I have come to wonder whether I
was not attracted above all to turning the weapons of publicity back

against the profit-motivated society that uses them, in a word to the publicity value of this 'counter-publicity' " (p. 182).

Just as the theme of *Hara Kiri* reflects an ambiguous approach to advertising techniques, so it betokens ambiguity in its author's feelings about musical comedy. Pierre speaks of appreciating "the marvelous stupidity" of the operetta form and of "the genre's possibilities for making people idiotic" (p. 189). He states categorically, "For I do not think, comedy in the boulevard theatre excepted, [. . .] that there exists a more adulterated, more mystifying, more demobilizing genre (I don't mince words, *I* don't!), in short a genre more likely to drown the everyday aspects of the class struggle than musical comedy (Phew!). Especially when, like me, one refers to the Hollywood version of musical comedy [. . .], in which counter-revolutionary noxiousness is multiplied by the disembraining mechanism of the American cinema, Yankee capitalism's instrument of dissemination number one, etc" (p. 186). In spite of this statement, he dedicates *Hara Kiri* to a Hollywood musical star and assures us, "there is on my part no irony (very much to the contrary) with respect to the musical comedy 'genre,' to which I owe those rare moments of pleasure which include *Cover Girl* and *Singing on* [sic] *the Rain*" (p. 190). Referring with characteristic discretion to "the joy I expect from my 'musical comedy' [. . .], despite its tragic aspects" (pp. 189–90), Pierre declares, "Writing *Hara Kiri or The Laws of Advertising*, I at no time had any pretension to creating a revolutionary work, but rather to questioning in myself that ambiguity to which I have admitted for a long time" (p. 187).

By José Pierre's own admission, his ambiguous attitude toward advertising accounts for the "bizarre attitude" of the hero of *Hara Kiri*. Hector enters publicity "as one used to enter the Church and he dies as a result of it. He dies perhaps because advertising is, perhaps, a slut, like the one (perhaps) who opens her bed to him. [. . .] You might say that his death is to be taken in fun. Yes, but only because every death, in the theatre, so long as it has not been decided that (as in old films) real bullets, real daggers, and real sabres will be used, is to be taken in fun" (p. 185).

What he has told us so far explains why, of the three plays in his *Théâtre*, Pierre regards *Hara Kiri* as "the most Brechtian." He alludes to "that ambiguity of Brecht's with respect to the theatre" and to "that mixture or rather that alternation of fascination and distrust which brings him sometimes so close to me" (p. 188). Yet even here the principle of ambiguity asserts itself as, remarking how much it pleases him to be expressing interest in Brecht three or four years after it was fashionable to do so, Pierre continues, "But, thinking it over, I wonder if (contrary to what Marx claimed to do with Hegel) I am not standing Brecht on his head, stroking him (big tomcat, veteran of the rooftops!) the wrong way." Typically, he poses a rhetorical question to which his reply is less than satisfactory: "But what is it that really triumphs here: theatre or advertising? Both, perhaps, as should be the case when cultural forms and cultural content are in agreement about keeping man in consumer society chained by his alienation. (Eh, what do you say to that? that's the stuff to give 'em, right?)" (p. 186).

It is in *Hara Kiri* no doubt that one is most readily made conscious of the influence of ambiguity upon the subject matter of a Pierre play and upon the impression it must communicate. And yet ambiguity is fundamental to drama as he conceives it. The contrast between the words meant to be sung in *Bonjour Mon Œil* and those that are to be recited may be plain enough for a reader examining the text rationally to grasp. He can be expected to detect a conflict between indoctrinated beliefs and liberative impulses. All the same, the dramatist's opposition to "natural" delivery of dialogue in his dramas makes it far more difficult for spectators to remain uniformly responsive to such a contrast and alert at all times to the conflict it signals. Should one say then that the playwright courts disaster? One might do so, if being ambiguous made *Bonjour Mon Œil* an exception among Pierre's writings for the stage. However, in the dialogue of *Le Vaisseau amiral* too Pierre shows himself quite content to let general meaning struggle for clear expression against unfair odds for which he is unquestionably accountable. He consistently demonstrates that, however much space his prefaces give to its discussion, manifest content in his theatre will never take better than second place to latent content. Meanwhile Pierre has no definite preconception of the latter. He leaves it to ambiguity to solicit the precipitation of unforeseen latent content, as he uses a mode of dramatic expression in which, consequently, ambiguous elements are no more a sign of technical ineptitude than they are signs of an impulse to emulate Brecht uncritically. In the work of this writer in whom, prefacing his *D'Autres Chats à fouetter*, a fellow surrealist, Robert Benayoun, has saluted "a perfidious but efficacious form of sabotage," in this co-organizer with André Breton of an international surrealist exhibition designed to stress surrealism's *écart absolu,* ambiguity is the principal claim made upon the attention of all who are sensitive to surrealism's ambitions in the theatre.

Jean-Jacques Auquier and Alain-Valery Aelberts

To renew fire. To provoke, salute
the *raw event*—the place *par excellence* of the theatre. At the very
root of everything that gives us a
reason to live.[1]

IN THE LAST THIRD of the twentieth century, the unperformable plays
of Robert Benayoun and Jean-Claude Barbé, together with the writings in dramatized form of Jean-Pierre Duprey, point to one line of
development that appears open to surrealism in relation to the theatre.
The theatrical work of José Pierre represents quite a different view of
drama. Composing his plays, Pierre takes into account and looks hope-
fully to the eventual participation of director, designer, and especially
actors, on whose cooperation he relies to bring to his work a dimension
on stage that it cannot have for those making contact with it only
through a reading of the text. He looks to theatre professionals to make
a contribution—all the more welcome for being in some respects un-
intentional—to the achievement of objectives that can be estimated best
by someone like himself, for whom theatre is not an end but one of
several pathways that may lead to the attainment of surrealist ideals. In
this regard, he comes to the theatre in a significantly expectant frame
of mind, comparable with that which led Alain-Valery Aelberts and
Jean-Jacques Auquier to write together *Cérémonial pour saluer d'Eruption en Eruption jusqu'à l'infracassable Nuit la Brèche absolue et la
Trajectoire du Marquis de Sade (Ceremonial to Acclaim from Erup-*

---

1. Alain-Valery Aelberts and Jean-Jacques Auquier, introduction to *Cérémonial
pour saluer d'Eruption en Eruption jusqu'à l'infracassable Nuit la Brèche absolue
et la Trajectorie du Marquis de Sade* (Brussels: privately printed, 1970), p. 21.

tion to Eruption into Unshatterable Night the Absolute Breach and Trajectory of the Marquis de Sade).[2]

The contrast is sharp between, on the one hand, the vagueness in matters pertaining to decor that we find in Duprey or the absurdities used by Benayoun to mock conventional stage setting and, on the other, the meticulous precision observable in a brief scenario, *Ra ma Chène*, that we owe to Auquier.[3] Whereas in their dramatized texts Duprey and Benayoun disdain involvement with questions of staging, Auquier carefully insists upon these. Nevertheless, in one way at least, the effect ultimately sought is the same. Like the other two, Auquier makes abundantly clear how little interest he has in communicating with us on the purely reasonable plane. He appears in fact to have taken care to eliminate means by which playwrights traditionally have made contact with their audiences. All the same, in his scenario he does not aim to appeal solely to a reader's imagination. Auquier wants to confront a public assembled to see his play performed with a visually compelling spectacle. For this reason, only staging can be expected to give *Ra ma Chène* its full impact. As is the case with José Pierre, we have to begin with Auquier by recognizing that he opposes any compromise with the inherited view of theatre, just as he is against submitting expression of surrealist ambitions to the familiar usages of his chosen medium. But at the same time, he looks to staging to play a part in transmitting a viewpoint to which surrealism lends significance. As he does so, he weighs the possibilities for bending the medium of theatre to surrealist demands, seeking to exploit those possibilities to best advantage.

Hung with black draperies, the stage is in semidarkness for the opening of *Ra ma Chène*. To the left, three people are seated at a circular table over which has been thrown a black cloth reaching to the floor. Each has his hands flat on the table and is staring at a skull placed between them. To the right of center stage, a coffin rests on two chairs. Behind the coffin's raised lid sits a man in dark clothing, invisible

---

2. This scenario was written between September and October 1968. It was dedicated to the Living Theatre and specifically to Judith Malina and Julian Beck. A revised version of the text was made in February 1969. The introduction to the version published in June 1970 marks certain departures from that prepared in 1969. The published version carries a preface by Henri Pastoureau and a poem by Gilbert Lely, to whom the scenario is now dedicated.

3. Jean-Jacques Auquier, *Ra ma Chène*, suivi de *La Mort plurielle* par Alain-Valery Aelberts (Brussels: privately printed, 1971).

but for his legs. The Airia from Bach's third Suite in D is audible as the man's white-gloved hands can be seen moving back and forth along the top edge of the coffin lid. The man speaks:

> You: the child-woman. Triumph of womankind.
> Anima,
> Conception,
> Fecundity,
> Lyricism,
> Poetry,
> Eroticism.
> You: another Yin-Yang, between Beryl and Ruby.
> Venus in the Lion.
> And me! Mercury lay in wait for *me* at the third dwelling.

Now he shouts, "Incest, beautiful as rape, spread throughout the sky." As he pronounces the word "incest," his legs begin to shake uncontrollably and his hands clench, ceasing to move across the raised lid. After the word "sky," he gives a raucous harrowing cry. We hear the music again, soon dominated by a woman's cry, more piercing and more harrowing than the man's. In altered tone, the man says, "After you womankind comes to an end." Having brushed the three skulls off the table with an identical gesture of the right hand, the characters seated stage left leave without a word. Meanwhile the man has slammed the coffin shut. His face is now visible, but his features are indistinguishable in the gloom that shortly gives way to almost complete darkness.

Like the regulation of every movement, the care taken in *Ra ma Chène* to control each visual and auditory effect is indicative of something quite different from respect for the customs dear to writers of realistic or symbolic drama. Everything Auquier prescribes contributes to deepening enigma, not to explaining what lies behind it. Essentially, his scenario exploits the theatre's potential for disorienting spectators, for submitting them to an imaginatively liberative experience over which reason is allowed to exercise no retarding influence. Although certain features of a conventional kind may hold our attention first, in this scenario—the use of skulls and coffin—they are not permitted to direct the play along the familiar channels with which the eye finds it natural to associate them. Where movement accompanies speech—the word "incest" inducing a trembling of the legs—the relationship between these two basic characteristics of dramatic presentation is not of a rational nature. It is one that cannot be interpreted with assistance either from everyday experience or from theatrical tradition, or even from common-sense speculation. From one end of *Ra ma Chène* to the other, the appeal Auquier makes to the eye and to the ear consistently calls for responsiveness to suggestion beyond the range of reason. This turns the theatre into something other than the place where the habitual or the representative is rehearsed. The stage now becomes the privileged locale where enticing hints at the unprecedented solicit and hold attention.

The modest proportions of Auquier's scenario could easily induce readers to give his project for the theatre less than its due, were it not apparent to anyone who turns to *Cérémonial pour . . . Sade* that, in the latter, Aelberts has joined Auquier in building upon certain fundamental principles laid down in *Ra ma Chène*. At the same time, publication of their *Cérémonial*, accompanied by an introduction, makes available to the public at large certain notes that give these principles clearer definition.

Radovan Ivsic found encouragement in Sade's *Aline et Valcour* to develop the central character of *Le Roi Gordogane* into a monster of superhuman proportions. A quarter of a century later, Aelberts and Auquier approach the Marquis somewhat differently. To them Sade is not just a man whose published writings constitute a rich source of invented characters. Like Ivsic, they are deeply impressed by the moral disorders that find illustration in these writings and wish to paint a faithful picture of them. However, they are no less responsive to evidence of such disorders in Sade's own conduct. Hence in *Cérémonial* they celebrate the life as well as the work of a thinker whose opposition to the moral and legal code of his day earned him twenty-eight years' incarceration in several prisons. They do not forget to incorporate into their text details of the Arcueil Affair that brought the Marquis to trial and condemnation for behavior foreshadowing that of his memorable heroes and heroines. In *Cérémonial pour . . . Sade* they aim at "a more intensely lived experience" (p. 20) through fidelity to Sade's life and writings. Hence their drama remains true to the spirit of *Ra ma Chène*, where the provocative word "incest" rings out and Auquier juxtaposes poetry and eroticism.

From its very first sentence, the introduction to *Cérémonial* treats Sade in the perspective all surrealists favor: "The phosphoric shadow of Sade takes possession of us like the night, bearing smiles, which encloses all crimes: irreducible, *mad love*" (p. 19). Aelberts and Auquier go on to praise "the incandescent language alchemy" of Sade's writings. Doing this, they lead us straight toward what appears at first paradoxical in their undertaking. The high esteem in which they hold Sade is beyond debate, of course. But so is their contempt for contemporary theatre, with which they associate mainly boredom and escapism, and where they are sensitive above all to an ambition to please "the fossilized flock." How then through the medium of theatre can they aspire to pay tribute fittingly to the author of *Les 120 Journées de Sodome?* More quickly than from reading the definitive version, we find an answer to this question in the 1969 typescript of their introduction. Here, noting that Louis Jouvet was a contemporary of Antonin Artaud's, Auquier and Aelberts condemn the former for declaring nevertheless that the essential thing in theatre is a text to be communicated by spoken words. "Odious," is their judgment upon this contention.

Aelberts and Auquier speak of their dramatization of Sade's life and works as "a first *attempt*." Commenting upon the effort they have kept in sight, they explain, "Our subject matter is *divergence*" (p. 20),[4] and continue, "We have tried only to create a certain degree of condensation of everything that, in the vast devouring Night of Sade, seems to us to constitute the warp and woof of life, of cruelty according to Artaud" (p. 21).

Originally *Cérémonial pour . . . Sade* was intended for presentation by the Pracina-Théâtre in Brussels. No mention of this occurs in the published version of the play. Yet we are hardly likely to fall into the error of concluding that Auquier and Aelberts reserve their text for reading only. Any doubt remaining after they have referred to Artaud and his Theatre of Cruelty is dissipated in their next paragraph beginning, "The text you are going to read must always be envisaged

4. In the final version, this sentence runs, "Notre propos est un propos d'*écart*." In the 1969 typescript, the last phrase is prolonged: "even if as absolute it cannot be justified." Evidently, the authors eventually decided that their reference to *L'Ecart absolu* would be too obscure for most readers to grasp. Incidentally, Aelberts and Auquier use the word *brèche* in the full title of their *Cérémonial. La Brèche* is the title of the French surrealist magazine of which Breton was editor between October 1961 and November 1965.

from the point of view of its representation on the stage—its primary destination" (p. 21). The authors inform us that allusions to action and even choreography have been kept as brief as possible. All the same, the difficulty facing the reader, who must represent their ceremonial mentally, has not escaped their notice. Numerous references incorporated into the text are designed to help evoke the mental images Aelberts and Auquier would like to generate. Everyone must understand, therefore, that such indications as *Cérémonial pour . . . Sade* provides exist only as points of reference. For example, the authors mention the costume devised by Jean Benoît in 1958 for his Execution of the Will of the Marquis de Sade,[5] but merely, they insist, to "indicate more clearly to which axis we refer." There can be no question of imitation, though: "It is absolutely not our intention to do over again what has been done. When we give a description of the dummy representing Madame de Mistival in tableau two, it would be inappropriate to show on stage a faithful copy of the ardent shrine by Adrien Dax from which it seems to derive. The latter is simply the support, the imagination's point of departure for representing this object."

Auquier and Aelberts are open to a contribution from imagination that can take either of two forms. They seek to promote active imaginative participation from the reader, as he watches their play enacted in the privacy of his own mind. At the same time, foreseeing adaptation of their text at the hands of a stage director, they gladly afford the latter the opportunity to transpose their drama to the theatre in a manner that will be productively imaginative. Ideally, the play Aelberts and Auquier project will take into account "the free and deliberate exercise of the imaginary *Book* that is in us all," just as much as it does "the director's gesture" (p. 21).

All this might be dismissed as presenting no novelty, as, in fact, a necessary condition to which every playwright must submit when he makes available to the professional and nonprofessional public a written text over which he ceases to have control, once it passes from his hands. In the case of *Cérémonial pour . . . Sade*, what is interesting is this. Auquier and Aelberts embark upon a theatrical endeavor resting upon unwillingness to leave anything to accident (they mention

5. See Alain Jouffroy, "Un acte surréaliste: L'Exécution du Testament de Sade," *Arts*, No. 754, December 23–29, 1959; J. H. Matthews, "The Right Person for Surrealism," *Yale French Studies*, No. 35 (December 1965), 'The House of Sade,' pp. 89–95.

Benoît's costume, devised to honor Sade, of which photographic records exist) and yet appealing at the same time to chance (they decline to authorize reproduction of that costume).[6] We are alerted to their intentions by a quotation extracted from Raymond Roussel's novel *Locus Solus*, which precedes the introduction to their *Cérémonial:* ". . . to oblige the dice to fall just right." The value they attach to this preliminary citation can be estimated from the fact that, absent from the 1969 typescript, it figures in the definitive text. Here it publicizes the dramatists' willingness to benefit, as José Pierre was prepared to do, even if in a somewhat different fashion, from whatever the process of staging may bring to the spectacle they have devised.

Leaving imaginative play enough freedom to enrich their text, while yet imposing upon it sufficient control to "oblige the dice to fall just right," Auquier and Aelberts are sensitive to the need for a fresh approach to certain aspects of theatrical spectacle that hold their interest above all: "It is the cry that needs to be reinvented, and movement, color, costume . . . within the original perimeter of incorruptible significations from which they cannot be cut off without by this very action being abolished" (pp. 19–20). They show their approval of Stéphane Mallarmé's argument, in *Crayonné au Théâtre*, that "a dancer *is not a woman dancing* . . . but a metaphor summing up one of the elementary aspects of our form, sword, bowl, flower, etc.," and that her performance suggests "writing with the body," which it would take paragraphs of dialogue or descriptive prose to render: "a poem freed of the apparatus of the scribe." Using dance in *Cérémonial pour . . . Sade*, Aelberts and Auquier give us to understand, they look to *l'écriture corporelle*, as Mallarmé spoke of it, to assume responsibility for transmitting poetry "on the level of remembered dreams." In other words, dance here is entrusted with the subversive role of communicating "the sovereign resurgence of all desires." As they make use of it, Auquier and Aelberts show themselves to be in agreement with Henri Pastoureau, who defines dance as "a coupling that is at the same time a ceremony."[7]

In their 1969 typescript, Auquier and Aelberts group together a

6. It should be noted that some modification takes place in the authors' thinking about their play. In the 1969 typescript, where a careful description of Benoît's costume appears in an appendix, Auquier and Aelberts insist that not a single detail may be changed.
7. See Henri Pastoureau, "Léxigraphie préalable," in *Cérémonial pour . . . Sade*, p. 16.

whole series of "preliminary remarks which it is essential to read," yet which they do not make accessible to readers of the published text of their *Cérémonial*. These notes include a section entitled "On the choreography," where the authors address themselves indirectly to the man who may eventually stage their play, warning him to bear in mind something Jean Genet wrote to Roger Blin, who put on his *Les Paravents:* "You must therefore lure the actors down into the most secret depths of their being . . . make them accept difficult procedures, admirable gestures that are unrelated to those they make in their own lives. If we oppose life and the stage, this is because we sense that the stage is a place neighboring death, where all liberties are possible." Taking the opportunity to stress how much importance they attach to Genet since Artaud's death—"the only poet in France to suspect what the theatre really can be, ceremonial and festival. The only one to whom we grant full licence to speak of it"—Aelberts and Auquier continue, "The body movements, the alphabet of gestures should be capable of reinvention each time in relation to the actors available." Then they call significantly for reflection upon their motives in leaving choreographic descriptions vague, and in "consenting deliberately before the void."

Among the preliminary remarks set down in 1969 is a section called "On the nature of the spectacle." Here Auquier and Aelberts admit that they are, at best, self-taught musicians. They could therefore not assume responsibility for writing music for their play, despite having thought more than once of doing so. "Hence," they explain, "the ambiguity, to a slight degree, of this scenario which tends toward theatre in the more or less traditional sense of the word, and toward one of the possible forms of modern opera (see, for example, Berio's *Laborintus*) [. . .]." Recalling that Michel Butor ("Opera, that is to say theatre") has equated theatre with opera, Aelberts and Auquier proceed to suggest that ambiguity in their *Cérémonial* may be attributed to his equation. They go on to remark that "this spectacle can be taken just as well in the direction of 'opera' if circumstances permit." Seen in the perspective of opera, therefore, "the sequences where no mention is made of music would have to be considered as so many empty or open spaces—a sort of nonwritten music, blank music [as we speak of a blank check]. To occupy these desert (but not deserted) spaces would be the task of the composer who *eventually* . . ."

Under the heading "On the music," the authors' notes explain that the composers and musical selections mentioned now and again in their text are simply those that came to mind as they wrote. A composer taking up *Cérémonial pour . . . Sade* would replace the authors' musical associations with a score that would be "perfectly rigorous and coherent." Only in exceptional cases, where choices indicated in the text "constitute veritable musical quotations," would these be "scrupulously respected." Once again Aelberts and Auquier reserve the right to direct response as they feel it appropriate, while yet adding, characteristically, "This said, imagination can be let loose."

The place reserved for music and dance in *Cérémonial pour . . . Sade* is a sign that Auquier and Aelberts do not deviate from their judgment condemning Jouvet's idea of theatre. It is as though they have elected to take as their motto a phrase extracted from Mallarmé's *Crayonné au Théâtre*: "a difference . . . Absolute." Crediting Mallarmé, before Edward Gordon Craig, Artaud, and Genet, with realizing that here lies the essence of theatre, Aelberts and Auquier give his plea for theatrical renewal an interpretation all their own, when they identify renewal with "some act sufficiently . . . *redoubtable*" (p. 19). What more redoubtable act could they commit, their undertaking implies, than confronting audiences with the message left to posterity by the author of *Juliette ou Les Prospérités du Vice?*

The purpose in view throughout *Cérémonial pour . . . Sade* is immersion of the audience in an atmosphere that is quite unique. If we are to evaluate the significance of the authors' intervention in the theatre, we have to consider the methods by which they believe their purpose can be served best.

As soon as one opens the text of *Cérémonial* it is obvious that Aelberts and Auquier share Breton's admiration for Sade's "deliberate transgression of the real and the plausible" and approve his use of "the phantasmagoria and terror of childhood." It is true they do not reproduce these phrases from Breton's *Anthologie de l'Humour noir* (p. 53). But the way their tribute to Sade is conceived testifies to agreement with Breton, whose comments are endorsed by the treatment they give their subject.

Ivsic followed Sade's example in giving the behavior of his monstrous central figure in *Le Roi Gordogane* a humorous aspect to which

Breton has shown that surrealists are particularly sensitive. Aelberts and Auquier, though, exclude humor and paint a portrait characterized by the sombre tones imposed by their view of drama as a *rite*. Operating to the disadvantage of humor and in favor of gravity, selectivity in *Cérémonial* points up the nature of the project to which Auquier and Aelberts devote themselves. At the expense of diversity, they seek to present a unified impression of Sade's achievement, offering this as exemplary.

Cérémonial pour . . . Sade is divided into tableaux. The authors' intention is not to separate their play into clear-cut segments, we read in their 1969 typescript, but to supply "a very discreet punctuation (a way of breathing, one might say)." In consequence, there is always the possibility that two tableaux may run one into the other. Above all, Auquier and Aelberts stress, there is never to be any hiatus, any interruption, however brief; "this is to say that no kind of intermission will be tolerated." Hence, once raised, the curtain never falls again until the show is over and no one remains in the auditorium.

The use of filters is to be avoided in *Cérémonial* so that there will be no variation in lighting from one tableau to another. Meanwhile the same white backdrop serves throughout. Thus the impression of continuity is enhanced. Sade's life and work are placed on the same plane of revolutionary affirmation. During the prologue the backdrop provides a convenient screen upon which a number of slides depicting sexual perversion are projected, to the accompaniment of a musical prelude (Ligeti and Berio are the composers specified). First we see stills from Luis Buñuel's films *Un Chien andalou* and *L'Age d'Or*, graphic works by Hans Bellmer, etc. Then Aelberts and Auquier pay tribute to Marcel Duchamp by showing a slide of his *La Mariée mise à nu par ses Célibataires, même*. When the music ends, we hear, "In nomine patris et filii et spiritus sancti," as the prologue comes to a close.

Now a Gregorian chant is audible while the lights come up very slowly to reveal, at the back of the stage and to the left, a sort of catafalque draped in black. In the foreground, to the right, a young girl in orange tights occupies a foetal position. She appears bald. Their backs to the audience, seeming at first to be cone-shaped inert objects, crouch several figures we take to be nuns. The light intensifies and they begin to move toward the catafalque, first slowly then more convulsively. The gloria fades away. A voice can be heard reading an extract from one of Sade's letters to his wife, beginning, "Yes, I am a libertine, I admit; I have conceived everything that can be conceived in that respect. But I certainly did not do all that I conceived, and certainly will never do so. I am a libertine but I am not a *criminal* or a *murderer*. . . ."[8] By the time the reading is over the nuns have reached the catafalque, have thrown off their outer garments, and are now recognizable as young men. Removing the cloth draping the catafalque, they uncover "a sort of metallic structure in the form of a reclining woman, dressed in a rudimentary costume." Studded with red-tipped needles, this structure is large enough for the actors to enter, as they do when Tableau 1 gives way to Tableau 2, showing the men executing a long series of body movements and gestures within the *woman-structure*. Two men bring on a large old packing-case around which everyone gathers.

The case is opened to reveal baroque ornamentation on the inside of its lid and two sides. When the front drops forward, several cushions can be seen. A number of actors install themselves upon these to enact a scene made up of passages taken from Sade's dialogued *La Philosophie dans le Boudoir*.[9] For this scene, the role of Eugénie, a fifteen-year-old girl who is to be perverted by moral re-education, falls to the *foetus-woman*. The young woman who proposes to take Eugénie's instruction in hand, Madame de Saint-Ange, is impersonated by an actress who was enclosed in the packing-case when it arrived on stage. Madame de Mistival, Eugénie's virtuous and pious mother, appears only at the end of the scene. She is represented by a dummy brought out, when needed, from behind the case by Mirvil, Madame de Saint-Ange's profligate brother. The dummy is described as consisting of a bust mounted upon a nondescript filiform structure, its face and torso covered with votive medals, devotional articles, and candles that have dripped wax.

At the very beginning of *La Philosophie dans le Boudoir*, Sade's ironically named heroine (Saint-Ange means Holy Angel) describes herself as "born for libertinage." She confides in her brother, "the more I ought to be reasonable, the more my damned head becomes inflamed and libertine" (p. 371). From one end to the other of *La*

8. The letter in question, which Sade called "Ma Grande Lettre," was written on February 20, 1781, while he was imprisoned in Vincennes. See Sade, *Œuvres complètes*, Vol. XII (1967), *Correspondance*, pp. 264–778. The quotations used by Aelberts and Auquier are taken from pp. 276–78.

9. The scene incorporates material taken from pp. 375–76, 392, 394, 401, 536–39, and 427 of *La Philosophie dans le Boudoir*, in *Œuvres complètes*, Vol. III (1966).

Philosophie dans le Boudoir conduct satisfying needs and bringing pleasures that only the imagination of a libertine could conceive is identified, in this way, with the overthrow of reason's restraints. This is why, in the context of theatrical innovation to which Auquier and Aelberts are dedicated, their first borrowing from the novelistic universe animated by Sade's imagination is especially revealing. At once it sets their drama in a perspective that eliminates concern for realistic convention, as it lays the foundation for a close parallel in *Cérémonial pour . . . Sade* between, on the one side, opposition to conventional social and moral precepts and, on the other, reason's authority. When Eugénie, rejecting her mother's appeal to return to the life of virtue she has known, shows her buttocks to the sodomite Dolmancé, the lights are extinguished and we hear "a polyphony made up of cries, groans of pleasure, panting, and curses." The packing-case is closed again and the *foetus-woman* resumes her original posture. From off stage comes a voice leaving no doubt that Dolmancé is enjoying Eugénie. As he glories coarsely in ejaculation, the first notes of Handel's Hallelujah Chorus are heard.

Words have pride of place in the second tableau. In the third they give way to movement. While some of the actors dance, others ceremoniously come to center stage bearing a construction called *phallic-object*, surmounted by an enormous flower. The object once in place, everyone joins in "a dance of ritual homage." This serves to link the scene utilizing elements from *La Philosophie dans le Boudoir* with Tableau 4. The latter gives us "a poetized account" of the Arcueil Affair, punctuated by the recurrent phrase, "This is orgasm"—

> ROSE KELLER
> He told me it was to tidy his room.
>
> SADE
> I gave her to understand that it was for a libertinage party.

From halfway through the tableau, the dialogue is accompanied by "a vocal polyphony" described as "very ceremonious." Meanwhile the dialogue is entrusted to actors who, as though sacrificing their individuality, gather together "so as to take on the value of a chorus." The effect desired is obviously an orchestration of statements, incomplete phrases, incomprehensible words, and cries, all culminating in "a long vocalic poem on the word ORGASM," delivered by Sade, Rose Keller, the Announcer, and a man impersonating the Law.

Tableau 4 solicits attention on the auditory plane only. Initially, the appeal of the next tableau is exclusively visual. Those on stage are joined by actors who have been off since Tableau 3. To begin with, all dance "to paroxysm." Then, with a ceremonious gesture that Aelberts and Auquier liken to that by which banderillas are implanted during bullfights, one of the actors withdraws two needles from the *woman-structure*. He uses these to pierce the flower at the tip of the *phallic-object*, releasing first a spurt of red liquid then of black. Only now do sounds begin to impinge upon our notice, as perforation of the flower sets off "sorts of liquescent cries" from the other actors. The people on stage move about in slow motion while a voice off reads a typical paragraph from *Les 120 Journées de Sodome*. Its effect, apparently, is to throw everyone into a frenzy—the *woman-structure* is destroyed. After a moment's darkness, the stage appears bare. We hear a second paragraph from *Les 120 Journées de Sodome*, read against muted background music, "Vivaldi or, better still, Mozart."

Tacitly at least, Auquier and Aelberts have admitted in their allusion to Benoît and Dax that they were open to influences from within surrealism, when writing *Cérémonial pour . . . Sade*. Use of music chosen to contrast with the violent readings of Tableau 5 suggests that inspiration came too from Buñuel, in a sequence of his *L'Age d'Or* for which, as it happens, the source was *Les 120 Journées de Sodome*.[10] Another reminiscence, emphasized by the dramatists themselves, occurs in Tableau 6. Here, muttering phrases from Sade's last will and testament, actors wrap a chain around the head of the *foetus-woman*, covering up her features so that she looks like the frontispiece designed by Jindrich Heisler for *La Philosophie dans le Boudoir*.[11]

Tableau 7 dispenses with words as, after simulating various hysteri-

10. On the use of *paso doble* accompaniment in the closing section of Buñuel's *L'Age d'Or* see J. H. Matthews, *Surrealism and Film* (Ann Arbor: University of Michigan Press, 1971), pp. 104–5. Incidentally, Buñuel uses Handel's Hallelujah Chorus to effect in his film *Viridiana*. See Matthews, *Surrealism and Film*, p. 156. See also André Labarrère, "La Musique dans les Films de Buñuel," *Etudes cinématographiques*, No. 20–21, 1962 (1), pp. 135–44.
11. In a footnote to their text Auquier and Aelberts openly admit to being indebted to Heisler, whose frontispiece, designed in 1943, is reproduced in the first number of *Le Surréalisme, même* (1956), p. 29.

cal convulsions[12] and emitting "cries and phonemes," the *foetus-woman* succeeds in liberating herself from the chain. She now uses it to encircle the *phallic-object*, strangling it while the crying of newborn infants is audible from off stage. As the lights go out we hear simultaneously the sounds of glass breaking, hysterical laughter, church bells, and parts of the Mass, said in Latin.

Mime is central in Tableau 8. Within a semicircle formed by the other actors, a man goes through the motions of finding and then strangling a woman whose body he subjects to necrophiliac violation[13] before, in Tableau 9, the other actors pursue him off stage. The principal feature of the new tableau is a parody of the Nativity in which Aelberts and Auquier deliberately seek that effect of accidental parallelism by which Buñuel alludes to Leonardo da Vinci's *Last Supper* in his *Viridiana*. Their Holy Virgin gives birth to a rat, while a thunderous voice off stage recites a phrase from *La Philosophie dans le Boudoir:* "and it is in the breast of a Jewish whore, in the middle of a pig sty that the God is announced who shall save the world!" The actor representing Joseph clutches the rat and rolls about the stage uttering guttural and whistling sounds. Two men dressed as stagehands draw screens in front of the Nativity while we hear music in which we can detect a Christmas carol.

In Tableau 10 the two stagehands will carry on a dialogue incorporating texts from *La Nouvelle Justine ou Les Malheurs de la Vertu*, *Histoire de Juliette ou Les Prospérités du Vice*, *Pensée*, and *Dialogue entre un Prêtre et un Moribond*, one of them taking the part of the dying man, the other playing the role of the priest:

> THE PRIEST
> You do not believe in God then? *At once from the wings [and an effort will be made to have some replies come from the auditorium]: "No! No!"; as an echo and in all sorts of tones.*
> THE DYING MAN
> No!

12. In 1929 Breton and Aragon celebrated "The Fiftieth Anniversary of Hysteria," in a tribute to the work of Charcot at the Salpêtrière Hospital. Their text is reproduced in Maurice Nadeau, *Documents surréalistes* (Aux Editions du Seuil, 1948), pp. 125–27.

13. As well as paying homage to Sade, Jean Benoît has created a costume in honor of France's most famous necrophile, Sergeant Bertrand. The costume was displayed at the eleventh International Exhibition of Surrealism (Paris, 1965). A color photograph, *Le Nécrophile*, appears in the catalogue *L'Ecart absolu*.

Parody reasserts itself in Tableau 11, where the *Missal* from which the celebrant reads texts by Sade, over an altar that is a woman's body, is a volume decorated with Man Ray's imaginary portrait of the Marquis.[14] Mockery of the Mass includes the lowing of cattle in place of ringing bells and a Host consisting of a banana between two tangerines, standing for the Trinity.

Tableau 12 begins with an enumeration of crimes that have made certain Popes stand out in history. Then the backdrop is brought into service again as a screen. Upon it, before a group of actors kneeling in attitudes of deepest piety, a picture of a Pope (John XXIII) is projected "in all his glory." Pontifical declarations by Pope Paul VI are received with applause. Then, imperceptible at first, a hole appears in the screen at the level of the Pontiff's genitals. As it increases in size a shower of rosaries, votive medals, and so on fall out of it onto the stage, where the faithful fight over them. As the peroration comes to an end, the audience hears "a cataract of *papal farts* metamorphosed in a simple manner,"[15] before the tableau closes on "a *concerto* of flushed toilets."

While the other actors tear away two layers of paper (one black, the other white) covering mirrors arranged all around the stage, so as to reveal finally a red layer, the man impersonating Sade recites sentences from *Juliette*, in Tableau 13. His voice sometimes appears to be coming from off stage. His last phrase gives prominence, like *Ra ma Chène*, to incest: "I dare assert, in brief, that incest ought to be the law of every government for which the basis is brotherhood." In the succeeding tableau he destroys signs bearing the key words upon which social order rests: money, family, army, country, God. Only the word "writing" resists his destructive fury.

In contrast with Tableaux 13 and 14, the next is quite complex. It calls for choreographic movement involving all the actors and for delivery in alternating voices of political pronouncements extracted from *La Philosophie dans le Boudoir,* from Sade's correspondence, and from

14. A sketch of Sade by Man Ray appears in the *Dictionnaire abrégé du Surréalisme,* ed. André Breton and Paul Éluard (Galerie des Beaux-Arts, 1938). Except for background detail, it is exactly the same as the *Imaginary Portrait of D. A. F. Sade* reproduced in the catalogue *An Exhibition Retrospective and Prospective of the Works of Man Ray,* Institute of Contemporary Arts, London, March–April 1959.

15. Auquier and Aelberts have in mind a passage from Stockhausen's *Kontakte* in its electronic version for "this pontifical offering quite rarely, we think, granted pilgrims."

his *Opuscules politiques*. It requires also that certain of the actors inscribe on the red-covered mirrors texts resembling concrete poems. These must incorporate the following key words:

COPULATION   LOVE
REVOLUTION   ANARCHY
LIBERTY   LANGUAGE
NATURE   ETHICS
REASON   GOD-CHIMERA

At the end of Tableau 15 we hear one of Sade's best-known statements, "Frenchmen, one more effort if you want to be republicans."[16] The sixteenth tableau continues to focus on Sade's role as a political thinker. A woman arrives, weighed down by a section of iron railing. This she sets up at various points as she moves about the stage, each time miming the opening of prison doors. We see no prisoners released, but hear the flapping of birds' wings and see, every time, one or other of the actors tear away the last layer of paper from his mirror. All this is easy enough to interpret so long as we have listened attentively to the extracts recited in the preceding tableau. However, the significance of Tableau 17 eludes anyone who is not acquainted with Sade's life history. It shows the Marquis attached by red, white, and blue ribbons to one of the mirrors, where he seems like a fly caught in a spider's web.[17]

While the dance opening the eighteenth tableau becomes wilder and wilder, the indistinct words going with it gradually become audible as "Revolution." Now two more Sade extracts can be heard. Taken from *Juliette* and *Aline et Valcour*, they reject laws as the instrument of despotism, arguing that free peoples must be self-governing. Thus Tableau 18 provides a coda to Tableau 17, which ended, "it is only in that instant when laws have been silenced that great actions have come

16. Cf. *Free Unions libres*, a collective publication by surrealists in England, conceived during the 1939–45 war, but published only in 1946. Here Dolmancé's discourse, "Français, encore un effort si vous voulez être républicains," from *La Philosophie dans le Boudoir*, is reproduced in English translation, pp. 42–45.
17. Sade was sent to Vincennes Prison for debauchery only four months after his marriage in 1763. He spent another five and a half years in Vincennes between 1778 and 1784, when he was committed to the Bastille. There he remained until 1789. He was transferred for an indefinite period to the insane asylum at Charenton-Saint-Maurice, just ten days before the storming of the Bastille, remaining there for nine months. The nature of his published work caused him to be returned to Charenton in April 1803. He died there in December 1814.

forth." The eighteenth tableau also introduces the two final ones, which are presented simultaneously, the stage being "symbolically cut in two."

On the left-hand side, Tableau 19 signifies the movement from anarchy to utopia, as conceived by Sade. The mirrors have disappeared at last. We hear an inflammatory quotation borrowed from *Juliette* before Sade begins "a long vocalic monologue in the manner of an incantation." This revives the actors who fell to the ground after their dance in the previous tableau. Little by little, forming a cluster of bodies around Sade, all "emit a sort of grand cantata of long sustained sounds imperceptibly changing register at long intervals." Eventually those surrounding Sade withdraw one by one, so that the chant dies down progressively into total silence. Meanwhile, to the right, Tableau 20 shows a figure dressed in a totemic costume described in enough detail to identify its resemblance to the one devised by Jean Benoît in tribute to Sade.[18] Now phrases uttered indistinctly in Tableau 6 become clear, as we hear from off stage the fifth and final section of Sade's will, expressing his wishes regarding interment of his body in an unmarked grave.

Once the reading is over, *Sade-Death* turns very slowly toward *Sade-Utopia*, while the sound of running water can be heard. When they are at last face to face, both fall to the ground, covered by Sade's cloak. A rhythmic cry from the assembled actors—"Fif . . ."—is completed over loud speakers: ". . . thly." And now a long sound of invariable pitch and intensity is audible, continuing until it becomes exasperating. Then a final phrase is heard, borrowed from Sade's biographer, Gilbert Lely: "EVERYTHING THAT SADE SIGNS IS LOVE."

From several points of view *Cérémonial pour . . . Sade* is an unusually well nourished work for a dramatic text of surrealist inspiration. Setting aside the close acquaintance with the writings of Sade revealed in it, we cannot but notice that it is quite exceptional among

18. Photographs of Benoît's costume are reproduced in Robert Benayoun, *Erotique du Surréalisme* (Jean-Jacques Pauvert, 1965), pp. 217 and 218. Front and back views of *Le Nécrophile* can be seen on pp. 228 and 229. Heisler's *Frontispiece* is reproduced on p. 213.

surrealist writings as we know them: it demonstrates a firm grasp upon the theatre as spectacle and illustrates careful concern for this aspect of stage performance.

Almost all surrealists see in drama a makeshift means, valuable only to the extent that the limits of the stage can be ignored or transcended. In contrast, Auquier and Aelberts are keenly aware that certain twentieth-century developments in theatrical technique lend themselves to an adaptation from which surrealism can expect to profit. They show themselves both willing to take advantage of these techniques—rising, for instance, above their predecessors' mistrust of Artaud, and recognizing what surrealists have to learn from Genet—and also capable of doing so efficiently. They prove they have not only a sharp eye for visual effect but also an ear attuned to the special contribution that sound may make on stage. Knowledge and appreciation of current developments in music make them unique among a group whose aversion to the medium has perplexed many an observer. Who else among the surrealists can claim to know the following well enough to draw upon their works for the purposes of dramatic presentation—Luciano Berio, Györgi Ligeti, Anestis Logothetis, Robert Moran, Hans Otte, and Karl-Heinz Stockhausen? For the first time used without a hint of irony, in *Cérémonial* music becomes a major factor in endowing a surrealist drama with its special atmosphere. No less striking than their familiarity with some of the innovative composers of the day is the fact that Aelberts and Auquier are willing to look outside surrealism for models, when calling for concrete poems in the fifteenth tableau of their drama. Paul Nougé may head the list, but nonsurrealists figure on it also: for instance, Ferdinand Kriwet, Jean-François Bory, Seiichi Niikuni. Similarly, realizing that cries and disconnected phonemes add to the effect their play will make, Auquier and Aelberts recommend imitation of Cathy Berberian's style, when it comes to delivering certain vocalic poems for which a place is reserved in their *Cérémonial*.

It so happens that the revised version of *Cérémonial pour . . . Sade* was made in the very month that the surrealist group in France disbanded.[19] The final revisions, made before the text appeared in 1970, were effected subsequently. Yet these brought no major changes in structure or orientation. Hence historical circumstance plays no signifi-

19. See the statement by Jean Schuster, "En Forme de Manifeste," in the literary supplement to *Le Monde,* October 4, 1969, p. IV.

cant role here. We have no right to consider that, preparing their text for publication in the total freedom guaranteed by a privately printed edition, the Belgians Aelberts and Auquier took advantage of a freedom of action they might have been denied a few years earlier—before the death of André Breton in 1966, shall we say. Had this been the case, then the scenario they wrote together would not have been significant in quite the way it is.

For reasons of their own, some more precisely formulated than others, surrealists have always tended in the main to deny theatre, even while availing themselves of dramatic form. As a consequence, some of the most noteworthy surrealist experiments in drama—certainly some of the most characteristic ones—betray their authors' abiding distrust of outworn conventions of drama and of those tendencies that limit the role of theatre to the imitation of reality. The distinction of *Cérémonial pour . . . Sade* is that in this text Auquier and Aelberts bring to the task of writing for the stage an open-minded attitude that allows them to foresee a fruitful reconcilation between the theatre's potential and the demands given priority in surrealism. Faced with the example they have set, surrealists to whom drama appears, even more than painting did to André Breton, "a lamentable expedient,"[20] may take heart.

20. In spite of this belief, Breton has devoted a volume to *Le Surréalisme et la Peinture,* running to more than four hundred large pages in its definitive edition (Gallimard, 1965).

Conclusion

What less do you want to know?
Haven't I dodged the question well enough?[1]

INTRODUCING his *Trois Scénarii*, Benjamin Fondane pointed out in 1928, "It is not, consequently, to correct the cinema, to make it better (*let it not become an art:* that is all we ask of it) that we propose in our turn this mortar destined to ruin a certain form of cinema in people's minds, to bring another into the world."[2] Without falsifying the views expressed in surrealism, and in Dada too, one could substitute the word "theatre" for "cinema" in Fondane's declaration. Like the Dada play, the surrealist drama generally implies a critique of theatre, based upon thoroughly anti-artistic principles. Nowhere have Dada and surrealism proceeded more ruthlessly than in the theatre to annex a literary genre to their own purposes. These are essentially nonliterary and anti-conventional purposes, vigorously opposed to drama as viewed traditionally. In one way, then, it is not at all surprising that both Dada and surrealism give less to drama than they take from it.

With neither surrealism nor Dada can there be any question of seeking to deduce or develop an aesthetic of the theatre. Indeed, the very contrary is the case. Even when there is no clear evidence of a destructive impulse venting itself upon conventional dramatic forms and usages, the Dada and surrealist plays reflect a neglectful attitude toward the theatrical mode, exerting influences that, by established codes, must seem primarily negative. No more than the Dada writer does the surrealist have an innate or inculcated respect for theatrical form. When he happens to make use of the dramatic framework, it is

1. Robert Benayoun, *La Science met bas* (Jean-Jacques Pauvert, 1959).
2. Benjamin Fondane, *Trois Scénarii* (Brussels: Espirit nouveau, 1928).

for reasons in which surrealist exigencies dominate. Conventional theatre patterns are borrowed, if at all, only with ironic intent and effect, in a manner that betrays the author's profound indifference to tradition. Tradition marks in Dada and surrealism boundaries that the playwright—so far as he thinks of them at all—has every intention of casting down. To grasp the significance of Dada and surrealism on stage, therefore, we must recognize that misuse of convention is a means for transforming drama into a vehicle better suited to conveying elements to which Dada and surrealism, each in its own way and for its own reasons, grant importance. Subversion rests upon the distortion and disruption of inherited theatrical practice. A man like Aragon, for example, tampers with the supposedly essential mechanism of drama, leaving his audience to wonder about the principles governing action, its location, and the characters involved in it.

When critics like Henri Béhar and Michel Sanouillet talk of this Dada sketch or that surrealist play as demonstrating real dramatic sense, it is far from certain that their enthusiasm would please the author of the work in question. In the case of surrealism, particularly, a true sense of drama may well be in radical conflict with the writer's most pressing needs. It is certainly a fact that, for Dada as for surrealism, professional competence in the theatre is no measure of success. Not until he had set aside Dada methods did Tzara write *Le Mouchoir de Nuages*, the most theatrical of his plays. Meanwhile Artaud and Vitrac—the surrealists most widely known for their interest in drama, the most dedicated of the group to making a contribution to the theatre—departed without regret or guilt from the standards laid down in Fondane's criticism of attempts to correct or better a familiar genre. Doing this inevitably made them outcasts from surrealism.

Of course, there is evidence enough of premeditation in *Vous m'oublierez* to dispose of the hypothesis that this is a text unworthy of serious consideration in relation to surrealism's ambitions in the theatre. To be tempted to dismiss what Breton and Soupault have done as just another product of automatism means losing sight of essentials. Even the decision to employ automatic techniques within the framework of theatrical composition represents a significant approach to drama and a noteworthy conception of how a play ought to make its impact. By the same token, when a surrealist speaks of having written an unperformable play, he is not guilty of seeking self-advertisement through paradox. The unperformable play announces a new kind of theatrical endeavor. Here, stripped of its stageable features, drama is set free to serve other purposes than those customarily reserved for it on stage. Now all suspicion regarding the possible influence, in shaping surrealist drama, of ignorance on the technical plane must be ruled out. We are confronted, in reality, with incontrovertible proof of an instinct to deny theatre, ingrained in the creative nature of certain writers who come to drama in a state of mind closer to hostility than to disrespect or mere indifference. Even in less violently anti-conventional mood, the the surrealist playwright uses coincidence, strange and inexplicable encounters—part of the stock-in-trade of surrealist writers—in a manner that detaches his play from theatrical tradition. He calls upon the *coup de théâtre* itself to assume a new role: to help defy credibility, instead of soliciting it.

The perspective upon theatre offered in this manner illuminates much that seems at first obscure in the drama of Dada and surrealism. Many short sketches of Dada or surrealist provenance strike some observers as exercises in anti-dramatic form, wilfully denied the chance to persuade us that we should take their authors' intentions seriously. Thus one hears Martin Esslin asserting, "Surrealism admittedly lacked the qualities that would have been needed to create a real Surrealist drama," and continuing with the argument, "but this may have been due as much to the lack of a real need for such a theatre on the part of the public as to a lack of interest or application on the part of the writers concerned."[3] The truth is, though, that surrealism followed Dada to this extent: it maintained a concerted attack upon the audience's privilege to judge the validity of theatrical experience. It is in the surrealists themselves, not in their audience (so far as surrealist plays have ever had an audience), that we must identify a limited need for theatre of the kind that Esslin has in mind. Surrealism has never wavered in its refusal to seek contact with the public at large. Georges Goldfayn speaks in typically guarded terms when he remarks, from the surrealist standpoint, "In the measure that one wants the crowd to make contact with certain works it is [. . .] through the theatre that this operation is most desirable, with all due reservations about the way this operation is conducted."[4]

3. Martin Esslin, *The Theatre of the Absurd* [1961], rev. ed. (New York: Doubleday, Anchor, 1969), pp. 348–49.
4. Georges Goldfayn, "A Voix très haut," *Médium: Communication surréaliste,* Nouvelle Série, No. 1 (September 1953), p. 25.

When we come to examine this "operation" and the motives lying behind it, we bring into focus the differences separating theatre in Dada from theatre as promoted by surrealism. Like Dada, surrealism gives attention to the conventions of theatre only to explode inherited forms of drama. In both Dada and surrealism, conventions subsist, where they are still visible, only to point in the direction the author has taken in forsaking tradition, leaving behind tracks by which we can detect the direction he has followed. But the Dada writer does not choose the same route as the surrealist.

Dada, as Tzara has remarked, "advocated confusing aesthetic categories as one of the most efficacious means of loosening that rigid edifice of art just a little [. . .]."[5] But Dada writers were not always sure—and certainly were not in agreement—about the ways in which such a "loosening" could be beneficial. They derived so much pleasure from destruction that they tended to find it fully satisfying in itself. Breaking down aesthetic categories remained in Dada a speculative undertaking having no precise motivation beyond dissatisfaction with current artistic modes. These appeared suspect to the extent that, like Tzara, the defenders of Dada found in them the hateful reflection of "the lies and hypocrisy of society." Hence the underlying impulse among Dada playwrights was to keep the public at a distance, to reject the audience, and to mock the basis of exchange upon which theatre had been assumed to rest.

Beyond any doubt surrealism gathered momentum in the theatre from what had been accomplished by Dada. If this had not been so, then we should be able to observe a much clearer division between Dada theatrical writing and the first plays deserving mention under the heading of surrealism. All the same, notable differences can be detected, once we view the experimentation of the early twenties in the perspective of surrealism's emerging plan of campaign.

Drawing distinctions here is not facilitated, though, for those who notice how the vocabulary of surrealism often overlaps that of Dada. Thus, for instance, Tzara as spokesman for Dada stresses the social significance of ambitions that necessarily have direct consequences for the theatre. And so does Breton, in his *Second Manifeste du Surréalisme:* "The problem of social action is, I should like to return to this and to insist upon it, but one of the forms of a more general

5. Tristan Tzara, introduction to Georges Hugnet, *L'Aventure Dada* (Galerie de l'Institut, 1957), p. 9.

problem [. . .] which is that of *human expression in all its forms.* Whoever says expression says, to begin with, language. You must not be surprised, then, to see surrealism situated first of all almost exclusively on the plane of language [. . .]" (p. 183). Years later Jean Schuster was to explain, "The value we attach to the emancipation of language is directly proportionate to the privileged place it holds in the continuum described by the adventure of the human psychism struggling with natural and social contingent circumstances."[6] Not until we realize how the same words can take on differing meaning, as Dada gives way to surrealism, do we find ourselves equipped to appreciate where surrealism marks a radical departure from Dada in the theatre. Thus the special function of drama in surrealism eludes definition unless we understand how the surrealists wish to emancipate language.

Surrealists protest everywhere against imposed convention and established technique. They believe that concern for these diverts attention from what really counts. Hence we progress best with the theatre as understood in surrealism when, instead of writing the surrealists off as ineffectual dramatists, we appreciate the following. As this is generally understood on the level of stagecraft, technical efficiency is not something a surrealist aspires to achieve. Lying elsewhere, his aims are not to be attained, he is sure, by the development of skills that theatregoers are used to considering basic to the playwright's art. What passes for hostility to familiar custom or even ignorance of it really denotes, in surrealism, a new scale of priorities. Quite different from the one usually applied in writing for the stage, the surrealists' scale of values gives precedence above all to the liberation of language. The result, so far as this interests us here, is affirmation of surrealism's independence from Dada in the theatre.

Denial of the long-established assumption that reasonable language is the most fitting medium for verbal communication between men—this surely is one of the "repulsions" that Artaud credited surrealism with registering. To the surrealist, language is not the faithful record of previously formulated thought, logically expressed so as to appeal to "dessicated reason." But this is true also of Dada. Where surrealism goes beyond Dada is in recognizing in language a means for stimulating thought in a manner considered valuable to the extent that words point forward, not backward. Surrealism locates mental, emotional, and

6. Jean Schuster, "A l'Ordre de la Nuit, Au Désordre du Jour," *L'Archibras,* No. 1 (April 1967), p. 8.

above all imaginative stimulus ahead, instead of behind us. Thus at the source of surrealism's revolutionary use of language in the theatre is a much more purposeful sense than in Dada of how dialogue advances, and why. No longer does dialogue work essentially to support and develop plot. On the contrary, to the degree that plot counts at all in surrealism, it tends to function mainly as a support for dialogue. The latter, meanwhile, pushes forward to a level of exchange where common sense and normal sequence surrender their claim to attention, either from the author or from his public.

Of course, one can recall a number of surrealist dramas that do not seem to follow this pattern at all. If, though, we divest ourselves of the habit of remembering plays for the stories they relate, we soon see that there are far less of these than we thought. The major discovery made in the name of surrealism is that theatre is compatible with poetry, as surrealists understand this, but that on stage it is frequently necessary to liberate poetry through language at the expense of drama. Hence surrealism's impact upon playwriting rests mainly upon diversion of theatre from dramatic to poetic ends. This is the significance of plot discontinuity and inconsistency in character and behavior, called upon to play their part in setting the theatre free from its restricted role as mirror to reality.

Time after time, in one way or another, dramatic necessity yields before surrealism's demands. Tonal variations give unwonted emphasis to conventional language in Artaud's *Le Jet de Sang*. Arbitrary manipulation of rhythm releases José Pierre's play from the limitations of realistic dialogue. Everywhere dramatic requirements are ousted by surrealism's needs, as when Vitrac grants words unprecedented freedom of action, or when Duprey allows drama to founder, as—by way of multiplication—he deprives his characters of definition. In reality, then, the idea of drama changes profoundly in surrealism. We can see this as well in the plays of Soupault and Breton as in Ivsic's. Drama is no longer resident in situation and character confrontation. It now lies in the struggle that either illustrates the potential of language for surrealist projection or lays bare the inadequacy of language to encompass all that imagination has to offer.

Advancing in the direction that surrealism prescribes very often means implementing procedures of an anti-dramatic nature. In other words, theatre in surrealism may be anti-theatre only incidentally, but still be essentially anti-traditional. It assumes its distinctive character thanks to obligations imposed upon the playwright to divert drama from its familiar course. To these he must submit as soon as he recognizes that surrealist aspirations impose the inversion of established modes of communication through language. Now less attention goes than in the past to action and the setting against which it used to be placed, for reasons of verisimilitude or dramatic intensity. This is because the surrealist form of theatrical representation casts the audience in the role of listeners far oftener than it asks them to be witnesses to events enacted on stage.

The lyrical phenomenon in poetry, as Breton understood it around 1920, not only requires a special form of theatre to give it expression. It also imposes special demands upon the listening audience, replacing conflict, as the theatre usually deals in this, with an emotional confrontation of an unprecedented kind. This confrontation defies elucidation according to the well-known values of the psychological theatre. It places comprehension, by the standards of what is customarily termed true-to-life behavior, second to glimpses of a world where reason does not hold sway—a world best recognized, it sometimes appears, from those of our dreams that challenge the limitations of visible reality.

This is to say that the surrealist who writes for the stage is motivated by a distinctive sense of responsibility to the public, whom he denies many traditional privileges. When he chooses to ignore the conventional barrier of the footlights, he is motivated not by whim or fancy, but by a need to stress something important to him: his concern for instituting a new relationship between what takes place on stage and the audience in whose presence it is enacted. His play speaks most directly to those who feel no regret at the elimination of the barrier erected by reason to keep the poetry of surrealist drama at a distance. Our need to *understand* with the reasonable mind, in a situation where we have been taught by past experience to find the theatre offering pleasures analogous to those of a spectator sport, impedes response on the poetic plane where surrealism aims to effect communication with its public.

Precisely because words lend themselves to projecting a mode of existence and a view of life beyond the confines of rationality, they give the surrealist some hope of precipitating poetry in the theatre. The ideal is not dramatic intensity, therefore, but poetic intensity. This means that a surrealist play is not didactic, or merely entertaining. It is essentially initiative. And initiation, after all, presupposes desire on the part of the initiate to be admitted to the privilege of sharing the experience he is being offered.

Theatre critics and historians tend to treat Dada and surrealism in a manner typified in comments made by Leonard Cabell Pronko, opening his book on the experimental theatre in France: "Jarry's revolt against bourgeois morality and prevalent theater values, drawing inspiration from the romanticism and bohemianism of the nineteenth century, led to the theater of the more organized revolt of Apollinaire's *Les Mamelles de Tirésias,* and the few dramatic efforts of dada and surrealism. By 1930, however, despite the efforts of Antonin Artaud, the lineage of Jarry seemed extinct, and it was only in 1950, with the performance of Ionesco's *Bald Soprano,* and three years later with Beckett's *Waiting for Godot,* that it became clear that the spirit of the avant-garde was still alive in the theater."[7] Pronko mentions by name not a single Dada play. Nor does he cite even one surrealist drama or sketch, whether written before 1930 or after. In fact, he honestly admits to being virtually without firsthand knowledge of Dada and surrealist plays.[8] It is clear that, when speaking of innovative French theatre in our time, Pronko judges dramatic activity upon the evidence of theatrical production alone. Hence he feels entitled to talk of "a silent pregnancy of almost twenty years," extending to about 1950. And this is why, presumably, he has no qualms about setting aside plays written in Dada and surrealism, when reviewing the development of twentieth-century vanguard theatre.

In a sense, Pronko administers a kind of rough justice. Dada rejected tradition, turned its back on continuity, denied all associations. No Dada writer could have behaved in a manner consistent with his principles, had he acknowledged, or sought to establish, or taken care to maintain ties with any mode of theatrical expression. As for the surrealists, it is significant that they were to pay far more attention to Apollinaire's description of *Les Mamelles de Tirésias* as a "drame surréaliste" than to the play itself.[9] Breton makes it quite clear in his

7. Leonard Cabell Pronko, *Avant-Garde: The Experimental Theater in France* (Berkeley and Los Angeles: University of California Press, 1962), p. 1.
8. Ibid., p. 213, n. 7.
9. Breton's first manifesto states that surrealism was named in homage to Apolli-

Entretiens that he responded most to Apollinaire the poet. Evidence suggests that surrealists in general agreed with him in finding little to admire in Apollinaire the playwright.[10] As for Jarry, his reputation in surrealist circles rests quite as much upon his novel *Le Surmâle* as upon *Ubu Roi*, where surrealists are impressed by the monstrous character of Ubu and by the humor with which he is presented, far more than by Jarry's theories about theatrical representation.[11] Any sense of taking his place in a theatrical tradition, however independent of mainstream developments, is foreign to the surrealist's experience, even though, like Aelberts and Auquier, he may on occasion find encouragement or incentive in something this or that individual has done before him.

Rejecting conformity—even the conformism of anti-conformity—is one thing. Escaping the consequences of existing in an historical continuum is quite another matter, of course. What is interesting is that the surrealists, who from the first made no secret of their awareness of taking their place after certain precursors whom they admired in poetry and painting, never troubled themselves about *situating* their experiments with theatre. They have been just as unconcerned to measure their influence on contemporary drama. The confusion occasioned by their disrespectful treatment of the theatre affords them more amusement than annoyance.

Special problems face anyone taking up the question of the influence exerted by Dada and surrealism upon the evolution of vanguard theatre in the twentieth century. At one extreme, the adjective "surrealist," for instance, is applied quite irresponsibly. Like its vague derivative "surrealistic," it is used all too often to cover any unexpected departure from the norm, whether it be unforeseen, weird, or merely odd. Thus its application in connection with the theatre is no more useful than in any other genre. To term Emilio Carballida "the first Mexican author to employ consistently a kind of theater that may be called fantastic, poetic, surrealistic—or simply nonrealistic,"[12] is to

---

naire (p. 38), but the insists that Apollinaire possessed not the spirit of surrealism but its "*letter*" (p. 39).

10. See J. H. Matthews, "Apollinaire devant les surréalistes," *La Revue des Lettres Modernes*, Nos. 104–7, 1964 (4), pp. 75–85.

11. See, for example, Jarry's articles, "De l'Inutilité du Théâtre au Théâtre," *Mercure de France*, September 1896; "Questions de Théâtre," *La Revue blanche*, January 1, 1897.

12. Margaret Sayers Peden, introduction to *The Golden Thread and Other*

achieve nothing. Nor is anything gained by referring to his first play as "a surrealist farce" when Carballida himself, acknowledging a debt to the seventeenth-century writer Sor Juana Inés de la Cruz, has classified it as an *auto sacramental*.[13] At the other extreme, excessive limitations too have their disadvantages. So we hear Martin Esslin, who mentions no surrealist writing for the stage after the twenties, nevertheless remark that the surrealists "were ahead of their time" (p. 349), without explaining how exactly the "chaos of pure automatism" (p. 332), which he identifies with surrealism in the theatre, has come to leave its mark on drama. "As for the theatre," observes Anna Balakian, "there have been so far more blueprints than real surrealist plays. One might say that no avant-garde play has remained completely unaffected by the precepts of surrealism; however, there are few truly surrealistic plays. Many named as such are rather Dada in their treatment of the absurd, whether as a corrective satire or as a caricature of irreversible traits in the human condition."[14]

Since Miss Balakian raises more questions than she answers, let us begin by remembering what theatre represents in Dada and surrealism. This means recalling that Dada and surrealist writers have asked drama to do certain things and to give up doing others. Hence there is something ironical to be noticed at this point. Dada and surrealist playwrights are not in the least interested in contributing in some way to the evolution of drama, but have found themselves doing so, all the same. Inevitably, they have left their mark upon the theatre because demands such as they bring to bear upon literary genres necessarily produce an interaction between content and the medium selected for their expression. Aspects of the theatre that have come under scrutiny in Dada and surrealism are—it could not be otherwise—among the basic features of theatrical tradition in Europe. And so however negative their approach, however haphazard their methods of dealing with the phenomenon of theatrical representation, however disinterested they have been in seeing through to logical conclusions some of the suppositions underlying their treatment of the stage play, Dada and surrealist

---

Plays by Emilio Carballida (Austin and London: University of Texas Press, 1971), p. xi.

13. "The plays range from the surrealist farce of 'The Intermediate Zone' [1948] to the grotesqueries of 'The Time and the Place,' [. . .]." *The Golden Thread and other plays by Emilio Carballida*, publisher's note.

14. Anna Balakian, "Dada–Surrealism: Fundamental Differences," *Proceedings of the Comparative Literature Symposium*, III, 'From Surrealism to the Absurd' (Lubbock: Texas Tech University, 1970), 25.

writers have helped inculcate a critical attitude toward drama that is characteristic of our time.

Yet only in exceptional cases can we speak of certain experimental dramatists as working on the periphery of Dada or surrealism and as having somewhat the same reasons for doing somewhat the same things —Georges Schehadé comes to mind, and one thinks too of the early plays of Eugène Ionesco.[15] But by and large, the distance separating Dada and surrealist ambitions from those that have gained popularity in the last quarter of a century is too great for direct influence to have been felt profoundly by writers whose ethical, moral, and existential preoccupations are so different from those upon which Dada and surrealism rest. As a result, one cannot fairly speak of influence or of ready imitation. One must speak instead of precedence and of possible borrowing. We can refer to similarities in the handling of material, but not to similar reasons for treating it in comparable ways. As a result, Dada and surrealism, which never consider stage technique of sufficient importance to be taken seriously, have earned themselves a place in the history of the evolution of modern drama by their innovative contribution to theatrical technique.

There is no need at this point to reiterate that any playwright true to Dada or surrealism must feel only indifference, if he sees his work granted attention by those for whom the changing face of drama is a matter of concern. His indifference is hardly an excuse, though, for the kind of distortion that some commentators apparently regard as

15. The surrealists' enthusiasm for early Ionesco plays is attested by François Valobre's article "A tout rompre," *Médium: Communication surréaliste* (Nouvelle Série, No. 3, May 1954, p. 7) on the occasion of the publication of Ionesco's *Théâtre* under the imprint Editions Arcanes (1953). Confirmation of their approval came the following January when *Médium*'s fourth issued carried Ionesco's story "Une Victime du Devoir" (pp. 38–40). (Dated 1952, this text was turned into a play the same year, being performed in 1953 and subsequently printed in *Théâtre*, Vol. I [Gallimard, 1954].) A year later Ionesco was saying, "What is comical is the unusual in its pure state; nothing seems more surprising to me than that which is banal; the surreal is here, within grasp of our hands, in our everyday conversation" ("Le Point du Départ," *Cahiers des Quatre Saisons*, No. 1, August 1955, as quoted by Esslin, p. 115). In 1957 Ionesco wrote his *Tueur sans Gages*, which Esslin regards as "probably his finest play" (p. 144), but which Ionesco himself has called "a step backward" and "superficial theatre" (in a broadcast during the BBC's Third Programme series *Art–Anti-Art*, 1959–1960; as reported in *BIEF: Jonction surréaliste*, Nos. 10–11, February 15, 1960, where a footnote signed by Gérard Legrand attacks the playwright: "A rhinoceros, no, but, at best, an ostrich"). To Robert Benayoun, attacking Ionesco for having written *Tueur sans Gages*, the word "pelican" seemed more appropriate. See "Eugene Ionesco ou le Pélican," *BIEF: Jonction surréaliste*, No. 6, April 15, 1959.

permissible, when Dada or surrealist writing for the stage needs to be mentioned. Prepared to admit that both Dada and surrealism have left something to the theatre, such observers appear alert only to what it suits them to see. It is noteworthy that Martin Esslin, for example, affirms that during the conversation between Patrice and the Author in *Les Mystères de l'Amour* "the basic theme of the Theater of the Absurd, the problem of language, is squarely faced" (p. 352). This may be true, even though Vitrac might have been just as disinclined to hear his work cited as a manifestation of the Theatre of the Absurd as, shall we say, Arrabal. What is important is that Esslin has nothing to say about Vitrac's play in relation to the problem of language as posed in surrealism. Moreover, ignoring Vitrac altogether when he finds it advantageous to do so, Esslin writes, "If a playwright like John Osborne, who usually works in a quite different convention, quite naturally starts a play like *Inadmissible Evidence* (1964) with a dream-sequence and no-one in the audience is shocked or surprised by such a device, this illustrate the degree to which the innovations of the drama-tists of the Absurd have become integrated into the mainstream of dramatic technique" (p. 379). In like fashion, Esslin talks of the music hall and the circus as presenting parallels with the dialogue between the two tramps in Beckett's *En attendant Godot* (Vladimir: "Charming evening we're having." Estragon: "Unforgettable"), when one might have expected Tzara to receive at least an honorable mention. It is not by ignoring Breton and Soupault that one sets the dialogue of Russell Edson's *The Falling Sickness* in true perspective.

Noting that Ribemont-Dessaignes's *L'Empereur de Chine* was per-formed in 1946 by Michel de Ré's *Le Thiase*, Michel Sanouillet ex-presses regret that it has not been staged since: "for a revival in today's context would make people realize not only Ribemont-Dessaignes's real dramatic gifts, but also the debt contracted by certain contempo-rary authors to this liberating theatre."[16] It would be hard to prove how many contemporary authors are indebted to Dada. But one must certainly give credit to Dada and to surrealism for bringing to the theatre an innovative spirit that initiated protest and reappraisal as these have become familiar to theatre audiences. It seems that Henri Béhar takes up the question more profitably than Sanouillet does, when he remarks apropos of the revival of Vitrac's *Victor:* "It will not be

16. Michel Sanouillet, *Dada à Paris* (Jean-Jacques Pauvert, 1965), p. 316.

surprising that the reception given Victor in 1962 should be very different from that of 1928."[17] We can agree with Béhar that the change in the public's attitude toward *Victor*—so far, that is, as we can infer this attitude from the comments made by drama critics at the time of the revival—marks not so much a sudden change of mind, but rather "a slow transformation of taste." However, to attribute this transformation, as Béhar does, mainly to Ionesco is to ignore Ionesco's avowed debt to surrealism, treating his theatre as though it had no roots in a past to which surrealism in the theatre belongs. The important thing, surely, is that when we look back, Dada and surrealist plays fall into place, in a pattern of theatrical evolution to which, whether they like it or not, their authors belong. If, indeed, some of the innovative features for which Dada and surrealism are directly responsible on the stage seem to have lost their ability to surprise, this is the price that experimentation must pay, when it is fruitful.

Commenting upon the revival of *Victor*, Jean Anouilh wrote in *Le Figaro littéraire* on October 6, 1962, "*Victor* is one of the three or four plays for which I would give half of what I have done . . . It should have marked a turning point. This is modern comedy. The people who didn't hear it have made us lose thirty years, waiting for Ionesco." Jacques B. Brunius gives a somewhat similar remark quite a different emphasis: "On the stage we had to wait until 1950 to see Eugène Ionesco gather the loose ends left dangling by Dada and Surrealism and accomplish what his predecessors had failed to achieve."[18] To place these two statements in their true perspective, we have merely to return to André Breton's praise of *Les Détraquées* as the only dramatic work he cared to remember, and especially to his parenthetical explanation: "I mean: written solely for the stage." It is not the medium but the use to which it can be forced to lend itself that interests the playwrights whose work we have been considering. Dada and surrealist writers attack the structure of drama because they have no faith in the viability of theatrical structure and hence have no ambitions to bring anything new to it. The surrealist, especially, is more concerned with what Breton terms "*poetic* intuition" than with consecrated literary modes. He recognizes, as does Breton, that the

17. Henri Béhar, *Roger Vitrac: Un Réprouvé du Surréalisme* (Nizet, 1966), p. 196.
18. From Brunius' contribution to the BBC's *Art–Anti-Art* series, as quoted in Pronko, *Avant-Garde*, p. 10.

intuition claiming his exclusive attention "wants to be not only assimilative of all known forms but boldly creative of new forms."[19] But none of these new forms could ever be an art form which, as Esslin has noted, "necessarily relies on constructive cooperation" (p. 319). Whatever Dada and surrealism give to the theatre, they give incidentally, neither by design nor by intent. The seeds they sow in the theatre produce a harvest that they are quite content to let others gather.

19. André Breton, "Du Surréalisme en ses Œuvres vives," in his *Manifestes du Surréalisme*, p. 363.